Media voices

Media
voices

The James Cameron
Memorial Lectures

edited by

Hugh Stephenson

First published in Great Britain 2001 by
Politico's Publishing
8 Artillery Row
Westminster
London
SW1P 1RZ

www.politicos.co.uk/publishing

A catalogue record for this book is available from the British Library.

ISBN 1 84275 007 0

Printed and bound by Creative Print and Design

Contents

Introduction
Hugh Stephenson

J AMES CAMERON died in January 1985 at the age of seventy-three. Spontaneously, hundreds of readers wrote to the *Guardian*, the paper for which he worked for the last ten years of his life, offering to support a fitting memorial. There cannot have been many journalists whose death caused such a reaction.

The late Tom Baistow, who as foreign editor of the *News Chronicle* had persuaded Cameron to join that paper, became the co-ordinator, with a number of Cameron's colleagues at the *Guardian* and elsewhere, of the idea that there should be an annual award to a journalist working for the British media whose work had been 'in the Cameron tradition', and an annual lecture in his memory. James Cameron had also worked often for the BBC, and its then Director-General, Alasdair Milne, gave the project his vigorous support. The result was the James Cameron Memorial Trust, funded almost wholly by an astonishingly large number of small personal donations from his army of friends and admirers. At Tom Baistow's suggestion, the Trust's activities have been arranged from the start by the Department of Journalism at City University, London.

1

Many such memorial trusts have quite a short active life, as the number of those with personal memories inevitably dwindles. It is a measure of Cameron's reputation that the annual event in his memory remains as vibrant an occasion as was the first in 1987. It is not just that he was a superb reporter and a superb writer during a golden age for foreign correspondents, though he certainly was for Beaverbrook's *Daily Express*, for *Picture Post* and for the *News Chronicle* in particular. As a reporter, he covered the Bikini atomic bomb tests, the independence of India and Pakistan, the election of President Truman, the Korean War, Albert Schweitzer in the Congo, Chairman Mao's China, the Vietnam War and much else besides. His books, particularly *Points of Departure*, live on as lasting evidence of his gift with words. But, beyond that, he had the ability to reach his readers personally, intimately and with humour, conveying his own wisdom and kindness.

This book reproduces all the annual memorial lectures so far delivered, except one: in 1998, Studs Terkel, the American historian and broadcaster and a close friend of Cameron, came from Chicago and gave an unforgettable performance on the theme of 'The journalist in flesh and blood'. The evening, however, was part reminiscence and part answers to questions from the audience and there was no editable text.

The other fourteen have been transcribed and edited for publication with a view to preserving their essential character as lectures rather than written articles; headnotes and footnotes have been supplied by myself as editor of the volume. It is appropriate at this point to acknowledge the generosity of the speakers in readily agreeing that all royalties from the sale of this book will go to the James Cameron Memorial Trust.

The subjects of the fourteen lectures in this volume were freely chosen by the lecturers themselves and were not planned to fit into a coherent pattern. Obviously, they reflect contemporary issues of concern to and about the media. As a body, though, two themes in particular recur.

The first is the degree to which the 1990 Broadcasting Act sacrificed public service broadcasting in this country on the altar of market forces. David Mellor, the junior minister at the Home Office directly responsible for the legislation, managed to get some marginal improvements in the original Bill past Margaret Thatcher, but that Act sent commercial television off in the direction of America, with audience size the overwhelming preoccupation and the viewer regarded as a consumer rather than a citizen. To protect its share of the audience, and thus the legitimacy of the licence fee, the BBC has gone more and more in the same direction.

The second theme is the running tension between protection of privacy and freedom of the press. There seems to be agreement that in this country we have the worst of both worlds. Having no written constitution, Britain has no constitutional statement recognising freedom of speech and freedom of the press as virtuous. This has made the media fiercely resistant to privacy legislation or any further restraint on what may be published, because it would surely be used by public figures to prevent legitimate scrutiny. But, having no privacy legislation, commercial pressures induce newspapers to publish intimate details of people's private lives without the slightest justification of real public interest. Governments have regularly wondered what to do about this problem and, having wondered, have decided to do nothing. It now looks as if it will be judges, rather than Parliament, who redefine privacy for the media as more and more cases invoking the European Convention on Human Rights find their way before the courts.

The Trust each year invites a distinguished panel to nominate a journalist for the annual memorial prize. Those serving on this panel at various times have been Tom Baistow, Roger Bolton, Michael Buerk, Henry Clother, Liz Forgan, Catherine Freeman, Sandy Gall, Geoffrey Goodman, Jeremy Isaacs, Martin Woollacott and Will Wyatt. The roll-call of recipients is as follows:

1987 David Hirst
1988 Michael Buerk
1989 Neal Ascherson
1990 John Simpson
1991 Robert Fisk and Charles Wheeler

1992 Bridget Kendall
1993 Martin Woollacott
1994 Ed Vulliamy
1995 George Alagiah
1996 Maggie O'Kane
1997 Fergal Keane
1998 Jonathan Steele
1999 Ann Leslie
2000 Jon Swain
2001 Suzanne Goldenberg

Hugh Stephenson
City University, London
November 2001

Ben Bradlee

Why governments lie

1987

Executive Editor of the Washington Post *from 1968 to 1991 and now the paper's Vice President At-Large, Ben Bradlee masterminded the Post's coverage of the Watergate scandal which led to President Nixon's resignation in August 1974 to avoid impeachment. Bradlee gave the first James Cameron Lecture in 1987 against the background of the Iran-Contra affair: the revelation in 1986 that alleged profits of $30 million from unauthorised arms sales to Iran had been used to finance covert assistance to the Contra rebels fighting the radical Sandinista government in Nicaragua seemed for a time to threaten President Reagan's position.*

I SHOULD LIKE to say up front that my qualifications for giving this first James Cameron Lecture are fairly suspect. I knew him only slightly. I have tried to overcome that obstacle by reading his books and by speaking about him to that sage American observer, Studs Terkel. 'All he was,' Studs said, 'was the

best journalist of the century as far as writing, style and content are concerned. Gentle. Sweet. Courageous. And a great man at the bar.'

I do know enough about the British press not to lecture you on how you should ply our chosen trade of journalism – what Walter Lippmann called 'a refuge for the vaguely talented' and what H. L. Mencken described as 'the life of kings'. The strengths of British journalism and American journalism lie in their differences, not their similarities. So I would like to speak from my own experience, with my own government and with my own newspaper, with the caveat that I have worked for only one daily newspaper in my lifetime. I would like to talk about government lying. Calculated lies. The wilful deception of the public for political ends, especially under the disguise of national security, and what an awful price we pay for such lies under any name: misinformation, disinformation, deceit, deception, or even economical with the truth.

In America, the press is curiously shy, even embarrassed, when faced with the need to use some form of the verb 'to lie', even now when public tolerance for the unexplained and for the unbelievable explanation is wearing thin. We seem to drop quickly into a defensive crouch, even when we are accused of abusing our power by not accepting explanations which often defy acceptance. We are, too often, close enough to the establishment ourselves to be comfortable in calling a lie a lie.

I am not talking about little lies, as in Vice-Admiral Poindexter

being asked to give up his job as National Security Adviser to return to active duty in the Navy. Little lies, as in we did not trade Soviet spy Sakharov for American journalist Danilov. Little lies, like Margaret Heckler has been promoted from Secretary of Health and Human Services to be Ambassador to Ireland. Little lies like that can take a long, long time to damage the bonds of confidence that link the people and the press and public policy, though damage they do.

Let us talk about big lies. Lies that change history. Two of them have to do with Vietnam, the war that so outraged Jimmy Cameron. A third has to do with the American spy Ronald Pelton, and a fourth concerns the various lies that blanket whatever the hell is the real truth about the Iran-Contra affair.

First, let me take you back to December 1963 and Tan Son Nhut Airport in Saigon. At the end of his first fact-finding trip to Vietnam for the new American president, Lyndon Johnson, Defense Secretary Robert S. McNamara was holding a press conference. He told reporters that he was 'optimistic as to the progress that had been made and could be made during the coming year' in the fight against the Vietcong. He was duly reported to an anxious world on that night's television and in the next day's newspapers.

Landing at Andrews Air Force Base outside Washington the next day, McNamara told another press conference that 'we have every reason to believe that [US military plans for 1964] will be successful'. Then he disappeared into a helicopter for the White House lawn and a one-on-one session with the President in the Oval Office. Also duly reported.

For seven and a half years, there was no report of the conversation that then took place between McNamara and President Johnson. Not until July 1971, and then only after the Nixon administration took the *New York Times* and the *Washington Post* all the way to the Supreme Court in a vain effort to keep them from publishing the so-called Pentagon papers, did we hear what McNamara really thought. Buried in those Pentagon papers (which so few people ever read) lay the revelation that McNamara had told President Johnson exactly the opposite of what he had told the press and, through us, the world. The Secretary of Defense returned from Vietnam 'laden with gloom', according to documents in the Pentagon papers. 'Vietcong progress had been great,' he reported to the President, 'with my best guess being that the situation has in fact been deteriorating to a far greater extent than we realized. The situation is very disturbing.'

Think for a minute how history could have changed if those comments had been made at Tan Son Nhut Airport, if those lies had gone unspoken at Andrews Air Force Base. Wonder where the true national security lay – in publishing the truth, in publishing lies, or in silence. Reflect for a minute on one of the eternal verities of our profession – insufficiently understood by us or by our readers – that the truth, the whole truth, emerges over time and that is the way it is supposed to be, as Walter Lippmann pointed out more than sixty years ago. The first crack out of the box, we don't get it all for lots of reasons, including the fact that people occasionally lie. It can take a long time to get it all – and get it right.

Now jump ahead some eight months to August 1964 – still more than twenty years ago – to an issue of the *Time* magazine of that month.

> Through the darkness, from the west and south, the intruders boldly sped. There were at least six of them, Russian-designed 'swatow' gunboats armed with 37-millimeter and 28-millimeter guns, and P-4s.
>
> At 9.52 they opened fire on the destroyers with automatic weapons, and this time from as close as 2,000 yards. The night glowed eerily with the nightmarish glare of air-dropped flares and boats' searchlights. Two of the enemy boats went down.

That is the kind of vivid detail that the news magazines have made famous. I do not mean to single out *Time*. On the same date, *Life* said almost the same thing and that week's issue of *Newsweek* has torpedoes whipping by US ships, blazing out salvo after salvo of shells. It had a PT boat bursting into flames and sinking. It had mountainous seas and swirling rains and everything that your English teacher loves to read.

Only one trouble. There was no battle. There was not a single intruder, never mind six of them. Never mind Russian-designed swatow gunboats armed with 37-millimetre and 28-millimetre guns. They never opened fire. They never sank. They never fired torpedoes. They never were.

It has taken twenty years for this truth to emerge. My authority is Admiral James Stockdale, who has written a fascinating book, *In Love and War*. Jim Stockdale was shot down over Vietnam a few days later and was a prisoner of the North Vietnamese for more than seven years. But on the night in question he was in a Saber jet fighter flying cover over the USS Maddox and Turner Joy. He scoured the seas for more than two hours and he is as sure as man can be that they were fighting phantom flips on a radar screen.

In case the Vietnam years have blurred in your minds, or even disappeared from your screens, may I remind you that this so-called Battle of Tonkin Gulf was the sole basis of the Tonkin Gulf resolution, which was the entire justification for the United States war against Vietnam. This non-event happened on 4 August. President Johnson went on television that very night to ask the country to support a Congressional resolution. The resolution went to Congress the next day. Two days later it was approved unanimously by the House and 88-2 by the Senate. The 'facts' behind this critically important resolution were quite simply wrong. Misinformation? Disinformation? Deceit? Whatever! Lies.

Reflect again how history could have changed if the Congress – and, more importantly, the people – of the United States had known that there was no Battle of Tonkin Gulf on 4 August 1964 and think once more of how long it took that truth to emerge.

The case of Ronald Pelton, the National Security Administration spy, is different in dimension and import, because the lies are more in the eye of the beholder than in any provable fact.[1] The most interesting aspect of the Pelton case is the fact that the top US intelligence officials were declaring information to be 'a matter of vital national security' when the Russians already knew it. In all my time in this wonderful business, I had never run into that anomaly before. I think the claim of national security is not true. I think it is alleged only to prevent government embarrassment. I think the true national interest is served by publication.

Some time in the late summer of 1985, the reporter Bob

---

1 Ronald Pelton was a former National Security Administration cryptographer, who in 1980 sold Soviet KGB agents in Washington information that US Navy submarines were successfully tapping the main Soviet communications cable on the bed of the Sea of Okhotsk between the missile submarine base at Petropavlovsk and the Pacific Fleet headquarters at Vladivostock. In 1985 he was arrested, following the defection of the senior KGB officer, Vitaly Yurchenko, and the following year was given three consecutive life sentences, plus ten years.

Woodward came into my office, closed the door and, almost in a whisper, laid out details of an American intelligence capability that blew my mind: the ability to intercept the most vital Soviet military communications being sent by underwater cable. He knew the capability and its importance. He knew the gadgetry, but he believed it to be ongoing. It was not, as we discovered later.

There never was the slightest question of publishing this story. We could identify no reasonable public right to know. In fact, we all agreed we had no such right and felt entirely uncomfortable with our knowledge. At the time – as more or less always in Washington – the President and the defence establishment were berating the press for publishing national security information with reckless disregard for the country's safety, even though most national security losses were self-inflicted by spies and zealots.

We even discussed trying to get an appointment with the President to inform him of our information and our concern. We scrapped the idea on the grounds that it would appear to be self-serving and grandstanding.

About that time I did run into the National Security Adviser, Vice-Admiral John Poindexter, at a dinner party and asked him for an appointment to discuss the same subject. We did meet and he suggested I talk to Lieutenant-General William Odom, the head of the National Security Agency. General Odom and I first met at his downtown Washington office in the shadow of the Executive Office Building on 5 December 1985. We told the NSA chief the detailed information we had, information we said that the Russians now had as a result of Pelton's treason. We said we felt extremely uncomfortable with this information, but we had it and the Russians had it. We asked why it should be kept from the American people.

General Odom shook his head in dismay. He said the information was still extremely sensitive. We did not know exactly what the Russians knew, he said. It was hoped, he said, that Pelton would plead guilty, avoiding any public discussion of the evidence against him. He looked us in the eye and told us that any story about this would gravely threaten the national security of the United States. We were to hear that claim many, many times in the next five months, as we tried to frame a story that would tell the American people what the Russians already knew – and only what the Russians already knew. We were determined not to violate the legitimate security of the nation, but we were equally determined not to be browbeaten by the administration, which has from time to time appeared to relish press-bashing, into not publishing something that our enemies already knew.

The weapons of any administration in this kind of a battle are formidable: presidents, admirals, generals, CIA directors, all telling you that publication would endanger the nation and the lives of some of its service personnel, and ultimately threatening to prosecute you for violating the law. These are red lights that a newspaper goes through only with a deliberate lack of speed.

From the first session with General Odom on 5 December to a final session with CIA Director Casey in the bar of the University Club on Friday afternoon, 2 May, the issue was joined. There were at least three meetings between Odom and one or more editors of the *Washington Post*. At least four meetings with Casey, one with Poindexter, one with FBI Director William Webster. (One afternoon Webster and Casey asked to see me urgently and walked through the city room into my office surrounded by bodyguards, while more than 150 reporters and editors watched in astonishment. The subject he wanted to raise was national security, but the area was Central America, not the Soviet Union.)

At each of these meetings, different versions of the Pelton story were discussed with the government officials. At various times, different versions of a written story were shown to them, something my newspaper rarely does in advance of publication. Each time, the officials invoked national security. Each time, the editors felt that national security was not involved, but were not one thousand per cent convinced that the Soviets knew every single detail of the *Post*'s story, and publication was delayed. At one time President Reagan, just back from the Japan Summit, called Katharine Graham, chairman of the board of The Washington Post Company, to impress upon her his views that publication of the

Post's story would endanger national security. How I would have loved to have listened in to that conversation.

That was the last red light. The *Post* withheld the story one more time and started working immediately on a new version that removed all the 'wiring diagram' details of the intelligence system. As a courtesy to the President, in the light of his call to Mrs Graham, the White House press secretary, Larry Speakes, was informed on Tuesday night, 27 May, that the *Post* was going to run its story with the wiring diagram details the next day, unread by any government official. It appeared the next morning under the bylines of Bob Woodward and Patrick Tyler.

Casey responded that day by saying that the CIA was studying the story to see whether it should be referred to the Justice Department for prosecution. And there the matter lay, until a few days later. In the middle of the Pelton trial, Casey and Odom issued a joint statement, warning the press against speculating about the Pelton evidence and, implicitly, threatening prosecution if it did. Warnings against speculation are the fabric of a *Pravda* editor's life. They are anathema in a free society and they were greeted as such by the American press on this occasion.

Pelton was convicted in early June, after seven days of testimony in a Baltimore courtroom, where the government laid out more information in a public forum about its most secret intelligence-gathering capabilities than at any time since the Second World War.

(Some of the testimony produced information that was not in the original *Post* article.)

The role of a newspaper in a free society is what is at issue here. Governments prefer a press that makes their job easier, a press that allows them to proceed with minimum public accountability, a press that accepts their version of events with minimum questioning, a press that can be led to the greenest pastures by persuasion and manipulation. In moments of stress between government and the press – and these moments have come and gone since Thomas Jefferson – the government looks for ways to control the press, to eliminate or to minimise the press as an obstacle in the implementation of policy, or the solution of problems. In these moments, especially, the press must continue its mission of publishing information that it – and it alone – determines to be in the public interest, in a useful, timely and responsible manner, serving society, not government.

That brings me to whatever history decides to call what is going on in Washington right now. Although the *Washington Post* has done landmark reporting in this case, we do not know what happened. We came to a dead end in our reporting whenever we got to those numbered bank accounts in Switzerland. It will take the power of subpoena to blast them loose and, without them, the truth will take forever to emerge. What we do know now is that almost everyone involved to date has lied, dissembled or taken the Fifth Amendment. I think it serves history to list some of these lies.

On 1 November 1985, President Reagan told reporters that there was 'no foundation' to reports from Beirut that former National Security Adviser Robert C. McFarlane had secretly flown to Tehran on a plane carrying American arms. This was a lie.

One week later, the President said: 'the charge has been made that the United States has shipped weapons to Iran as ransom payment for the release of American hostages in Lebanon . . . those charges are utterly false.' This was a lie.

Six days later, the President said: 'everything that we sold them could be put in one cargo plane and there would be plenty of room left over.' This was a lie.

In the meantime, the President told the world that no third nation was involved in any shipment of arms that might have taken place. Another lie.

Before they were silenced by their attorneys, Admiral Poindexter and Lieutenant-Colonel Oliver North took similar liberties with the truth. The cost of these lies will be borne by us all. The last national poll taken by the *Washington Post* earlier this month shows that 65 per cent of Americans believe that the President is lying about the Iran–Contra affair, an increase of 16 percentage points in less than four weeks. (The public is apparently less upset than I am about the price democracy pays when its leaders lie, for the same poll showed that 66 per cent of Americans thought President Reagan was honest.)

It feels to me – as the eminent American baseball player Yogi Berra put it so well – that it's '*déjà vu* all over again'. It reminds me of Richard Nixon looking the world in its television eye and saying he was unable to tell us about Watergate because it involved matters of national security. (My personal all-time favourite lie!) If the truth does in fact set man free – as the Bible attests – then man is enslaved by silence.

Denis Forman

How many miles to Babylon?

1988

Chairman of Granada Television from 1974 to 1987 and Deputy Chairman of the Granada Group from 1984 to 1990, Sir Denis Forman has been one of the leading figures in the independent television industry. His 1988 Cameron Lecture was given at a time when the Conservative government led by Margaret Thatcher was working on what became the 1990 Broadcasting Act, the avowed purpose of which was to bring market forces to bear on that industry and to break up the 'cosy duopoly' of the BBC and ITV companies.

WHEN I WAS asked if I would deliver the second James Cameron Memorial Lecture I instantly agreed, out of affection and nostalgia for that name. More sober thoughts were to follow. I picked up James's books one by one and began to realise the impossibility of doing justice to the master.

'Master' is no cliché in this context. I know of no journalist of our generation who came within a mile of Jimmy for elegance, wit, penetration and speed. In particular, I know no one who could pick up the phone in a bar in Patagonia or Ulan Bator, a bar that had yielded up a good part of its stock during the course of the evening, get through to the copy desk and reel off, with no apparent effort, a story which in the *Guardian* the next day would read like an essay that had been polished and re-polished in the quiet of a Hampstead study. So I came to the conclusion that I must abandon the lecture form, in which my performance must fall so lamentably short of his standards. Instead I would tell you of a strange experience that recently befell me, and which may not be altogether irrelevant to the world he and I inhabited together, nor to the present discontents of those of us who work in the media today.

This experience was due to Elmer Rice. In 1930 he wrote a now forgotten book about the golden age of the silent movies. In the book, *A Voyage to Purilia*, the author was transported by magic into the land of the silent film where, like a man from Mars on Earth, he observed the customs and mores of the inhabitants. As he moved around Purilia he found young girls tied to railway tracks all over the place, policemen who tripped over their feet and fell into barrels of whitewash, highways clogged by strings of vehicles pursuing each other and so on. Over the whole scene presided the Presence – a voice from the sky – explaining in authentic subtitle style the nature of what was going on.

Let me take you to join Elmer Rice in Purilia for a few moments. He was about to sit down to supper in a simple farmhouse kitchen. A jovial-faced fellow in overalls approached the table, stumbled over a rug and lurched against the sideboard, dislodging a plate which fell upon his head and broke into a dozen fragments. None the worse for that, he took his place briskly at the table and tied an enormous napkin under his chin as the Presence remarked: 'Jim Sloan, the hired man, never ate peas for fear of cutting his mouth.' Also at the table were a beautiful young girl and her mother. These were members of two of the distinctive castes of Purilian society. The mother was an Umbilican, the most venerated of the social classes. These were sweet-faced gentlewomen, with soft white hair parted in the middle, wearing simple black dresses and a shawl thrown over their shoulders. The other belonged to the Pudencian class of young and beautiful girls, whose essential distinguishing characteristic was virginity. Rice explains that maternity in Purilia is in no sense a biological function. Both virginity and maternity were metaphysical states, with no progression from one to the other. 'It would be sacrilege to suggest a Pudencian was capable of maternity or that an Umbilician, in achieving maternity, surrendered her virginity.'

And so his voyage went on. He became locked into a major plot (one of a thousand going on around him) and gradually grew accustomed to the realities of Purilian life. I do not dwell upon

Purilia for its own sake. I do so because of what it did to me. Recently I re-read the book and one night, after laying it aside, I found myself transported, not into the silent movies of sixty years ago, but into a familiar yet strange land of today. The first thing I noticed as I drove into London was the surprisingly large number of houses with acrid smoke pouring out of the ground-floor windows, which the Presence informed me was caused by the low combustion level of rubber foam furniture, a fact confirmed by several fire chiefs who appeared in front of me by magic, urging a ban on all such material. Then almost every street I passed seemed to have suffered a recent bomb explosion or a burst water main. I quickly gained the impression that the main characteristic of this strange country, which I discovered to be named Mediana, was its lack of normality. Trains, for instance, had usually either run into the buffers or broken some speed record; aeroplanes were likely to have hijackers aboard, a defective undercarriage or were lying in little pieces on the ground; and boats were commonly either sinking or showing the scars of recent aerial bombardment.

Everyday life, too, seemed to have its eccentric twists. Births were commonly multiple, anything over three at a time being the most common. Single births tended to be many weeks and sometimes months premature, or else the result of some monkey business with test tubes or borrowed ovaries. Most babies in Mediana appeared to spend the first few weeks of their lives in oxygen tents. In an effort to discover how the ordinary citizen viewed this gloomy scene, I entered several private houses in the suburbs and dormitory areas only to find the householders, usually a married couple, on the verge of tears. In nearly every case, a baby had been abducted, a child had gone missing, or a relative was being held hostage.

I also discovered that the common illnesses of Mediana were not the flu, arthritis or bronchitis, but appeared to be AIDS, radiation sickness, or the critical malfunction of those parts of the body which required the extraction of an organ from a dead person and its insertion into a live one. The human kidney, when defective, appeared to occupy a great deal of attention. It was, however, puzzling to know how all these medically interesting patients were cared for, because every hospital ward appeared to have been just closed down and doctors and surgeons were seldom seen at work, but spent all their time talking to us about shortages of money and nursing staff.

Determined to escape from this scene of doom and despondency, which I learnt was called New Storia, I drove several hundred miles to a city, which was much talked about, named Soapstown. Here were a number of tight-knit communities, one populated by sturdy northern characters, who were inclined to utter phrases no longer much used elsewhere such as 'Jam Butty' and 'Ecky Thump'. Another was made up of a colony of Cockneys, although in some cases their cockney accents barely disguised their upper-class origins. Both of these communities had certain traits in common: they appeared to live their lives in only three sites, their own homes, their places of work and the public house; they never appeared to go more than a mile from this basic triangle and, although sometimes it was alleged that one of them had gone to Majorca or Paris, there was never any evidence that this was actually so. Their overriding characteristic was a passionate interest in each other's personal affairs. 'Did you hear that our Joan has got her cards now the boss has taken up with your Lily' is the sort of greeting a citizen generally received on entering the pub. Serious crime was rare, but the incidence of minor deceits and infidelities which caused suspicion, rumour, separations, reunions and domestic crises was high. Indeed, they made up the whole of life. I found the activities of Soaptowners quite fascinating.

As I journeyed on through Mediana, I encountered briefly the region of Teledrama where the inhabitants appeared to live their lives in cycles, starting as a humdrum family or business group and, during an hour or ninety minutes, becoming enmeshed in crime, espionage, drug running or in sexual encounters of a complex nature. As each cycle gathered pace, the visages of the participants became gaunt with worry, fear or jealousy and the cycle generally ended with an orgasm of emotional *Sturm und Drang*, often involving murder. The survivors, however, and even the resurrected corpses, would cheerfully regroup, assume different personas and embark on another cycle, never seeming to have learnt a single thing from their previous experiences. Nevertheless, again I found Teledrama an exciting and stimulating place.

I also passed through the animal kingdom of Safariland, where pretty well every creature was tearing another one to pieces, through the Juvenile Territories in which all adults seemed to wear an ingratiating smile and speak in words of one syllable in a sing-song voice, and next Grandstandland, where in every direction people were feverishly playing all manner of games, very large persons indulging in wrestling and darts, and very small ones turning cartwheels on canvas mats to the strains of Ravel's *Bolero*, with a resident Presence giving an hysterical account of all these doings in a voice often so highly pitched as to indicate that ritual castration was a requirement of his profession.

By now my journey was gathering speed, because I could descry in the blue distance the great mountain ranges above the plains of Mediana where lived the Mediamen themselves. This was the master race with the power to control all that I had seen. They plotted the course of affairs for months ahead, for instance, in Soapstown but, if they so wished, they could wipe out a whole community in an instant. (Indeed, this had just happened to a popular roadhouse I had visited, perhaps because so many visitors dropped in for a chat without making use of, or paying for, any of the services offered by the establishment.)[1] The Mediamen's city lay at the summit of a mountain range and their offices were housed in large irregular structures, which looked as if they had been built by termites. In the public part of the city stood the largest edifice of all, whilst in the private part were fourteen or fifteen piles of varying sizes. Between the artists' quarter and the slums were the huts and caravans of a newly arrived type of Mediaman, known as the Independent Adventurers.

I called first at the huge offices of the Public Service Mediamen, the IEC (the Inform and Educate Corporation), and was very civilly received. It was immediately clear on reaching the upper floors, however, that the community was in a state of consternation. Men, and more occasionally women, burst through doors, their arms full of files, their brows furrowed, talking in emotional tones: 'If he insists on moving the weather forecast to 2.30,' I heard one say to another, 'we shall all resign.' Small groups in earnest conversation dispersed with furtive looks as I approached and everyone listened somewhat apprehensively to the voice of the Tannoy, which from time to time would enjoin one string of initials, which I took to be a person, to be in touch with another.

---

1 The long-running ITV soap opera *Crossroads* was axed in 1987. It was revived by Carlton TV fourteen years later.

My host, an apparently cheerful elderly fellow, was accompanied by a silent young man, who sat behind him. Both were apparently oblivious to the mood of their colleagues and they began by quizzing me about my journey through Mediana, showing an interest only in those activities controlled by their own organisation – the Public Service. Here I was at something of a loss, for I had been unable to distinguish between public and privately controlled activities in what I had seen in, for instance, Soapstown and the Newstoria Region. But I told them that I was enormously impressed by the vigour, variety and efficiency of all the activities I had witnessed.

Thus, after a general exchange, it was possible for me to ask my hosts why the building appeared to be in a state of ferment. 'Ferment?' he said. 'Oh, no. The IEC is changing course, it is true, and that gives rise to a good deal of discussion, but it is a change for the better. We are all tremendously enthusiastic about being a leaner, tighter, more efficient organisation. That is what all the excitement is about. Look,' he said, waving an arm to the window, 'there is a symbol of the new IEC.' I looked out and saw on one side of a courtyard some ragged workmen chucking a lorry load of worn-out abacuses on to a bonfire, while opposite there were a number of white-suited operatives erecting a gigantic VDU. 'On that screen', he said, 'it will be possible to punch up instantly the hourly productivity of any one of our 50,000 employees, the cost against budget of any of our activities, the wind strength in the central Pacific and the exchange rate of the yen. Everywhere we are cutting costs and installing modern business methods.' But then, as he proceeded to tell me about the wonders of the Marketing Department, his voice began to falter and he slowed to a stop. He had become deadly pale and I offered him a swig from a flask of brandy, which I had about my person. He drained it in a gulp and, putting his head in his hands, he burst into tears. 'You look like a kindly, trustworthy person,' he said between sobs. 'I will tell you all. I am an elderly broadcaster, one of the old guard. They have given me this temporary Public Relations job, but the Department for the Disposal of Aged Broadcasters is on my tail day and night. They will get me sooner or later.' I expressed my sympathy and gently asked him to tell me the whole of his story.

Little by little the full picture was revealed. It appeared that there was an authority superior even to that of the Mediamen, which resided in the capital on the summit of the highest mountain in the land. This power went under many names – Parliament, Government, the Administration, the Cabinet – but my new friend, for some unknown reason, referred to it as 'Her'. In ancient days, the Superpower had acknowledged the sovereignty of the Mediamen over Mediana, requiring only a degree of consultation on the appointment of the Council of Elders and holding in reserve certain powers that were never used. So things had gone along happily enough and the Mediamen, in those days known as

Broadcasters, had formed a sort of club or masonic circle, whose purpose was to ensure that all the activities in Mediana were designed to reflect their own image and, thereby, to nurture a better, more civilised and more cultured society. But, since the Golden Age of Broadcasting, two things had happened. A new class of Broadcaster had sprung up, who had introduced into Mediana the idea of Pleasure and who also took a keen interest in the revenues from the sale of products to interested parties. Yet this had not proved to be any lasting disaster. The Public Mediamen found some virtue in the Pleasure principle and had adopted it in quite a large measure; and the privateers had come to accept many of the values of the IEC.

But worse was to follow. The Superpower began to show signs of wishing to diminish the sovereignty of the Public Broadcasters. There were two main reasons for this, he explained. First, it had traditionally been accepted that the Broadcasters were free, nay even in duty bound, to offer, without fear or favour, a running critique of the Superpower's performance in the business of government. But gradually the Superpower had become impatient of criticism and now required unquestioned support for all their policies all of the time, interspersed with frequent flattery and, at least twice a year, a sustained bout of adulation. At first the Broadcasters had resented this loss of freedom and had continued stubbornly on their customary course. In the face of impending conflict, they became a little rattled and made a sufficient number of operational errors to give the Superpower a sufficient reason to move in to set things right. This they did by packing the Council of Elders with their own agents, disposing of the paramount leader and imposing a new ideology.[2] This involved an entirely alien and harsh economic regime for Mediana. 'Terrible things,' said my friend, 'are now happening. Yesterday,' he sobbed, 'the Enterprise Department sold the Holy Grail of Broadcasting to the Japanese for half a million dollars – the Holy Grail, which has stood in the boardroom since broadcasting began.'

I listened to this recital with some surprise and, while my friend blew his nose and wiped his eyes, I asked whether some of these changes might not be to the benefit of Mediana. Was it not possible that the Old Broadcasters were something in the nature of cultural zealots, who wished to impose their ideology on Mediana just as he alleged the Superpower did today? I had heard him use a phrase 'The Brute Force of Monopoly', which had grated somewhat upon my ears. He drew himself up and replied: 'No. It was and is the prime duty of Public Broadcasters to elevate public taste and

2   Alasdair Milne, Director-General of the BBC from 1982 to 1987, had several passages of arms with Margaret Thatcher's government, especially over the BBC's coverage of Northern Ireland. He never established good relations with the new chairman of the BBC Board of Governors Marmaduke Hussey, appointed by the government in 1986. Milne resigned in January 1987 'for personal reasons'.

awareness, to educate, inform and entertain them.' 'Then,' said I, 'was it not perfectly natural for any Superpower to require a subject state such as Mediana to show loyalty and support for its policies?' Again he assumed a Napoleonic pose and replied that indeed there were many examples of a Superpower using the media in its support, but these were mainly to be found in dictatorships such as had existed in a place called Europe before the Second World War and today in an Eastern bloc. Many aspects of these governments, including control of the Media, were, he said, generally thought by civilised persons to be abhorrent.

I thanked him for his frankness and asked if I should now go and talk with the Private Sector. He was discouraging. 'They are all at sixes and sevens over there,' he said. 'They are busy trying to repel the Independents and at the same time the Superpower is putting the whole of their present system under review. They are in confusion. They have no coherent view and there is a split between those who are in Satellites and those who are not.'

'Satellites,' I said, 'what are they?' He groaned. 'As if we hadn't enough on our plate,' he said. 'The Superpower is going to start up a whole new range of Media activities in the sky and also under the earth. Some of the skymen will be foreign,' he said sourly. 'Not from our Mediana at all and likely to be common.'

'I have a final question,' I said. 'What about all that admirable activity I saw in Mediana? How will that be affected by all the problems you have described to me?' 'Oh, that will go on pretty much the same for a while,' he said. 'We can't give much attention to it at the moment.' 'But surely,' I said, 'the activities of Mediana must be of interest to the Superpower?' 'They couldn't care less,' he said. 'So long as there is plenty of political support and we toe the new economic line, they're happy. They like us to keep in a bit of sex and violence, because they think it's a vote winner for them to oppose it.' I could see he was a soured man and, inwardly, I was determined to discover for myself what indeed was the true attitude of the Superpower.

As I got up to leave, a message flashed up on the VDU between us. It read: 'Would ADG PR2 please report to ADG DOB1. I could see the blood drain from his cheeks and, as he tottered towards the door, I feared for him. The quiet young man in the corner now put his hand on my arm. 'Don't pay too much attention to him,' he said. 'He's one of yesterday's men. Come with me and I will show you what you should see.'

We took the lift to a lower floor and instantly I was aware of a changed atmosphere. Busy groups of people were debating in conference rooms, walking in and out of each other's offices, moving purposefully about the corridors, talking and arguing in an eager and good-humoured way. I asked him who these people were. 'These are the Creative Classes,' he said, 'the people who actually create and control everything that goes on in Mediana.

First, they deal in written predestination – it's called scripting – and then their scripts are brought to life'. I asked him if there were creative groups with the same dynamic energy in the Private Sector. 'Indeed there are,' he said, 'and amongst the Independents too. Collectively it is the Creative Class that has made our Mediana the prosperous and happy place it is. It is generally recognized,' he said, with the hint of a complacent smile, 'as the best and most successful media country in the world. It is the envy of the universe.' 'Good gracious,' I said, 'what a contrast with the mood upstairs. How does the management stand in these matters? Will they ensure that the Creative Classes are allowed to continue to thrive?' 'For a time,' he said, 'The management of all the media groups will do the best they can. But they may lose the will to support the Creative Classes or, indeed, they may not be allowed to retain sufficient resources to do so. Their problem lies with the Superpower.' 'But surely,' I replied, 'the Superpower must be delighted by the success of the Creative Classes.'

He looked at me quizzically. 'Not so,' he said. 'The Superpower is not pleased. Not pleased at all.' 'But why on earth not?' I said. 'Because,' he replied, 'Mediana does not conform.' 'Conform to what?' I asked. 'To their religion,' he said. 'Come with me and all will become clear.'

As we left the building, he explained to me that the land through which I had travelled and which had impressed me so much was only one part of Mediana, Mediana TV, and that there were two adjacent provinces, Mediana Sound and Mediana Print. We would fly over these two territories. Indeed. before long. we were airborne over all the kingdom of Mediana Sound. I learned that Mediana Sound was, if anything, in a greater state of chaos than Mediana TV. At one time, apparently, the province of Sound, which was the oldest part of Mediana, was run on the traditional public service lines, but now the Superpower was making it conform to the new religion. He explained that central to this religion was the holy concept of competition in the market place. The Superpower's belief in this was absolute and brooked no exceptions. Mediana Sound, which had for centuries been administered by two landlords, both agents of previous Superpowers, would now be put up to tender in small lots for a large number of would-be landlords to bid against each other. There would be eager competition for the choicer parcels of Sound land. 'But will that improve things?' I asked. He looked at me quizzically. 'We must wait and see,' he replied.

By now we had crossed the frontier between Mediana Sound and Mediana Print and my companion pointed out that this country was sharply divided between a populous plain teeming with workaday life and a high plateau where the upper classes resided. The plain, he said, was known as T&B land. I asked him to explain these initials and he blushed modestly, saying only that the initials referred to certain protuberances on the female form. Few young females in that part wore many clothes above the waist, and the men, if their torsos were well enough developed, had a tendency to walk around in jockstraps.

When I expressed my astonishment and said that I had seen no evidence of such licence in Mediana TV, he only smiled and bade me observe the well-clad and sober figures on the Plateau. These were quality citizens, he explained, not numerous, but wealthy and loyally supportive of that small part of Mediana Print that was not T&B. I asked about the Superpower's policy on ownership here and he replied that it was much more relaxed. Even before the advent of the new Superpower, the competitive principle had been widely accepted. 'So', said I, 'there will be a very large number of landlords each owning a small parcel of Print.'

'Well, not exactly,' he said. 'Recently one or two rather thrusting landlords, some of them from abroad, have bought up huge estates. One in particular has become such a dominant figure that the name of the capital city has been changed to Rupertsville in his honour.[3] He owns large properties both in T&B land and on the Plateau. 'Why, then, does the Superpower acquiesce in monopolistic ownership in Print, while striving to abolish it in TV and Sound?' I asked. 'There are several reasons,' he replied. 'First, the

3 A reference to Rupert Murdoch, whose News International Group owns the *Sun*, the *News of the World*, *The Times* and the *Sunday Times* and who became a political supporter of Margaret Thatcher after she was chosen as Conservative Party leader in 1975.

major Print landlords hold their monopoly by means of an understanding with the Superpower that they will give it unquestioning
political support at all times. This is of great value to the Power,
because the rest of Mediana, including some of the smaller
landlords in Print, has not yet learnt the advantages of behaving in
this manner. Second, the Print landlords have blazed the trail of
reform in working methods, which has greatly improved their
position in the market place. They have made millions redundant.'
(I noticed that my companion appeared to cross himself whenever
he mentioned what he regarded as a holy word, but the movement
he made was nearer to the sign of the dollar than to that of the
cross.) 'Third, there is no nonsense about public service in Print. Its
ethic is pure and unalloyed commercialism, particularly in T&B
land, and this, of course, accords with the Superpower's highest
principles.' 'This raises several questions,' I began, but he laid his
hand on my sleeve, saying: 'My friend, I think it would be advisable
for you to ask any further questions of someone in real authority
in the capital city. Pilot, to Babylon please!'

I asked him why the capital was so named. 'Our capital was
recently renamed in honour of the city which marked mankind's
discovery of the virtues of the market place,' he said. 'Babylon
stands for the beginnings of civilisation, namely the dawn of
economic competition.'

Soon we alighted at a private airport, transferred to a limousine and drove through a city where the older buildings seemed ill cared for and crumbling, but amongst them bright new cubes of glass and steel sprang up towards the sky. We drove past the State Art Gallery and the National Cathedral, both desperately in need of repair, and drew up in front of an exceptionally large cube of shining glass. We alighted and were ushered into a large office of which the walls, the ceiling, the floor and all the fittings were made of steel. Behind the steel desk sat a middle-aged, well-dressed man, unremarkable in any respect except for his eyes, whose gaze, through steel spectacles, transfixed me as soon as I passed through the door. He waved us to a seat.

I introduced myself and asked him what role, evidently an eminent one, he played in Babylonian affairs. 'In Babylon, Public Relations is a security matter. My identity is of no importance,' he replied. 'You wish to ask me some questions?' 'Sir,' I said, 'as a lifelong practitioner in another place, I would like to congratulate you on the excellence of your Mediana TV and to ask you about your plans for its future. I was deeply impressed by the activities I saw in Mediana itself and even more so by the enthusiasm and quality of the Creative Classes in Media City. I am sure you will want to make certain that this great enterprise . . .' 'You must understand,' he interrupted, 'that the activities you see on the screen are not important. What is important is that for many years the Mediamen have been acting wrongly. They have been uncompetitive, uncommercial, they have provided a last refuge for evil labour practices. Their methods are not cost-effective and their productivity index measured against Print is low.'

'I am sure you are right,' I said, 'and your new measures will greatly improve all these faults, but is there not a danger that, with the introduction of so many new activities, so much new technology and so much more competition, there will not be enough resources to go round and that the present Creative Classes will be unable to sustain the wonderful range of activity in Mediana that goes on today? Might it not be that, as in the region of Print, T&B, which is cheap and often used as an effective agent of commercialism, will move in?' 'T&B is appreciated by the man in the pub,' he replied. 'We do not discourage it. But we will not allow Pornography of any kind whatsoever. We want complete deregulation and complete freedom for any kind of activity that is not Pornography and does not subvert the security of the state, which means, of course, the security of the Superpower. You should know that the expression of any view critical of the Superpower is now a serious infringement of our new Official Security Act.'[4]

'But supposing that activity in Mediana becomes less interesting, less varied, more boring, more commonplace than it is today,' I said, 'would that not worry you at all? Surely there are other values

4   A reference to what became the new Official Secrets Act 1989.

in life as well as efficiency? No one would think of privatising the State Art Gallery, for instance, or the National Church. They offer values that are not dependent upon the market place.' 'The State Art Gallery,' he said, rummaging in a drawer and throwing a brochure down in front of me, 'is about to be dealt with. Look at that. Next year a competitive gallery will be set up on an adjacent site.' (A glance at the brochure showed that over the entrance to the new gallery a huge screen would display animated examples of great masterpieces. I saw that in Piero Della Francesca's *Baptism of Christ* real water would drip from the bowl held on high by St John and a live dove would flutter over the head of the Saviour.) 'The year after,' he said, 'we will privatise the State Gallery. It will be sink or swim.' 'How do you mean, sink or swim?' I asked. 'If the State Gallery goes down, it will have to sell off its assets,' he replied. 'You mean the pictures, the National Collection?' I asked. He nodded.

'But the whole point of a State Gallery is surely to acquire and show pictures . . .' Again he interrupted me. 'The National Church,' he said, 'will be privatised in 1994. We will start by floating off the Church Commissioners one year before that. They have property assets worth more than £500 billion. There should be no problem in arranging a flotation. The Church of Rome – a little more difficult. We are presently negotiating with the Vatican to make it a wholly owned subsidiary of our International Communications company, or we may float it off independently on the USM. We are determined to improve Rome's competitive position in relation to the National Church. The smaller churches – Quakers, nonconformists, chapel and all of those – will each be privatised locally. Like the buses.

He appeared to regard the interview at an end but, making a superhuman effort to keep hold of my sanity, I asked if I might be allowed one final question. He looked at his watch and nodded. 'I am deeply impressed by your dedication to your principles,' I said, 'but they do, after all, apply to the means of doing something. Competition and efficiency cannot be ends: what is your ultimate purpose? What sort of lives do you, the Superpower, want your citizens to enjoy? Plato told us to seek goodness and beauty. Bentham believed in the greatest good of the greatest number. Christ said we should love our neighbour. When your citizens are all fully efficient and competitive, when they have reached that perfect state, what values will you seek for them then?'

He gazed at me sternly for a few moments and then slowly said: 'There are some questions the mere posing of which is an act of impiety.' At that, the light began to fade, the spokesperson, the steel office and the city of Babylon itself dissolved into mist and I knew that my journey was over.

Louis Blom-Cooper

The right to be let alone

1989

Louis Blom-Cooper is a distinguished lawyer and public servant who has served on innumerable commissions and inquiries; he became a QC in 1970 and was knighted in 1992. He served as chairman of the Press Council from 1989 to 1990, during the last days of that body: with the newspaper industry on notice that it was 'drinking in the Last Chance Saloon', he had been brought in to make self-regulation publicly credible. In 1990, the Press Council was disbanded and suceeded by the Press Complaints Commission.

T HE PRESS IS overstepping in every direction the obvious bounds of propriety and decency. Gossip is no longer the resource of the idle and of the vicious, but has become a trade, which is pursued with industry as well as effrontery. To satisfy a prurient taste, the details of sexual relations are broadcast in the columns of the daily papers. To occupy the indolent, column upon column is filled with idle gossip, which can only be procured by intrusion upon the domestic circle. The intensity and complexity of life, attendant upon advancing civilisation, have rendered necessary some retreat from the world, and man, under the refining influence of culture, has become more sensitive to publicity, so that solitude and privacy have become more essential to the individual; but modern enterprise and invention have, through invasions upon his privacy, subjected him to mental pain and distress, far greater than could be influenced by mere bodily injury.

Nor is the harm wrought by mere invasions confined to the suffering of those who may be the subjects of journalistic or other enterprise. In this, as in the other branches of commerce, the supply creates the demand. Each crop of unseemly gossip, thus harvested, becomes the seed of more, and in direct proportion to its circulation results in a lowering of social standards and of morality. Even gossip apparently harmless, when widely and persistently circulated, is potent for evil. It both belittles and perverts. It belittles by inverting the relative importance of things, thus dwarfing the thoughts and aspirations of people. When personal gossip attains the dignity of print, and crowds the space available for matters of real interest to the community, what wonder that the ignorant and thoughtless mistake its relative importance. Easy of comprehension, appealing to that weak side of human nature which is never wholly cast down by the misfortunes and frailties of our neighbours, no one can be surprised that it usurps the place of interest in brains capable of other things. Triviality destroys at once robustness of thought and delicacy of feeling. No enthusiasm can flourish, no generous impulse can survive under its blighting influence.

Those are not my words, although they reflect, with an elegance of language – if somewhat redolent of the Victorian age – that I could not emulate, what is a generally held public perception of some sections of the press in Britain today. The words, in fact written in 1890, were the prolegomenon to the most seminal article in a legal periodical. They were prompted by the experience of two graduates of the Harvard Law School at the nuptials of one of them. Samuel D. Warren later became a professor of law at that renowned academic institution, and Louis D. Brandeis a Justice of the Supreme Court of the United States. They were arguing that the common law of England was available and ripe for development in establishing a cause of action for invasion of privacy.

Stimulated by the Warren/Brandeis article, the protection of privacy in the United States has been achieved through a complex intermingling of common law and state and federal legislation. These provide Americans with a right of privacy against intrusions of government, private institutions and individual citizens. The Supreme Court has also created a constitutional right to privacy in a series of cases in which the Court established 'privacy zones' relating to place, persons and relationships. These decisions are aimed at state and federal infringement. But the protection of privacy from intrusion by private institutions, such as the news media, and individual citizens has been left to state legislatures and the law of torts.

Invasions of privacy by the news media pertaining both to unsolicited and unwanted publicity and to the public disclosure of frequently accurate but acutely embarrassing personal facts confront two principles. The news media's obligation to gather and disclose information – the public's right to know – clashes with the countervailing concern of the individual to retain control and confidentiality over personal details. How to reconcile these two legitimate interests poses a dilemma for any adjudicator, be it a self-regulatory body like the Press Council or the courts of law. An analysis of the American jurisprudence reveals that the courts have accorded the news media a preferred status over the individual citizen's right of privacy. There is currently a debate in academic legal circles in the United States as to whether changes need to be made in order to redress the balance of perceived inequities.

These transatlantic voices have been only mutedly heard in Britain. The tort of invasion of privacy as such has not existed in common law. The English courts have declined to recognise one and Parliament has not spoken on the subject, although there is now to be an independent review by a committee 'outside of Government' into privacy and related matters.[1] [On the subject of privacy there is a fundamental difference between the common law of England and that of Scotland. By contrast with England, Scottish authorities assert that even though there is no conclusive judicial precedent, there is no reason why a Scottish court should not give a remedy for an infringement of privacy simpliciter. By the law of Scotland (unlike the law of England) it is not necessary for conduct, in order that it should qualify as an actionable wrong, to be assignable to any particular legal category; and in any event, certain invasions of privacy would support an *actio injuriarum* or an action for *convicium* (a form of action akin to defamation but is defeated by proof that the words complained of were true).]

Does the American experience indicate the replication of the tort in England? Is the English law of defamation and the evolving jurisprudence on confidentiality adequate to protect individuals from incursion by the media into their strictly private affairs? The nub of the action for defamation lies in the publication of falsehoods which damage a person's reputation. That is why truth is a complete defence, although, be it noted, not to a charge of criminal

---

1 This was a departmental inquiry which became known as the Calcutt Committee after its chairman, Mr (later Sir) David Calcutt QC, which reported in 1990 (Cm. 1102).

libel. If the defendant proves the accuracy of the allegations, the law gives the plaintiff no civil remedy. It is, of course, not necessary to prove the literal truth of the words written or spoken, but sufficient that the substance or sting of the allegation be demonstrated. But the law of libel is framed in terms of someone's reputation in the eyes of his fellow citizen. Unlike privacy, it is unconcerned with an individual's sense of his own dignity.

The concept of privacy was thought to be synonymous with the protection of private property and ownership. But Warren and Brandeis argued powerfully for expansion of nineteenth-century common law remedies against physical intrusion and proprietary interests into a much broader legal right – 'the right to be let alone', to echo the famous phrase first coined by Judge Cooley in his textbook *Cooley on Torts* (1888). What the two authors had in mind was the creation of a legal remedy against both unwanted and unwarranted publicity and the public disclosure of private facts, which were being threatened by the developing technologies of photography and mass circulation publications. The essence of this right of privacy was thus unrelated to either property rights or reputational interests. Instead, the harm inflicted on the individual was the unauthorised publicity accorded to truthful facts or accurately described events by the newspapers at the time. The injury was to the person, or as Warren and Brandeis phrased it, to the 'inviolate personality'.

Privacy is normally understood, therefore, as a value asserted by individuals against the demands of a curious and intrusive society. Privacy rests upon an individualistic concept of a society and is antipathetic to corporatism. Consistent with this basic understanding, the function of the common law tort of invasion of privacy is the protection of subjective interests of individuals against injury to the inner person. It provides redress of injury to a person's emotions and mental suffering. The English common lawyer would have insisted that privacy was possessed by every Englishman, but would deny actionability for any invasion of privacy, solely on the grounds that the law gave no remedy in damages for wounded feelings. In a libel action, damages for mental distress may, however, be awarded, although this would be a rare and subsidiary consideration [Fielding v. Variety Inc. (1967) 2 QB 841, 851]. If it were otherwise, publication to the plaintiff alone would suffice to mount an action for libel, and that is not English law.

The seed sown by Warren and Brandeis did not bear immediate fruit in the development of the law of torts in the common law world. In the United States, it had to wait for the outstanding work of William Prosser of the University of California Law School, the dean of tort scholars, who in 1960 took the privacy right and proceeded to classify it into four separate actionable wrongs, which has subsequently featured in successive restatements of the law of torts, in the case law of State Courts and in State legislation. Two of the four categories of actions which raise tortious invasions of privacy are strictly derivations of other rights, and are misplaced under the concept of privacy. The two are: intrusion upon an individual's seclusion or solitude, or into his private affairs; and appropriation, for the appropriator's advantage, of the individual's name or likeness.

Apropos intrusion, where there is an unauthorised entry upon land or premises in the possession of an individual, the latter may bring an action for trespass to land. There are two problems associated with this remedy. First, the remedy is available only to a person having legal possession of the land or premises; a guest in the hotel or private house, or a patient in hospital, is not protected. Second, since trespass to land involves an unauthorised entry physically on to the land, the action will not be available to a person whose home has been spied upon from outside his property (except possibly the public highway) by someone using a telescopic camera or a long-range hearing device. The Royal Family can testify to the immunity from legal action of many a press photographer whose camera telescopically captures the unwary prince or princess.

Appropriation involves the exploitation, usually for commercial gain, of the individual's name or likeness, and is therefore, again, a violation of a property right. It suffices to say that the law provides an effective remedy for a variety of situations, albeit outside the realm of torts. The law of copyright covers most photographs of an individual. Special protection is provided, substantively, to the voice and likeness of actors, singers, musicians, dancers and other artistic performers. Another class of people to whom a special remedy is afforded are persons engaged in business. Unfair competition may be penalised, either by way of the tort of passing-off or as an offence under Trade Descriptions legislation.

The two remaining categories are, on the other hand, facets of a single concept of privacy and may be treated together. The two are: the public disclosure of embarrassing facts about an individual; and publicity which places the individual in a false light in the public eye. Dean Prosser accepted that the so-called 'false light' category approximated to the law of defamation, a recognition of the affinity between libel and privacy. The remaining category – the public disclosure of private facts or personal information which an individual would prefer to keep to himself and not share with others – represents the core of the concept of privacy, since it relates to the expectation of privacy inherent in the notion of the 'right to be let alone'. This distinct right of privacy has taken a firm root in the United States. In the leading US Supreme Court case in 1967, Justice Fortas said that the exact scope of the right of privacy varied in the respective jurisdictions, but that, simply stated, it was the right 'to live one's life as one chooses, free from assault, intrusion or invasion except as they can be justified by the clear needs of community living under a government of law' [Time Inc. v. Hill 385 US374 @ 413 (1967)].

The right of privacy is thus conceived not as an appendage to some other pre-existing law, but as one which is *sui generis.* A publication can tell the truth and yet be a breach of privacy. It may involve no transgression of the laws relating to confidentiality but still amount to a breach of privacy. Whatever its origins or derivation, the right to privacy has nevertheless more than a superficial affinity to the law of defamation.

The injury caused by an invasion of privacy in fact bears a striking resemblance to the harm for which a remedy is provided in the law of defamation. Both touch on wounded feelings. The principle upon which the law of defamation rests, however, covers a different aspect of human response. It deals exclusively with damage to reputation, with the injury being caused to the victim in his external relations with his fellow men and women. The matter spoken or written about a victim, however widely circulated and however inappropriate for publicity, is actionable in law only by its having a direct tendency to injure him in social intercourse. What is not part of the tort of defamation is the impact of that publication upon the victim's self-esteem or upon his psychological susceptibilities. The rights and wrongs associated with the law of defamation are by their nature material, and as such are mere extensions of the law's protection of proprietorial interests as conditions necessary, or at least promoting worldly prosperity or economic advantage. Hurt feelings *per se* are not the object of the law's protection. However painful publicity may be, and however invidious may be the publisher's action, the suffering is *damnum absque injuriarum* (harm befalling a person without legal wrong) unless the act is somehow otherwise unlawful.

The application of the libel laws in practice may reveal a rather different story. One suspects that juries are not slow to convert what is merely capable of bearing a defamatory meaning into a defamatory statement whenever they detect some offensive invasion of privacy. What may be no more than an affront to one's dignity is readily transposed as a danger to reputation. When, moreover, it comes to the question of damages, an element – often a substantial element – in the amount awarded by a jury is a penalty for improper disclosure of intimate details of an individual's life. Who can doubt that a high proportion of the half a million pounds awarded to Jeffrey Archer reflected the jury's disgust at the motive and manner of media intrusion into Mr Archer's private life?[2] If that is a proper conclusion to be drawn from one of the few cases that have been litigated through to the

---

2 Jeffrey Archer resigned as Deputy Chairman of the Conservative Party in 1986 after two newspapers printed allegations that he had paid a prostitute to go abroad to avoid her involving him in a scandal. The following year a libel jury awarded him damages of £500,000 against the *Daily Star*, following evidence from his wife, Mary, which persuaded them that he was not the kind of person who resorted to prostitutes. John Major made him a life peer in 1992, but in 2001 he was convicted of perjury in the 1987 libel case and sentenced to four years in jail.

trial court stage, how frequently do these factors influence, if not dictate, the settlement of libel actions and the amounts paid out to those willing at least to issue writ, without the intention or means of seeing the litigation through to the ultimate trial stage? May it not be that, lurking within the interstices of the litigious process in libel, there lie the principles of privacy at work. Until we know a great deal more about the nature of the workings of our defamation law from the bulging files of the legal departments of national and regional newspapers and magazines, the suspicion must remain mere speculation. The need for research under rigorous methodology in this area of socio-legal activity is pressing. Until we are all better informed about these matters, we will have to take policy decisions upon the law as expanded in the textbooks rather than from the law in action. I merely assert, without the ability to adduce evidence to support it, that the libel law in action contains the seeds of a public desire to protect by legal remedy the privacy of the individual.

The English law of defamation claims to afford adequate protection from unjustified vilification in public. The line of demarcation between justified and unjustified disclosure is, however, drawn strictly between truth and falsehood. Statements about a person's private life can be freely made so long as they are substantially true. It matters neither that the information contained in the statements is scurrilous, nor that the publication is concerned with the private life of a public figure or an obscure citizen. It has to be observed, however, that the public figure's reputation is more likely to be exposed, and hence needing to be protected, than is that of the publicly unknown person, although the 'unknown' has his privacy within his own immediate neighbourhood. There is the crucial question: is the line of truth the proper demarcation between what is a justified or an unjustified publication?

Some Anglo-Saxon systems provide that a defence of justi-fication (or truth, as the Faulks Committee on Defamation recommended in 1975 that it should be renamed) should not succeed unless the defendant proved not only that the words were true but also that there was a legitimate interest of the public in being informed about the subject matter published. Such a provision, were it to become part of English law, would assimilate the civil action for libel to that of the criminal law. Proposals along these lines have been suggested from time to time, precisely as a means of remedying the omission of any cause of action for invasion of privacy. Both the Porter Committee on Defamation, which reported in 1948 and provided the basis for the Defamation Act 1952, and the Faulks Committee considered that the defect sought to be remedied by such a change in the law ought, in relation to serious repeated libels, to be left to the tender mercies of the criminal law, even though the penal sanction today is palpably quiescent (not to say obsolescent) and wholly unpredictable in outcome and relief to the victim. In less serious and unrepeated libels, the two committees, in unison, thought that matters should be left 'to the regrettably less efficacious sanctions of good taste and to the internal control of the press'. The efficacy of editorial and proprietorial self-discipline and the newspaper industry's self-regulation appears to be insufficiently appreciated by legislators in 1989, if the current parliamentary scene is anything to judge by.

What, then, of the proposal, given the unacceptability of the alternative? Would it place too great a forensic burden on newspapers locked in libel litigation? If such changes were made in the law of defamation, it would equilibrate with privacy, since the latter, by general accord, will always provide a defence of legitimate public interest in disclosing private information.

US law relating to libel suits confers much less protection to the individual against defamatory statements than does English law. US laws require private plaintiffs to prove at least that the defendant publisher was negligent with respect to the falsity of the words used. Plaintiffs who are public officials or public figures must prove even more, that the defendant knew the statement to be false or had serious doubts about the truthfulness of what he was publishing. This stringent provision in libel actions is simply a healthy recognition that some factual error is inevitable in the hurly-burly, if not the hugger-mugger, of the market place in public affairs. Discussion of public affairs must have some 'breathing space', or 'margin of editorial judgment', if it is to be vigorous and vital. The Defamation Act 1952, as an exception to the English rule that whoever defames another is strictly liable unless he proves the substantive truth of his statement, incorporates the notion of unintentional defamation. But the statutory provision is cumbersome in its phraseology and has in practice provided little relief from strict liability. (The Faulks Committee could discover only one reported instance where the provision had been used.)

For the same reason, that speakers and writers on public affairs must be given a wide berth for honest error, the US courts have recently abandoned the evidential rule which so dominates the English libel scene. In England, the burden of proving justification (or truth) of a publication rests on the defendant. The effect of the English rule is for the court to treat any statement sued upon as presumptively untrue – a presumption which gives undue preference to the private interest in clearing the defamed's name as against the public interest in free speech. This sanction has the undesirable, if not unintended, consequence that when the defendant is unable to discharge the burden of proving the truth of his statement, the plaintiff walks away from the courtroom with his pockets bulging, but without having cleared his reputation because doubt remains about the truth. In many cases, the burden of proof is immaterial. But when the truth is improvable, or where the evidence of veracity is evenly balanced by evidence of falsity, the assignment of the burden is decisive. The American laws choose to give freedom of expression the benefit of the doubt, and to oblige the plaintiff to establish the falsity of the impugned statement. Under the English system, the maintenance of a person's good name gets the benefit of the doubt.

The Faulks Committee roundly rejected any suggestion for change of the English rule, which it regarded as sound in principle. The Committee proclaimed that the rule tended 'to include a spirit of caution in publishers of potentially actionable statements which we regard as salutary. Such a shift would severely upset the balance of the law of defamation against defamed persons.' A responsible press is an undoubtedly desirable goal, to be fostered and encouraged by the law. But responsibility cannot be inculcated in an enterprise that must intrinsically be unregulated by governmental authorities or legal control.

In a legal system that endorses and encourages freedom of expression in the shape of uninhibited reporting of, and commenting upon, public affairs, there is always the countervailing need to protect the victims of unsolicited and undesired invasion of privacy. Hence the shaping in America of the English common law in the hands of state legislators and judiciaries, and the generating of a tort of invasion of privacy. But it is vital to acknowledge that it was a need perceived within the framework of the reputational interests protected by the law of defamation. The affinity of the two – privacy and defamation – leads in reality to their intertwining. This is not a novel idea. Under the Roman-Dutch system of law, the two remedies are encapsulated in the Lex Aquilia, which provides an *actio injuriarum*.

The *actio injuriarum* in Roman law – I derive my source, appropriately, from the Institutes of Justinian – is an action for outrage, insult or wanton interference with rights, for any intentional act which shows contempt for the personality of the victim in a way that lowers him in the estimation of others. This concept has been adopted by the Roman-Dutch legal systems. The contemporary action is for a violation of rights relating to personality, dignity or reputation, only the last of which replicates the Anglo-Saxon action for defamation. The unauthorised publication of a personal matter is *prima facie* an aggression upon the person's dignity. It is not always actionable. Much depends upon the circumstances of each particular case, the nature of the published matter, the personality of the individual, his station in life, his previous habits with reference to publicity and the like [O'Keefe v. Argus Printing and Publishing Co Ltd 1954 (3) SA 244, 249].

The emerging experience of the American law of privacy is that it is grappling with the problem of finding a consensus about its precise ambit. Difficulties have been encountered in reconciling the tort with the public's right to know. Whether the media publish accurate, but often embarrassing, facts about a person, or whenever personal information is published which an individual prefers not to be shared with the general public, a conflict instantly arises between competing social values. The difficulty is not so much in devising criteria for impermissible disclosures, as in spelling out the right balance between the individual citizen's interest in being 'let alone' and the legitimate public interest in finding out. It is neither entirely easy nor unduly difficult to construct tests of 'legitimate public interest'. A public interest instantly arises by reason of some public office or position that an individual is holding (though less certainly by virtue of his tenure of such office in the past); or by reason of his conduct in the public domain; or by reason of his involvement in a public event, such as an accident on the road. But the inquiry cannot stop at that point; otherwise private life would end where public life begins, an unacceptable proposition. There must be a secondary step in the process of balancing the competing values. The question posed is: how far are disclosures about a person's private life relevant to his public role. Is the publication of a person's visit to a brothel permissible if the person happens to be the local vicar? The answer is not easily provided and will, ultimately, depend on the circumstances, including the religiosity of the readership of the publication.

These are questions of social values, rather than of legislative techniques. Parliament must decide which social value should prevail. The Press Council has for many years adjudicated on complaints of breaches of an unwritten ethical code of journalistic practices. Since 1976, it has consistently affirmed its Declaration of Principle that outlaws invasion of privacy unless the particular invasion is outweighed by the public interest in its publication. Only a small fraction of the total number of complaints received have related to alleged infringements of privacy that would not also be susceptible to actions for libel. The adjudicatory process of the Press Council does not formally separate out the two concepts. The issue of reputation is regarded as an aggravation of the unjustified disclosure of information.

The argument for not recognising a general right of privacy in English law is that it would create an undesirable fetter upon the freedom of the press. The fact that this prediction is not borne out by experience of the right of privacy in the United States is due to the less restrictive American law of libel. The sensitivity in America towards the freedom of information is reflected in the two, limited legal incursions upon unbridled freedom of expression. In England, there is less such sensitivity in the contemporary law of defamation and an absence of any protective device for strictly private affairs. There is thus an imbalance of competing values on the one hand, and an absence of any resolution of the same values on the other.

The first thing to do is to acknowledge the imbalance in the one (the law of defamation) and then to address the omission in the other (a law of privacy). The definition of defamation, as realised in the English jurisprudence, has remained stubbornly undefined, either by case law or by statute. The broad definition is that a defamatory statement is the publication to a third person of matter which in all the circumstances would be likely to affect a person adversely in the estimation of reasonable people generally. The Faulks Committee adopted such a definition in recommending statutory enactment. It added that it agreed with the Younger Committee on Privacy in 1972 that the 'concepts of defamation and of intrusions into privacy should be kept distinct from one another'. Certainly, so long as the law of defamation is constructed in terms exclusively of reputational interest, it will inevitably be conceived as distinct from, or as possessing only a superficial affinity to, privacy.

It is interesting to observe that the government's approach to these issues accords more with my views of the close relationship of protection of a person's dignity and his reputation. At the second reading of the Protection of Privacy Bill on 27 January 1989,[3] the Minister of State at the Home Office, Mr Tim Renton,

---

3 A Private Member's Bill introduced by the back-bench Conservative MP John Browne. It did not reach the statute book, but the wide cross-party support it attracted was one of the main reasons why the government set up the Calcutt Committee.

commented on the danger of legislating for privacy in isolation from the related areas of the civil law, and that the interface between privacy and defamation was, in principle, clear-cut. The announcement of the independent review appears to mirror that approach.

If injury to reputation is properly to be treated as an adjunct to the individual's self-esteem, there could be a single tort of protection for the person. The definition of this tort, which would be an amalgam of defamation and privacy, would run along these lines. Any unauthorised use or disclosure of personal information, calculated or intended to cause or which did cause distress, annoyance or embarrassment, or damage the reputation of another, is actionable, unless otherwise justified on the grounds of the nature of the personal information and the legitimate public interest (if any) of such information. I suggest that the law would, thereby, be according overdue recognition to the need to redress dignitary harm as well as proprietary harm.

Before engaging in the process of synthesising defamation and privacy, one must not be in doubt as to the elements of privacy, so as to identify the commonality of the two. Privacy, however legally defined, is crucial to the human psyche. Three interrelated and overlapping themes are essential components.

First, there is control: the individual's ability to exercise authority over personal information and its disclosure. The emphasis is placed on the individual's right to select what private facts and what concept of 'self' will be presented to the rest of his fellow men. The right to be let alone must initially be self-circumscribed.

Second, privacy is integral to the development and maintenance of social relationships and to the values associated with these – confidentiality, trust and loyalty. Privacy acts as a catalyst for the human need to form and sustain stable interpersonal relationships. As one psychologist put it: 'If the various needs and motivations that lead us into forming social relationships constitute the bricks of social life, then privacy and its relative aspects contribute to the mortar.' Privacy cements social intercourse. Publicity of private affairs will threaten these relationships if they exceed the bounds of permissible public curiosity.

Third, privacy has a role in the growth and sustenance of intimate personal relationships, particularly sex-related activities that are almost universally conducted in private.

A hundred years ago, Warren and Brandeis, with great foresight, appreciated that the individual's privacy was threatened in the future by an alarmingly curious and intrusive society. Recently, an academic lawyer from the University of California (the Prosser stable) has summarised a century of US experience that we would do well to heed, for it provides a lesson for the laws of both Anglo-Saxon systems. Professor Robert C. Post concluded his extensive survey, 'Privacy, Civility and the Common Law', with these words:

The ultimate lesson of the tort, then, is the extreme fragility of privacy norms in modern life. That fragility stems not merely from our ravenous appetite for the management of our social environment, but also from the undeniable prerogatives of rational discourse. From within that discourse, the way of life which happens to constitute us and to bestow our privacy with its meaning is merely arbitrary, a matter of aesthetics or instinct. And so we are led to attempt to rationalize the value of privacy, to discover its functions and reasons, to dress it up in the philosophical language of autonomy, or to dress it down in the economic language of information costs. But this is to miss the plain fact that privacy is for us a living reality only because we enjoy a certain kind of communal existence. If we cannot acknowledge and preserve that existence, the privacy we cherish will vanish.

Liz Forgan

Freedom of expression: the worm in the bud

1990

Director of Programmes at Channel Four from 1988 to 1993 and Managing Director of Network Radio at the BBC from 1993 to 1996, Liz Forgan is now a freelance writer and broadcaster. Her Cameron Lecture, given at a time when the media in general and broadcasters in particular seemed to be facing mounting demands for more statutory and institutional restrictions, called for an affirmative statement of the case in favour of freedom of expression.

THIS YEAR'S James Cameron Memorial Lecture should have been a party: a joyful celebration of the ending of systematic press and television censorship across Central and Eastern Europe and the beginning of a new age in South Africa.

Who would have thought last year that a journalist would become Prime Minister of Poland, a playwright President of

Czechoslovakia, and that an explosion of freedom would have brought forth newspapers, magazines, radio and television programmes, clattering out all across the Soviet Union and Eastern Europe, taking in great gulps of freedom and shattering forty years of censored silence in a few dizzy weeks?

But, as those who complain about the media often observe, journalists never stay long with the good news. Show us a thousand acres of perfect rose bushes and we will head straight for the single, solitary worm in the single, solitary bud. It is not that we cannot see how lovely the thousand acres are, how perfect the roses, how sweet the smell. It is just that the worm is so much more interesting and maybe important to report.

So let us leave Eastern Europe and survey the thousand rolling acres of British liberties. Beautiful roses. Well-established stock. Strong growth. People come from all over the world to admire them and, indeed, we admire them quite a lot ourselves. But let me pull aside one leaf here to show you the little worm just beginning to crunch its way into the juicy new shoots. I observe that in this bud there is a worm and, since I am more of a journalist than I am a poet or a horticulturist, it is the worm I am going to concentrate on today.

To abandon metaphor and be precise, I am talking about half a dozen measures by which freedom of expression has been eroded in Britain in the past eighteen months and about the overriding flaw in our legal framework that has permitted those erosions to take place and will continue to do so unless we confront it.

Now let me be clear. I mention Eastern Europe and the Soviet Union only to make a real gesture of celebration at the extraordinary inrush of liberties there and a tiny ironic reference to the flow of the tide in the opposite direction in Britain, a country where freedom of expression is supposed to be part of the water supply. As John Betjeman put it:

> Think of what our Nation stands for
> Books from Boots and country lanes
> Free speech, free passes, class distinction
> Democracy and proper drains.

I do not believe that there is a conspiracy to gag the press. I do not believe that wicked men or women are intent on carting us off to the Lubianka. I do not believe that David Waddington[1] and Nicolai Ceaucescu[2] are brothers under the skin. We have a thriving and plural press. We have scurrilous magazines and hard-hitting political journalism in the press and on television. We can see

1 Home Secretary from 1989 to 1990 in the final stages of Margaret Thatcher's government. He then became a life peer and was Governor of Bermuda from 1992 to 1997.
2 Romanian Communist Party leader from 1965, overthrown and executed with his wife in 1989.

lampoons and sexy films and knockabout and satire, *Satanic Verses* and Dennis Potter and the National Front, and we are a very mature and confident democracy in which none of this breaks too many windows and all is right with the world. But I do believe that we are growing careless. I do believe it is time to pay attention to a precious thing for which others fought and suffered, and which we are in danger of failing to value properly. I do believe we need to reassert three simple propositions and then make sure they are never again permitted to slither back into ambiguity.

The first is that freedom of expression is a necessary condition of a free society. You cannot eat it and it will not necessarily stop awful things happening. But with freedom of expression there is a chance of the system righting itself; without it, you get first inefficiency and finally tyranny, and in the end you can't eat, either.

Franklin Delano Roosevelt had his priorities straight in his address to Congress in January 1941:

> In the future days which we seek to make secure, we look forward to a world founded upon four eventual human freedoms. The first is freedom of speech and expression.

My second proposition in need of rehabilitation is the old English idea, carried by the founding fathers to America along with other useful things like universal suffrage and disestablishmentarianism, that freedom of expression is effectively guaranteed only by the doctrine of no prior restraint. In other words, let me publish and be damned, if I deserve it; but damn you if you think you can censor me before I have spoken.

The third idea, which everyone involved in these arguments needs to remember, is that the claim to freedom of the press or media exists only as an extension of the general right of freedom of expression. Journalists deserve no special protections. The point about freedom of expression is not to have more interesting newspapers (or even more commercially successful ones). It is to have a clean and honest society in which the citizen on whose ballot democracy depends has access to the information he or she needs to cast that ballot in a meaningful way. So there is no argument about the interests of the media versus the public interest. The former only has any claim to legitimacy in so far as it represents the latter. The only relevant balance to be struck is that between good done by disclosure and good done by restriction; and the only measurement of both is the public interest.

The trouble with Britain is that, almost every time we are called upon to sit down and judge where the public interest lies in a case of conflict between free expression and restraint, we make the wrong decision. And the main reason for that is that we have never got around to enshrining our commitment to freedom of expression in statute law. Scour the books. Consult the wisest lawyers. It is nowhere to be found except in a common law notion, which is sometimes said to be so deeply ingrained in this aspect of English justice that it is unassailable. Maybe so, but it is noticeable that every time anyone suggests assailing it by means of new legislation they go ahead and do so with the greatest of ease.

I do not want to enter into the arguments about whether this statutory Ark of the Covenant should take the form of Article 10 of the European Convention or a Bill of Rights or something more akin to the First Amendment to the American constitution. That game is more fun for lawyers than it is for journalists, and besides it takes ages to play.

I simply want to observe that without some clear, unequivocal statement in statute which says that this society requires, first and foremost, a right of freedom of expression as a guarantee of all its other liberties and that it shall prevail over all other interests, unless specified reasons justify an exception, we shall go on putting the cart before the horse, the boot on the wrong foot and the burden of proof on the wrong shoulder. We shall go on tackling every question backwards and in isolation without a conceptual framework in which to resolve what are admittedly often extremely difficult problems. And we shall go on taking what are, in my opinion, fatally wrong decisions, because we have got our centre of gravity in the wrong place.

This lack of a solid baseline of principle has led us into serious mistakes with the new Official Secrets Act, the Security Services Act, with the *Spycatcher* affair, with the Sinn Fein ban.[3] We came within a whisker of real trouble with the Broadcasting Bill and are not out of that particular wood yet.[4] I am worried by what I am starting to hear come out of the Calcutt Committee on Privacy.[5] Every single

3 The 1989 Official Secrets Act was an attempt by the government to make it easier to bring charges of breach of official secrets after a number of cases where juries had failed to convict under the 1911 OSA, notably in the 1984 case against Clive Ponting, a civil servant in the Ministry of Defence who had leaked information about the sinking of the Argentinian cruiser *General Belgrano* to the Labour back-bench MP Tam Dalyell during the Falklands war. The *Spycatcher* affair involved the doomed legal attempts by the government in 1986 and 1987 to prevent publication, first in Australia and then in Britain, of the memoirs of Peter Wright, an ex-MI5 officer. In October 1988 the Home Secretary Douglas Hurd, using powers under the BBC Licensing Agreement and the Broadcasting Act 1981, stopped the BBC and the commercial broadcasters broadcasting direct interviews by members of Sinn Fein. The ban was circumvented by using actors with Irish accents to dub the words spoken on to the interview footage.

4 At the time of this lecture in March 1990, the Broadcasting Bill was still going through Parliament. Before its enactment in November that year, the government conceded some amendments, though its anti-public service broadcasting thrust was not changed.

5 The Calcutt Committee produced its report on privacy and related matters at the end of 1990 (Cm. 1102). It was critical of the Press Council and sceptical about self-regulation in general, but came out against legislation to introduce a new tort of infringement of privacy. It proposed its own Code of Practice for the press and indicated that, if the industry was unable to prove within eighteen months that it could get its self-regulatory act in order under a new Press Complaints Commission, such regulation should be put on a statutory basis.

one of those instances represents a genuine problem for a free society. It is not simply a case of bad guys winning over good guys, but a real conflict between two good and proper interests. My complaint is that, when such conflicts arise, one of those interests – the public interest in free expression – always suffers because it is not spelled out anywhere that obliges us to take it into account, if we are considering eroding it even for some good purposes.

Let me give you some examples. Example number one: It is beyond all question true that large numbers of people are deeply offended and outraged by the sight of Gerry Adams appearing on television and speaking on behalf of terrorists and murderers of innocent civilians and military bandsmen.[6] So what do we do? We decide to end their pain and restore to them the right to watch their television sets in peace once more by banning the voices of a legally elected political party that represents a substantial proportion of the Northern Irish electorate from the principal medium of mass communication. And we do it at a stroke by order of the Home Secretary under a section of the broadcasting legislation that gives him absolute power to prohibit any broadcast without further Parliamentary approval. We do it in a heated emotional atmosphere and those who protest are accused of advocating civil rights

---

6 Gerry Adams has been President of Sinn Fein since 1983. In 1989 ten Marine bandsmen were killed in an IRA attack on their barracks in Deal, Kent.

for terrorists. Nowhere in British law is there any requirement on the Home Secretary to demonstrate why his decision to end the offence to some should prevail over the duty to all to report properly one of Britain's most sensitive political stories. He is not required even to consider the effect on the British electorate's right to be fully informed about a matter on which it casts its votes, pours out its taxes and sends its sons to risk their lives.

In order even to have the argument, it is necessary to pursue a fruitless and expensive gallop through every stage of the British legal system, to the High Court, the Court of Appeal and the House of Lords, all of whom have absolutely no option but to find in favour of the Home Secretary, because there is no challenge in English law to his power. Only having exhausted domestic remedies can the thing be taken to Europe. There for the first time the Home Secretary's action has to meet the challenge of a stated right to free expression in Article 10 of the European Convention. Of course, even there it is a right hedged about by exceptions, but at least the argument can take place in a judicial context, with warring principles being seen to clash and be judged against each other. Meanwhile, incidentally, the *Independent on Sunday* can run a most sympathetic three-page cover story on Gerry Adams, with charming colour pictures and speculation as to whether history will or will not show him to have been a great man.

Example number two: Something had to be done about official secrets. The law was unworkable. We had Sarah Tisdall, Clive Ponting, Cathy Massiter, Peter Wright, Colin Wallace, Fred Holroyd[7] – all putting individual conscience or self-interest (depending on your point of view) above their duty to Ministers and their loyalty to their employers. Now, despite the Home Office's insistence that the new Official Secrets Act is a liberalising venture, we have a situation where even the most virtuous of whistle-blowers, trying to draw attention to the rankest iniquity, risks the full force of the criminal law and the removal of his job and pension if he dares to breathe a word of his knowledge in public. Not only is there no requirement on Ministers to consider the public interest in disclosure. Public interest is deliberately excluded as a defence for the whistle-blower. No one imagines it is an easy task framing legislation that will effectively protect the legitimate secrets of the state and the legitimate need of any organisation for reasonable confidence in the loyalty of its staff, while at the same time protecting proper, healthy freedom to reveal matters of public interest. All the more reason why we need some adversarial forum in which to test such proposals against the opposing

7 All self-appointed 'whistle-blowers' in the civil service, the security services or the army who fell foul of Official Secrets legislation or regulations between 1980 and 1990.

interest. What statutory guarantee of freedom of expression did the government have to satisfy or show reasons for overturning when it framed this Act? None whatever.

Example number three: We are clearly going through an exceptionally nasty period in the history of our tabloid journalism. Lies, cruelty, viciousness and sleaze characterise some publications that call themselves newspapers, and shame for them attaches to all of us. Lives of innocent individuals are ruined; public figures are victimised; sensibilities are coarsened and cheapened; and the currency of free speech is devalued. But, though I have great respect for Calcutt and his committee currently considering the possibility of instituting a tort of invasion of privacy to counter these abuses (a tort which, incidentally, is apparently now being considered also in relation to broadcasting, even though the Calcutt terms of reference were explicitly in relation to print), I am worried that they are considering them in relation to no statute on freedom of expression. I have no doubt that the Calcutt Committee is paying attention to its members' own notions of freedom of expression and that they will seek to strike some sort of balance to their satisfaction between whatever those notions are and the harm perceived to be done by intrusion on the part of unscrupulous reporters. But again it is the cart before the horse. The burden of proof on the wrong shoulder. Give us a clear, unequivocal statement of a primary right to free expression and then we can have sensible arguments about whether it is right to make exceptions in pursuit of other good aims. But let us have that First Amendment, or that Article 10, or whatever form it is to take, out there on the table at the start of the argument. Until it is there, anyone who cares to see clearly where the priorities for a free society lie should treat with the utmost suspicion and reluctance proposals for torts of invasion of privacy, right-of-reply legislation, bans on Sinn Fein spokesmen and other such *ad hoc* restrictions.

In both press and broadcasting, the 'media policemen' and quangos are proliferating in the name of consumer protection. They are currently seen as defenders of the helpless individual in the face of an all-powerful and uncaring media. What has gone virtually unremarked is the extent to which they constitute, in fact, an institutionalised erosion of the freedom of expression which should belong to us all. Without a proper baseline against which to weigh the claims of those who would censor or restrict or protect, there is a real danger that, while individual interests may get a more attentive hearing than ever before, the wider public interest in a free press may be at risk. So, before we welcome more codes of practice and more statutory arbitrators as being *ipso facto* on the side of goodness, truth and beauty, let us just stop and consider the downside for a moment.

At least the oldest of these policemen, the Press Council under its chairman Louis Blom-Cooper, has real competence and experience, both legal and journalistic, to call upon in the exercise of its duties. Its new Code of Practice, in its final form, is an improvement on early drafts, which were so framed as to oblige the journalist in almost every case of conflict of interest to show cause why free speech should prevail.

But the Press Council still appears determined to proceed with one proposal that comes perilously close to pre-publication censorship. It intends to invite people who fear that a paper may be about to infringe the Code to telephone Ken Morgan, the director. Though at this stage he cannot have the slightest clue about the rights or wrongs of the matter, he will undertake to have a word with the offending editor to let him know that a complaint has been made in advance of publication. Persistence might result in a more critical attitude on the part of the Press Council, if the complaint should eventually be upheld. Shame on you, Louis! That is unworthy of a lawyer and a journalist of your quality.[8]

I do not envy the Press Council its job at this moment. Sections of the press have apparently gone out of their way to earn the maximum possible opprobrium. Threats of draconian legislation unless the press sets its house in order are not safely to be dismissed. But let us not, as part of the solution, lose hold of the fundamental

8 A version of such a 'hotline' was tried by the Press Council's successor body, the Press Complaints Commission.

guarantees of free expression and let us get all this in proportion.

The year 1989 saw what was described as a record number of complaints to the Press Council. The total was 1,484 for all newspapers and magazines, national and regional. Of these, a total of 73 were upheld, including 47 for the whole of the national press, daily and Sunday combined. For next year, the Press Council is asking for a budget of £1 million.

The Broadcasting Complaints Commission at £200,000 for upholding 24 complaints of unfairness or invasion of privacy by television or radio is cheaper than the Press Council. Which is better value I leave to others with less of an axe to grind to judge. But, perhaps because its procedures are informal, it is sometimes hard to discern the public interest that derives from its challenge to the editorial freedom of those who come before it. (There are no rules of evidence, no opportunities for cross-examination, and the parties to the complaint rarely meet or communicate directly.)

Plymouth Sound radio station recently had a complaint against it rejected by the BCC, but was still ordered to purchase advertising space in the local paper to publicise this finding, because the BCC considered that not enough people would hear it if it were simply broadcast on the station itself. Earlier this year the BCC found that a Channel Four documentary, *Seal Mourning* (incidentally an international prizewinner), had been unfair to the British Fur Trade Association, despite the fact that neither the Association nor any of its members had been referred to in the programme. Our latest complaint was, ironically, against *Hard News*, a programme that ventilates claims of abuse against the press. It came from someone who, while perfectly entitled to appeal for protection to the BCC, might nevertheless not seem to be precisely the sort of victim it was set up to protect – Dr Vernon Coleman, the *Sun*'s doctor. What on earth are we doing setting up quangos and spending public money for this kind of exercise? Where is the public interest in commissioning Lady Anglesey to protect the *Sun* against Channel Four?[9]

The Broadcasting Bill, heading for the statute book this autumn, was once going to usher in a multichannel age of 'light touch' regulation, pluralism and choice for the viewer. In the end, it is heading towards a more complex net of controls and restrictions on the content of programmes than we ever had before. The Bill invents a wholly new broadcasting policeman in the shape of the Broadcasting Standards Council. It also lets the real policemen further into the control rooms of television by introducing the criminal law for the first time into the difficult area of taste, judgement and the balance between reporting the truth and inciting a breach of public order. And it restates a narrow, rigid

9 The Marchioness of Anglesey was Chairman of the Broadcasting Complaints Commission from 1987 to 1991.

definition of balance in programme content that is quite inappropriate for a multichannel service aimed at grown-up viewers.

The extraordinary Clause 145, which would have given a fairly
junior policeman the right to come and ask us on his own sole
authority for scripts, tapes and film in advance of transmission if
he thought an offence under the Obscene Publications or Public
Order Acts might be about to be committed, has now been
dropped from the Bill after a hoo-ha. I am sincerely delighted
about that, but at the risk of sounding ungracious I have to observe
that the fact that we could possibly have considered popping in
such an outrageous provision in the first place only goes to
underline my principal theme – that freedom of expression is
dangerously unsafe in our hands until someone makes this sort of
thing an infringement of a statutory right.

In the matter of what broadcasters call 'due impartiality', David
Mellor[10] has decided that the antique notion of having to achieve a
balanced viewpoint across each individual series of television
programmes must be carried on lock, stock and statutory barrel
into the new era of pluralism. The obligation to balance every
series of programmes has proved unduly rigid for a four-channel
system. It is just perverse for a system where there will be more tele-

---

10 At the time, Minister of State at the Home Office with responsibility for piloting the
Broadcasting Bill through Parliament.

vision channels than national newspapers. Of course, that does not mean that the idea of fairness in public service broadcasting has become old-fashioned. But this literal, censor's approach, counting minutes and reducing intellectual argument to a game of eenie meenie minie mo, is a cause of amazement to our European colleagues and should simply have been thrown out as an anachronistic and unjustifiable infringement of freedom of expression.

I am afraid that Channel Four has already flouted this rule under the existing Broadcasting Act, innocently supposing that no one could seriously intend to limit television's freedom in this mechanical way any longer. In 1986, when clearly the liveliest political arguments were taking place on the right of British politics, we transmitted a series (in clear defiance of the Broadcasting Act) called *The New Enlightenment*, six prime-time documentaries in which there was probably no voice to the left of Nicholas Ridley.[11] It was fascinating, important, highly relevant to the main agenda of British politics at the time. But no one could possibly have called it balanced: it was the right arguing with the ultra-right. Not only would it have been irrelevant and irritating to stick a Labour or Liberal Democrat voice into

11 Tory politician on the right of the party, a junior member of Margaret Thatcher's government from the beginning in 1979 and a member of her Cabinet from 1983 until forced to resign in 1990 because of an interview published in the *Spectator*, which suggested comparisons between the German Chancellor Helmut Kohl and Adolf Hitler. He died in 1993.

the series, it would positively have prevented the job of description, argument and analysis that it set out to tackle.

I told myself and the Independent Broadcasting Authority that elsewhere on Channel Four people who wanted to spread out a left-wing vision of the world were also free to do that. We agreed that the viewers were more than capable of understanding what was going on and needed no artificial balancing voices forcibly imported to protect them. The series went ahead and no one took the IBA to court. I wonder whether we would have got away with it had the thrust of the series been to the left.

Reckoning that the new Bill should be properly drafted for modern times, we and the IBA both proposed an easing up of the rules. To no avail. Due impartiality across a series remains, maybe all the more rigid now that it has been reaffirmed. So what am I going to say when one day, as they surely will, someone comes to complain that Channel Four's *Business Daily* has never once featured the suggestion that the pursuit of profit is not axiomatically praiseworthy? Shall I stick Dennis Skinner[12] in there amongst the merchant bankers for a statutory one minute thirty seconds of denouncing the stock market?

12 Labour MP for Bolsover since 1970, a man of emphatically independent and radical views who describes himself in *Who's Who* as being of 'good working-class mining stock'.

The Broadcasting Act 1990 is going to be even more restrictive of free speech than that of 1981. Let me give an example of what I mean. In 1983, Channel Four transmitted a programme called *A Gentleman's Agreement*. It was about so-called video nasties, unbelievably unpleasant films that used to be widely available from video shops, garage forecourts and the local newsagent, full of sadistic violence often associated with the rape or murder of women.

The point of the programme was to inform the general audience about the nature of this material, freely available despite the 'gentleman's agreement' of the more respectable video dealers. We interviewed some of the most enthusiastic consumers of the stuff – including families with junior-school-age children, one of the dealers and the NSPCC. We reported on the campaign against video nasties which was then just being launched. It was the first many people had ever seen of what was to be found in a video nasty. And it shocked them. There can be little doubt that the film helped to prepare the ground for the debate that led to the Video Recordings Act. There were obvious difficulties in making such a programme for transmission on television. They are the sort of difficulties that current affairs producers routinely run into in this area of subject matter. In order to convey truthfully what sort of material was being included in video nasties, you had first of all to acquire large numbers of them to carry out proper research. Then it was necessary to show some of it to the audience: if not the nastiest bits, at least sequences that were nasty enough to give the audience real understanding of how far we had come from Hammer House of Horrors.

In order to tackle the makers and vendors of the videos, reporters had to confront people who were not in the least anxious to appear before a television camera. Children had to be interviewed and asked questions about their viewing of gruesome and sexually explicit material. Lots of problems. A sensitive subject that could easily go wrong. Lots of 'shock horror' in the press, including an attempt by a suspicious Mary Whitehouse[13] to get the programme banned before transmission.

Under the Broadcasting Act 1981, the programme required close attention from a senior editorial figure at the Channel and from a counterpart at the IBA. Rather more than a routine operation, but clear rules, clear lines of communication and a clear sense of common purpose between the broadcaster and the regulator. To get that same programme on the air under the new 1990 Act will be another thing altogether. We shall be dealing not with one but with four other bodies, two different codes of practice and the criminal law. Where there was clarity, there will be the following

13 Since 1965 a tireless campaigner against what she sees as falling standards of taste and decency in broadcasting, and founder of the National Viewers' and Listeners' Association.

confusion. The new Independent Television Commission must see that nothing is included which offends against good taste and decency. It must also see that due impartiality is observed in matters of current political controversy. In the new age of broadcasting, the ITC does not see programmes before transmission, so we must scan their guidelines, perhaps ask their advice and make a judgement about where they draw the lines.

In another part of the forest, however, and operating to another set of guidelines, is Lord Rees-Mogg's new Broadcasting Standards Council,[14] charged with being a 'focus for public concern' about the broadcasting of sex and violence, and having its own statutory right to scrutinise our editorial judgements, regardless of whether the ITC agrees with us or not. If we get on the wrong side of it, we can be forced to broadcast an 'adjudication' about our shortcomings which could gravely damage the faith of our audience has in the editorial integrity of Channel Four. The BSC's Code of Practice is rather wordier than the IBA's present guidelines, but says, for example:

> Although broadcasting is only one of a series of influences
> operating in society and the extent of its power uncertain,

14 William Rees-Mogg, editor of *The Times* from 1967 to 1981, was Vice-Chairman of the BBC from 1981 to 1986 and was made a life peer by Mrs Thatcher in 1988. He was the first chairman of the Broadcasting Standards Council from 1988 to 1993.

it shares a duty to avoid anything which might incite to crime and so aggravate society's problems. It has the . . . duty of doing nothing in its portrayal of violence which might put at greater risk or further distort vulnerable sections of the community.

Well, I am not sure where that leaves our video nasties, but in future we will have to take a guess.

The Broadcasting Complaints Commission does not publish a Code of Practice, for which some of us may be thankful. But it does have a mandate to investigate complaints about invasion of privacy or unfair treatment. It is not very likely that it will look with sympathy on a complaint from a video-nasty maker, but in the light of recent practice, we cannot rule it out.

So, with our three-headed Cerberus of assorted regulators, ITC, BSC and BCC, all barking noisily at the gates, can we now get on and make the programme? Well no, just one other matter, I'm afraid. Since the new Broadcasting Bill has concluded that three regulators are not enough and that we need the criminal law in here too to keep the tide of broadcast filth at bay, we now have a technical problem. It is an offence to possess obscene material even if you do not intend to publish it. So it is going to be difficult for us to research this programme properly without putting ourselves at risk of a criminal prosecution for having filthy films in the filing cabinet, even though only thoroughly blameless fragments of them will ever reach our screens. You will understand that by this time, with criminal penalties left hanging over us (and the police could still raid the place with a magistrate's warrant under the Obscene Publications Act), we are now in a league that requires me, as Director of Programmes, to inform the Channel Four board about this affair before we can go into production.

How would the board have reacted in 1983 if I had spelled out such risks in advance? Who can say? It is exceptionally courageous, experienced and tough in these matters. But, on the whole, boards of most broadcasting organisations are not ideally placed to take such routine editorial decisions. They tend to be businessmen, teachers, artists, trade unionists, shareholders: invaluable for keeping a broad sense of direction and good management, but not experienced in the stresses and strains of current affairs journalism. It certainly will not improve the chances of getting difficult or dangerous programmes made in future, however clearly in the public interest.

If this story seems long in the telling, it is nothing compared to the actions it will take in real life to get slightly controversial programmes transmitted. In the new age of broadcasting, where fewer and fewer programme-makers are protected by the security of a permanent institution around them, this kind of time is dangerously expensive. Who is going to go on trying to get programmes of this kind on the air, if you are going to have to go through this assault course before you can even start? Independent producers live on programmes in production, not on ideas that are dawdling about waiting to reach the starting gate. Who can blame them if they opt for making nice, simple feature programmes instead? Even directors of programmes get fed up with the hassle in the end and start dreaming of interviews by Jimmy Young[15] instead of a constant hail of sandbags. Is this what the public really wants from its television?

God knows, there is plenty wrong with newspapers and television, but we are in danger of permitting ourselves to be swept along on a fashionable tide of panic. The worst problem with the British media, press and broadcasting, is not the vulgarity, cruelty, intrusion or even lies of the tabloids. It is not sex and violence on television. It is not the invasion of privacy or the ungracious refusal to acknowledge fault. All those ills are there and we must address them, but they are not the worst threat.

The worst threat to the public interest – the true, general, long-term public interest – is the laziness of some journalists. It is the impoverishment and cowardice of some newspapers and broadcasting institutions. Above all, it is wanton carelessness with the precious right of free expression. We are trailing it in the mud. We

15 Presenter of the *Jimmy Young Programme* on BBC radio since 1967.

are trampling carelessly over it. We are sacrificing long-term health for short-term problem-solving, and we are content to see a large hole in the middle of the legislative framework on which our liberties depend. We are chipping bits off, or letting others chip bits off, the first freedom. We should realise what is going on and stop it.

Godfrey Hodgson

Truth, journalism and the Gulf 1991

For both journalists and the military, the Gulf War in 1991 raised all the old issues of conflicting interests. From the perspective of a senior journalist responsible for a national newspaper's coverage, Godfrey Hodgson – then Foreign Editor of the Independent *– analysed the ways in which this war was different. In addition to his time on the* Independent, *Godfrey Hodgson was the* Observer's *Washington correspondent from 1967 to 1971, has worked for the* Sunday Times *and is an authority on American politics.*

J AMES CAMERON reminded us that 'journalism is not and never has been a profession'. We are, he said, 'at our best craftsmen, and that is by no means an ignoble thing to be'. In looking back at the coverage of the Gulf War, it would be presumptuous of me to analyse the successes and failures of individual journalists or papers in detail, as if this were a script for *What the Papers Say*. Instead, I want to do two things: first, to try to put the coverage of the war into a historical context; and, second, to draw out some of the issues it has raised for members of our craft.

Perhaps rather surprisingly, I take as my text for the historical background to the journalism of the Gulf War the words from a Ministry of Defence document entitled 'Proposed Working Arrangements with the Media in Time of Tension and War'. In that paper, written in 1988, you will find the following sound common sense:

> It is often impractical to attempt to define too closely in advance the arrangements under which any particular event will be reported by the media. This is particularly so in the case of armed conflict. The operational and environmental circumstances cannot be foreseen with any accuracy; and the nature of the conflict cannot be pre-determined.

It has become almost banal to observe that news media, like generals, always prepare for the last war, not the next. It might be more accurate to say that newspaper editors and television executives, like uniformed officers and civilian officials in defence ministries, do try to imagine how the next conflict will be different from the last, but end up being taken by surprise just the same. Certainly the conflict in the Gulf, in its 'operational and environmental circumstances', was not at all like Vietnam, or Grenada, or Panama, or the Falklands. Nor was it much like the all-out war in Europe between Nato and Warsaw Pact forces, overshadowed by the danger of escalation to the nuclear threshold and beyond, that preoccupied those in London who sought to draw the lessons of the Falklands and those in Washington who were determined not to repeat the mistakes of Vietnam. It was not even remotely like the eight-year war fought between Iraq and Iran.

However courageous and effective the British contribution, we should never forget that the Gulf War was an American war. It was started and ended on the orders of the President of the United States. It was fought under the command of an American general, largely by American airmen, sailors and soldiers, in the main with American weapons and according to an American plan. And, incidentally, what a masterly plan it was. In terms of information, too, Washington was in the lead. In Washington, as memories of the Second World War and Korea recede into the historical past, it was the lessons of Vietnam that were most vivid to those, both military officers and civilians, who decided how the war was going to be reported.

For many in the American military – and even more, perhaps, among the conservative Republicans who have made up the last two administrations – Vietnam was a humiliating disaster for American armies and one that was largely caused by journalism.

There are those of us who believe that the United States's aims in Vietnam were undesirable, unattainable, and never coherently explained. We take pride in the way that, in the beginning, a handful of reporters – David Halberstam of the *New York Times*, Neil Sheehan, Malcolm Browne and Peter Arnett of the Associated Press, and a few more – began to report the war as reflected by their own growing doubts. First, they began to ask whether the war was being won as easily as they were being told. Then they began to ask whether it was being won at all. They moved on to ask whether it ought to be fought at all, and in the end some, though not all, of them campaigned openly against it. At the same time, television brought the war and its horrors into every American home. It was 'the living-room war'. It was also the 'open war', as Morley Safer called it, 'the first war fought without censorship'. It was as a direct consequence of the fact that newspapers and television were freer than ever before to report the war and all its horrors, more graphically than any previous war, that the American people lost heart and eventually forced the politicians to acknowledge defeat.

That, in simple terms, was the conventional wisdom in Washington when the Gulf crisis began. The thesis itself is too simple. For a start, it is not true that the media in general were biased against the Vietnam enterprise. In the beginning, only a tiny minority of reporters were critical, even by implication. And it is far from likely that, if only the media had followed the official line under Presidents Johnson and Nixon, the United States would have been able to snuff out the Vietcong rebellion. Still, what is relevant here is that many senior American military men in 1990, including General Colin Powell and General Norman Schwarzkopf, were junior officers in Vietnam. They and many like them believe that their achievements were somehow sabotaged by the media. And they were absolutely determined that the same thing would not happen in the Gulf.

The Vietnam War was not, of course, the first war fought without censorship. But what was far more important in practice than the absence of censorship was the access that reporters, hundreds and, in the end, thousands of them, had to the fighting. You could go to Saigon and you might be snowed under with misleading information by the Military Assistance Command, Vietnam, at its famous 'Five o'Clock Follies'. But there was nothing to stop you hitching a ride on a helicopter and flying to where operations were going on, to see for yourself.

It has been usual to attribute that access to the American belief in the freedom of the press, as enshrined in the First Amendment to the constitution. Certainly there does exist in the United States, even in the military, a 'First Amendment culture' that makes people more willing than their equivalents in Britain to acknowledge at least the theoretical existence of a 'right to know'. But that had comparatively little to do with the reasons why it was possible to report the fighting in Vietnam. After all, the famous Cable 1006 from the Pentagon, which laid down the information guidelines for the war in 1962, said that journalists

> should not be transported on military activities of the
> type that are likely to result in undesirable stories and
> should be advised that trifling or thoughtless criticism of
> the Diem government would make it difficult to maintain
> co-operation.

It was, in part, the fact that the United States did not control South Vietnam, that the US forces were guests, however over-mighty guests, that made access to the war so easy. Even if the American military command had wanted to control access, or to institute censorship, it could not easily have done so without a damaging public row that might have upset Congress, the one thing the administration and the generals could not afford to do.

I have said that I do not agree with those who believe that reporting was what lost the United States the Vietnam War. But it has to be conceded that, from the point of view of the American high command in Saigon by early 1968, the reporting was certainly not helping. A series of vivid images – thatched huts casually burned by an American with a zippo lighter, a Vietcong suspect executed in the street, a child running down a road screaming because she has been burned with napalm – were seared into the American consciousness. At the same time, the increasingly sceptical tone of newspaper reporting shook the public's certainty about the war. In the end, those who thought the war was wrong on principle, added to those who believed it was a mistake because it was unwinnable, became a majority that the politicians could not withstand. In any case, after the fall of Saigon in 1975, coming as it did after the fall of Richard Nixon the previous year – which was also widely attributed to a media plot, when in truth newspapers and television were doing their job as it ought to be done – there was widespread resentment of the media among the military and in conservative political circles, a conviction that many journalists were at best irresponsible and at worst disloyal. Like many ideas and fashions, that suspicion of the press has crossed the Atlantic and become part of the culture of many conservative politicians and journalists here too.

Help was to come for the beleaguered American military, though, from the last place they would have expected: from Britain. Relations between the media and the civilian and military 'author-ities' during the Falklands conflict in 1982 were, on the whole, so bad that they provoked an unusual amount of soul-searching and self-criticism in Whitehall, expressed in no fewer than six official or commissioned inquiries into what went wrong and what ought to be put right. Nevertheless, there was one aspect of the Falklands experience that was meat and drink to the Pentagon. The reporters who were able to travel with the Task Force to the South Atlantic could not have been more totally dependent on the military authorities if they had been in the glasshouse. They were cooped up on shipboard for 8,000 miles and many weeks, unable to learn anything of the fighting when it began, except by courtesy of the naval and military authorities, and unable to transmit what they might learn, except over military communications.

For the Pentagon, the lessons of the Falklands were reinforced by those of Isreal's Operation Peace in Galilee in 1982. It is true that, in September, the massacre at Chatilah and Sabra, reported by journalists such as Robert Fisk, dealt a grave blow to Israel's reputation for civilised behaviour in warfare. But, before that, the Israeli system for helping, manipulating and ultimately controlling journalists through escort officers was seen by defence officials in Washington and London as an answer to their problems.

So, when in 1982 President Reagan decided to invade Grenada, the military decided to do exactly the opposite of what they had done in Vietnam. They imposed a news blackout, not only on reporters but, in the early hours, on the administration's own spokesmen as well. Hundreds of reporters, assembled on the nearby island of Barbados, went wild with frustration. When some of them tried to charter small boats to get to Grenada, one American admiral ordered naval patrols to shoot at any such craft.

In London, meanwhile, the lessons of the Falklands were being digested. The military and civilian officials were aware that what had enabled them to control the media in the Falklands was the total control they had enjoyed over access to a battle. Much thought was devoted to the problems that might arise if war were ever to break out on the Nato central front, where hundreds, even thousands, of journalists would have access to the battlefield.

As the Ministry of Defence document already quoted put it, however, the 'operational and environmental circumstances' of war 'cannot be forecast with any accuracy'. Vietnam had been fought in a land of jungle and paddy fields, controlled by a nominally independent ally. The enemy were guerrillas, supported by a powerful neighbour in North Vietnam, and with an even more powerful sponsor, China, in the background. The American phase of the war alone lasted for more than a decade.

The Falklands war was fought by a small, professional tri-service expeditionary force in a British dependency in the chill South Atlantic autumn. The combat, though sharply contested, was essentially one-sided and over in weeks. From the point of view of the news minders, however, the Argentinians were able to inflict enough bad news to pose serious political and morale problems. It was necessary to ask whether a style of news management that just about worked for a quick victory would not have proved catastrophic if the conflict had been protracted and the result seriously in doubt.

It was this sequence of utterly different 'operational and envi-ronmental circumstances' that both those journalists and those in government responsible for coping with them had in mind when the next war broke out, not in crowded, temperate Central Europe, but in one of the harshest, emptiest and, at the same time, most explosive regions on earth. The United States, moreover, found itself faced with the need to cater for its own aggressive, pluralist journalists in a host country that normally maintains total control of the media; and, as the leader of the coalition, for both the British, with their separate journalistic traditions, and the French, who in the event went to great lengths to demonstrate their unwill-ingness to take Anglo-Saxon briefings on trust.

Traditionally, the American attitude to journalism, reflecting the protection accorded to the freedom of speech in the First Amendment to the constitution, has been relatively permissive; the British attitude, relatively restrictive. The difference is neatly illus-trated by the contrast between the US Department of Defense's guidelines on information and those produced by the British Ministry of Defence:

> A free flow of general and military information will be made available, without censorship or propaganda, to the men and women of the armed forces and their dependants ... Information will not be classified or otherwise withheld

> to protect the government from criticism or embarrass-
> ment . . . Propaganda has no place in Department of
> Defense public affairs programs.

That, at least, is the theory as espoused by the Pentagon. Contrast
that with a contemporary statement of principle from the British
Ministry of Defence:

> The function of the public relations staff is to keep the
> public informed of defence policy and events and of the
> activities of the armed forces . . . At the same time the
> Defence public relations staff has to create a favourable
> climate for such activities . . . The aim . . . is to be both
> informative and promotional.

There is another difference. The American statement was itself
released to the public; the British statement was secret and covered
by the Official Secrets Act.

Nevertheless, in August 1990, when the Pentagon and the
Ministry of Defence, in company with the Saudi government, were
bracing themselves for the arrival of what might be hundreds of
war correspondents, the policy they hammered out between them
inclined closer to the magnetic pole of British restriction than to
that of American openness. A senior Ministry of Defence official

told me in an interview that: 'The US looked at the 1982 Falklands experience and said, that's the way to do it, and that is how they played it in Grenada and also in Panama.' It seems an interesting example of the Anglo-American special relationship at work.

The defence planners had a number of special problems to confront in the Gulf. The war would take place from the territory of the Kingdom of Saudi Arabia, traditionally suspicious and restrictive of Western media. In the international hotels of Riyadh and Dhahran, journalists would be able to evade all censorship with direct-dial telephoning or by 'tandying' their stories direct from portable computers. Away from base, journalists whose news organisations could afford the cost, some $25,000, could use satellite phones. Television news crews could take advantage of new, miniaturised technology, more portable than anything available even in the early 1980s. Finally, there was real concern for the safety of reporters. The Iraqi army looked formidable. Iraq was known to have Scud missiles and two longer-range variants, which – for all the Western headquarters knew – might be adapted to fire chemical or even bacteriological weapons.

Looking at all these problems and contingencies, the solution the military adopted was a pool system. Pools are a familiar, if not deeply loved, device in both American and British journalism. The idea is that, if there are physical or other difficulties about admitting to an event all the journalists who want to cover it, a small group is admitted on condition that their copy, or their pictures or television film, is made available for all. Something similar was done in both the First and Second World Wars. Still, the circumstances in the Gulf were different, in several respects. Since 1918, and even since 1945, the news media have multiplied exceedingly. For a major news event, such as a world economic summit, it is not unusual for 2,000 or even 3,000 journalists to turn up. When television takes a major interest, even those numbers will be far surpassed. For an American presidential nominating convention, for example, each of four US television networks will show up with well over 1,000 reporters, executives, technicians and other staff.

In the Gulf, it was possible to control total numbers, thanks to the reluctance of the Saudis to grant visas. In October, indeed, the Saudi government proposed to allow no more than forty-two correspondents of all nationalities in theatre. In the end, there were seventy-five British journalists given visas for Saudi Arabia, not counting TV technicians, and comparable numbers from the other countries that had contributed troops to the coalition. The American contingent, while larger, still fell far short of the number news organisations would have liked to send, not to mention the large numbers of freelances and representatives of smaller outlets who would have liked to have been there. In fact, a number of distinguished American magazines, including *Harper's*, the *Village Voice* and the *Nation*, are suing the US government for failing to meet their requests for accreditation. One estimate in the *Washington Post* of the total number of 'correspondents, photographers, technicians, secretaries and "gofers" of every description and from all parts of the world' who were in theatre puts their total number at 1,152 – a bit more than a squad, but still far short of the mob that will show up for the Tory party conference this year or the Republican national convention next year.

The Ministry of Defence started off on the wrong foot by announcing the composition of a naval pool. Though the names were supposed to have been drawn out of the hat on a chance basis, it just so happened that the lucky newspapers – *The Times*, the *Sunday Telegraph* and the *Daily Express* – were just the ones that a slightly old-fashioned military man might have wanted to choose. Newspapers that were excluded, including the *Independent*, made vigorous representations at ministerial level. The Ministry of Defence then called in the Newspaper Publishers Association to do the actual choosing, but inevitably damage had been done to media confidence in the fairness of the process.

The intention was to create half a dozen 'media response units' – pools that would be given access to the two British armoured brigades, to three RAF bases and to the Royal Navy respectively. These were to have been supported by a 'forward transmission unit' (FTU) at divisional headquarters to pass copy and television film back to London. In the end, this FTU became a seventh pool of six BBC, three ITN, one IRN and Phillip Stephens from the *Financial Times*.

The pool system did not work well. The military were slow in getting them organised. Long before the air war began on 16 January, many news organisations, including the *Independent*, had made their own dispositions. Besides correspondents in Egypt, Jordan, Turkey, Bahrain, Israel and Baghdad itself, we decided to send four reporters to Saudi Arabia – Robert Fisk, Charles Richards, Richard Dowden and in our defence corre-spondent, Christopher Bellamy. None of these was included in pools (though one reporter for the *Independent on Sunday* was). Instead, our correspondents made their own arrangements, with notable success, for covering the war. Bellamy remained, until the end, covering the headquarters in Riyadh. Richards succeeded in joining an American pool, with the First Cavalry. Dowden and Fisk operated like two one-man Long-Range Desert Groups and with brilliant success. Without wishing to embarrass our friends, we were also able to make use of inconsistencies between the visa policies of different Saudi authorities and the considerable freedom of action which appears to be possessed by a substantial number of members of the extended Saudi royal family.

I cite our own arrangements at the *Independent* because I know more about them, but in greater or lesser degree a number of serious newspapers decided that they could not afford to rely wholly on the pool arrangements. In our own case, in about six weeks with an average of more than four Gulf pages a day, we used pool copy on fewer than half a dozen occasions. There were other problems with the pool system. Journalists included in pools appear to have resented those excluded. On one occasion, Robert Fisk reported that 'an NBC television reporter who was part of the [American] military pool tried to obstruct us with the words: "You [expletive deleted], you'll prevent us from working. You're not allowed here. Get out. Go back to Dhahran."' The reporter then summoned a military officer and the 'unauthorised' reporters were sent packing – at the request of their 'authorised' colleagues. So much for the simple-minded notion that all journalists display solidarity against governments.

When it became apparent that some enterprising journalists were nonetheless succeeding in evading the pools and the rules, the authorities' response was sometimes heavy-handed. Robert Fisk reported in a discussion on BBC *Newsnight* on 6 February that, in order to get to the front, he often had to drive into the desert to avoid checkpoints specifically set up to prevent journalists travelling. On 18 February 'media guidelines' were distributed, banning 'non-pool and unescorted civilian media personnel' from a 100-kilometre radius around al-Khafji and from Hafr al-Batin and other areas; and prohibiting reporters from wearing nuclear-biological-chemical protection suits. Although many news organisations (including the *Independent*) provided reporters with their own protective suits, this appeared to threaten exposure to chemical warfare as a sanction for enforcing the press pool arrangements.

Meanwhile, the American media were, if possible, even more discontented with the arrangements made for them to cover the war. As early as 20 January, four days after the beginning of the air war, Malcolm Browne, one of the journalistic heroes of Vietnam, complained in the *New York Times* that 'for the first time since World War II [American] correspondents must submit to near-total military supervision of their work'. He quoted a United States Air Force general, who began his briefing of the reporters in Riyadh as follows: 'Let me say up front that I don't like the press. Your presence here can't possibly do me any good – and it can hurt me and my people.'

On 4 February, R. W. Apple Jr. of the *New York Times*, one of the most respected and most experienced reporters present, wrote from Riyadh that 'the fissures of a new credibility gap have opened before the Persian Gulf War is a month old'. Many of the more than 500 reporters there, he said, 'express intense dissatisfaction with the quality of information furnished to them by the United States command and even more with restrictions on their ability to go see for themselves'. He complained that briefers in Riyadh gave only 'skeletal' details of military activities, often withholding information already reported from the field, or alternatively refused to discuss matters already confirmed from the Pentagon in Washington. Sometimes information was withheld, Apple charged. Sometimes incorrect information was given out, for example when it was contended that US Marines had played no significant part in the battle for al-Khafji, when in fact two Marine units were present on the ground and Marine helicopters, artillery and tactical air units played important parts in the battle.

Part of the problem, Apple suggested, derived from the poor quality of the briefers. At the beginning, the US command briefings were given by lieutenant-colonels, but later their place was taken by generals. On 1 February, when a brigadier-general was fielding the questions, the atmosphere in the briefing room, according to Apple, 'became so sour that General Schwarzkopf, who was watching on television, called in a number of reporters for an off-the-record session'. Subsequently, briefings were conducted by a senior Marine general in Washington and frequently by General Schwarzkopf himself in Riyadh.

Short as the war was, a number of acute issues or dilemmas arose. The most important was the presence in the enemy capital, Baghdad, for most of the war, of a small group of newspaper, radio and television reporters. The Iraqi government, obviously well aware of the value of public relations, allowed a limited number of reporters visas and put them up in the Al Rashid hotel in the centre of Baghdad. They were allowed to move around the city to a limited extent and were given occasional briefings by senior staff of the Information Ministry. When filing or broadcasting, they were censored by 'minders' from the ministry.

They were also guarded by officials from the security service. Indeed, when they were expelled from the country (some of them were later readmitted), it appeared to be as a result of the victory of the security men over the men from Information. On occasion, the Western reporters were taken to particular places, inside or outside Baghdad, which the regime wanted them to see. Three of these visits, in particular, caused a degree of controversy. On 8 February, Patrick Cockburn reported in the *Independent* that journalists had been taken to see a bridge in al-Nasiriyah, where forty-seven civilians had been killed by allied bombing. Later, however, once outside Iraq, other reporters stressed the presence of soldiers among those hit.

Second, the foreign reporters were shown what the Iraqis maintained was the only factory in the country for manufacturing baby milk. The allied command maintained it was a chemical weapons factory, though later there were reports – apparently inconsistent with both accounts – that a Geiger counter, smuggled into the vicinity of the factory, recorded intense activity, suggesting that the facility was connected with nuclear research.

A third, if anything more controversial, issue arose when the reporters were taken to what allied military spokesmen insisted was a military headquarters, hit by bombing, and reported that more than a hundred people had been killed there, many of them women and children. It appeared that, whatever military function the building may have had, it was also used as a shelter by families, perhaps those of high military or civilian officials.

The issue that aroused the most passion, though, was the presence in Baghdad and continued broadcasting of Cable News Network and its correspondent Peter Arnett, a New Zealander who, like Browne, made his reputation in Vietnam. Part of the criticism derived from professional envy. CNN alone had been allowed by the Iraqis to install a 'four-wire' – a direct two-way voice link. From rival television networks, compelled to rely first on operator-placed calls that never came, and then – after the bombing knocked out even that – on CNN itself, there were dark charges of baksheesh and political favouritism. In the United States, there was concern that CNN, watched by Saddam Hussein and George Bush alike, might be transmitting raw data. Robert Fox, in the *Daily Telegraph*, protested that 'the rise of CNN marks a change in television journalism, where spectacle and the personality of the purveyor now precedes the dull but necessary sorting of rational fact. We are now in the era of the reporter-performer and the age of the journalism of narcissism.' A more serious charge was that CNN, and presumably other media with correspondents in Baghdad, was in danger of supplying valuable information to the Iraqis. A Conservative Member of Parliament, Sir Patrick McNair-Wilson, wrote to the Prime Minister suggesting that there should be a single channel of information for both the American and the British press, with a single spokesman 'controlling information'. The media feast, Sir Patrick wrote, 'is both unhealthy and potentially dangerous and, if things do not go well, could be especially bad for the morale of families and troops'.

The high profile of CNN may have obscured a more general issue. There were those who believed that reporters who remained in Baghdad were at best helpless victims of Iraqi propaganda and manipulation, if not worse. (The *Sun* called them 'the enemy within'!) My own view is that this not only underestimated the professional skill and scepticism of reporters like Arnett, John Simpson of the BBC and Patrick Cockburn, but also did not allow for the extent to which reporters in Dhahran, Riyadh and Jerusalem, and indeed in London and Washington, were also being exposed to partial truth. The sharp change in the way Western briefers presented the air war, first exaggerating its success, then deliberately playing it down, illustrates the value of having an outside source of information, however controlled or censored.

Things, of course, went remarkably well, for the allies. The air war was virtually unopposed, the ground battle – which many observers had predicted would be long and costly – was over in four days with fewer than a hundred allied fatalities. Scud missile attacks on Israel and Saudi Arabia were terrifying, but no chemical weapons were launched. The remarkable thing is that, even so, relations between the media and the generals were so bitter. If the war had gone on longer, if the coalition had sustained heavy casualties, if the morale of the Arab members of the coalition had ever been shaken (as many predicted it would be), it is plain that relations between the generals and the journalists would have deteriorated to a point where Vietnam would have seemed like a love feast.

How serious, after all, were the journalists' complaints? Some certainly dismissed their colleagues as whingers. Richard Harwood, a former managing editor of the *Washington Post* (and a former Marine), spoke of the press corps' 'self-pitying mob psychology'. 'They spend hours bitching at their lot,' he wrote on 10 February, 'nurturing paranoias, muttering about "censorship", desperately reaching for inconsistencies in the daily feedings by their briefers and handlers.'

Such unsympathetic voices remind us that the relationships between the military and the media, or between the media and government, in a time of war are not those of simple antagonism. This is no 'zero-sum game', in which two sides push doggedly like two armies to capture turf from one another. Some journalists denounce pools. Some fight to get on them. Some believe it is right to report from Baghdad. Others see that as 'the enemy within'. Meanwhile, the men on whom the reporters depend for their information are equally divided. Military officers are often keener than their civilian masters to let reporters talk to their men, knowing that it will be good for morale.

Finally, contrast the American Air Force general who said he didn't like the press because 'your presence here can't possibly do me any good' with what for me is the abiding image of the war, more significant and in a way more ominous than the most terrible images of Iraqi cruelty or allied ruthlessness. It is a photograph of General Schwarzkopf in his element, taking questions from television reporters at a briefing. Like a teacher in the classroom, he reaches with his arm over the noisier pupils in the front row to take a question from the back. This is the conqueror in his late twentieth-century glory: not dominating a mettlesome horse, like Napoleon or Wellington; not poring over his maps and his order of battle like a Moltke or an Eisenhower; but caught by the cameras in the quintessential action of the modern commander. For, terrible as is the price a General Schwarzkopf can exact from the enemy, he knows that the decisive front is at home.

Uncongenial and troublesome the reporters may be, but the modern general needs them. 'I don't know what effect these men will have upon the enemy' he might say, as the Duke of Wellington did of his soldiers, 'but by Gad they terrify me!' Locked in this reluctant embrace with powers who need him almost as much as he needs them, for his part the modern journalist in time of war needs a redoubled vigilance against manipulation, a reinforced confidence in the usefulness of his craft. Never, I believe, has that vigilance, that independence of spirit, been more needed than at this very moment, as the coalition's armies stand by while Saddam Hussein reimposes his brutal domination in Iraq by the well-tried methods of barbarism. For most Western media, the story is that the war is over and our boys are coming home.

For journalists who respect their craft, the war is never over.

Tom Bower

Robert Maxwell:
a very British experience

1992

Tom Bower's biography Maxwell the Outsider *was published in 1988, before Robert Maxwell died and despite sustained efforts by him to prevent it appearing. After Maxwell's death and the subsequent exposure of his fraudulent business practices over more than forty years, the inevitable question was: how could the regulators and the media have let him get away with it for so long?*

HOW, ONE WONDERS, would James Cameron have summarised the Maxwell saga – a series of events which continue to provide a rare insight into the nature of Britain?[1] Undoubtedly, he would have noted the ironies and the hypocrisies

---

1 As his publishing empire crumbled, Robert Maxwell's body was found in the sea off Gran Canaria in the Canary Islands on 5 November 1991, having fallen unobserved from the deck of his motor yacht at some point in the night.

which Maxwell's death highlighted. The partisan rhetoric, which demanded change but has resulted in 'politics as usual'; and the call for new ideas, which has evaporated into inactivity.

Cameron would have noted the exposure of dishonesty. Not just Maxwell's, but the dishonesty of some of those people who willingly served Maxwell as employees: the dishonesty of those who served as his professional advisers; and the dishonesty of his accomplices, who failed to exercise their supervisory powers. But, above all, I would like to believe that Cameron would have noticed the extraordinary distortions which have enveloped this saga ever since Maxwell's death. The image presented is of a buffoon, a tyrant and crook acting either alone or with a tiny handful of sycophants. It is an image proposed for self-protection, not only by those who served him, but, more importantly, by those whose duty it was to prevent Maxwell's crimes and should now have the responsibility to pursue his accomplices. The sentiment that Maxwell was a 'one-off', an aberration, is supremely convenient for those who are to blame, but it is a distortion, an easy retreat from the anger sparked in the weeks after his death, amounting practically to a cover-up. Altogether, it is symbolic of the culture of inactivity which Maxwell exploited for his profit and which makes his career a uniquely British experience.

Let me digress for a moment. There was one brief, even glorious, momen in the aftermath of Maxwell's death that I think even he would have appreciated. Remembering Maxwell's own boasts about how he fought from Normandy to Berlin and had for ever after savoured the moment when he walked among the ruins of Hitler's bunker, I seized the opportunity, just before the auction of its contents, of an exclusive visit to Maxwell's penthouse flat in the *Mirror* building.

After a four-year battle, here was my equivalent of a visit to the Führer's bunker – the powerhouse of the disgraced empire. There, beside the emperor's huge bed, I spotted Maxwell's own *Mein Kampf*, the authorised biography *Maxwell* by Joe Haines. For nearly a decade I had researched the history of postwar Germany and, in particular, both the allied failure to remove incriminated Nazis and the allied reinstatement of Nazis to power after 1945.

A British war crimes investigator once revealed to me his method of interrogation. It was 1945 in Hamburg. On the other side of the table sat the former Nazi apparatchiks, accused of atrocities. 'I was just obeying orders,' pleaded those same Nazis who in past years had boasted of unlimited power. Uniformly, they cried that they had been fooled, cheated and robbed by a brilliant confidence trickster. On the interrogator's desk was a statue of Hitler. At a suitable moment, he turned the statue around. On the base was carved the phrase 'I too was just obeying orders.' I have been particularly struck by the similar shedding of responsibility by those who worked with Maxwell and who were, by any objective definition, his incriminated accomplices.

Among the most insidious developments in Britain over recent years has been the disappearance of any sense of shame by those responsible for misdeeds. Ministers do not resign when caught lying. Civil servants scurry for cover when exposed for duplicity. Industrialists and bankers stay in their jobs when their profits collapse. The question of the responsibility for Maxwell's frauds is critical. Had Maxwell lived and been prosecuted, undoubtedly he would have blamed the political and economic system. He would have pointed to the past and blamed perpetual persecution. Above all, I have no doubt, he would have cast the blame on dozens of his advisers – in fact, on all those who took his money, including his senior employees. Hence the relief that many of them must have felt at having escaped incrimination by Maxwell. And hence their chorus of mitigation that they, too, had been fooled and had acted in ignorance.

But should their responsibility disappear just because of Maxwell's death, while his legacy remains? The issue of responsibility for the whole of Maxwell's rise and fall (and his second rise and fall) mirrors a fundamental weakness within our culture that needs to be addressed, especially since the pensioners suffer while some of the Maxwell family provocatively continue to enjoy the fruits of his crimes.

It is six months since Maxwell's death, yet not one government or private agency has completed any investigation into his crimes – with the exception of the parliamentary inquiry and report into pension laws. Two inquiries are still under way. The most obvious is being conducted by the administrators – the accountants – but, because they are acting on behalf of the creditors, they are severely limited. The second is by the police. Despite their protestations of activity, few can have much confidence, considering their record in the Blue Arrow and Guinness cases, that their efforts will compare favourably with their equivalents in New York.[2] There has been hardly any sustained complaint or even comment regarding their inaction. Instead, the sentiment throughout all Four Estates seems to be either that the Maxwell story is 'off the boil'; or that it is confined to the plight of the pensioners.

If that sentiment persists, then we shall miss the opportunity of understanding the unique nature of the Maxwell experience. For the same institutional impotence that allowed Maxwell three times in his career to perpetuate frauds without punishment and failed to protect his victims would now seem incapable of launching an efficient investigation into his crimes.

---

2 Fraud charges were eventually brought against Robert Maxwell's two sons, Kevin and Ian, and a third Maxwell director, Larry Trachtenberg. In 1996, after a trial lasting 131 days and costing over £25 million, all three were found not guilty. The case dealt a blow to the reputation of the Serious Fraud Squad.

Of course, there are frauds in every country, but I do not believe that there is another equally prominent example of a conman being allowed to perpetuate his art – so publicly – three times within living memory. The understandable and normal reaction to exposure of serious fraud is to examine and sometimes change laws and improve professional standards. But that, I believe, ignores the essence of the Maxwell experience: namely that in 1971 Maxwell had been investigated by the Board of Trade and then subsequently by the police for fraud. Overwhelming evidence of his crimes was produced and yet he was not prosecuted.

Then, twenty years later, there was again a Maxwell fraud. The evidence is overwhelming. This time there is no formal inquiry and once again both the police and the prosecutors dither about pursuing those responsible.

I shall reflect upon the role of newspapers and journalists within this culture of inactivity: are they accomplices or victims? But first let us consider Maxwell. His achievements were considerable – not merely his path from extreme poverty to wealth in a foreign country, but all the other aspects of his exceptional, multifaceted career. Without him there would not have been a major scientific publisher in Britain. It says much about Britain that the company he created, Pergamon Press, is now owned by a Dutch competitor. It says much about Maxwell that he rescued the British Printing Corporation, the nation's largest printers, from bankruptcy because no one else dared. And it says much about Britain that Maxwell was the first decisively to challenge the printers' blackmail.

Only Maxwell, it seemed, was willing to buy the *Daily Mirror*. Its former owners looked at practically any solution, including doing a deal with a man they did not trust, to get rid of what they regarded as an albatross round their neck. And only Maxwell seemed to understand ten years ago how the world's media would be dominated by a handful of international conglomerates, as he ambitiously bid to join that select few. Maxwell's failure to establish his corporation as one of the world's ten biggest means that Britain's newspapers and TV stations now risk becoming pawns in an industry dominated by American, French, German and Italian giants. If this sounds congratulatory of Maxwell, I think it is important to recognise the other side of his successful exploitation of Britain's culture of inactivity. It was Britain's loss that it could not harness the good and prevent the bad.

Maxwell's life and career were a succession of challenges, each more extraordinary than the last. Each of those challenges confronted an essential aspect of British society: and in each Maxwell was, either immediately or eventually and in his own terms, the victor. By that definition, therefore, Maxwell left behind a succession of the vanquished: sometimes to Britain's benefit, sometimes to its detriment, but always as a remarkable reflection on and, too often, an indictment of Britain since 1945.

In essence, Maxwell's fortunes, political and financial, were earned by exploiting British weaknesses. It is my contention that those who believe that Maxwell abused Britain's tolerance and sense of fair play in allowing a penniless refugee to become an army officer, an MP and, after his resurrection, a media mogul misunderstand that it was the flaws and not the favours of British society that allowed Maxwell ultimately to steal nearly £2 billion.

Britain's failure to address Maxwell's sins during his lifetime is consistent with the continuing failure now to launch an official investigation into how the regulatory system failed to prevent his crimes and consistent with the explicit decision by the government, the City and the professions to avoid those fundamental reforms which could prevent the next round of frauds.

Instead of taking seriously the issues of solving the problems exposed by Maxwell's life, we have seen his former employees vying to tell stories about the horrors of working for the man or seriously bidding to take over the remains of his empire. So, in his death as in his life, Maxwell continues to expose Britain's frailties, its amateurism and its pretensions.

In the role of dishonour, the first target is the easiest to consider – the City and the financial community: the obvious culprits. There is a strong school of thought among so-called respectable circles in London which argues that it was wrong to prosecute in the Blue Arrow or Guinness trials because the alleged crimes were common practice and probably not even real crimes at all.[3] Considering the leniency of the sentences, the judge in the Blue Arrow trial seemed to sympathise with that opinion.

Among the consequences which this school apparently ignores is that, by its narrow definition of corruption and by its wide tolerance of malfeasance, it does not aid business but, on the contrary, leads directly to its collapse. In London, one example of the consequence of failing to prosecute the corrupt is the perilous state of the Lloyd's insurance market. In world terms, an example is the collapse of the Soviet economy.

In respect of Maxwell, City bankers were just behaving naturally – fools easily parted from other people's money. But the real culprits in the City were those appointed to regulate and supervise

3 In 1989 the employment company Blue Arrow made a £837 million rights issue (at the time the largest ever made) to finance its takeover of the US employment agency Manpower. The issue was massively undersubscribed, but a press release was put out stating that almost half the issue had been placed and that the rest had been sold on the stock market. Four Blue Arrow officers were found guilty in 1992 of conspiracy to defraud by misleading the stock market. In the Guinness case, the chief executive at the time, Ernest Saunders, and three other figures prominent in the City were found guilty in 1990 of charges ranging from false accounting to theft and conspiracy for acting together to bolster the Guinness share price artificially during its contested takeover bid for the Distillers Company in 1986. Their initial appeals against conviction failed, but later the European Court of Human Rights ruled that their trial had been unfair as they had been forced to provide Department of Trade and Industry inspectors with evidence that had then been used against them.

the financial system. For example, John Morgan, the chief executive of the Investment Management Regulatory Organisation (IMRO), and George Nissen, its chairman, were paid handsomely to ensure the safety of the pension funds. They failed to perform their task and the consequences are now plain. Yet not only have they failed to submit their resignations, but the body politic in Britain has not demanded their dismissal.

The City establishment's attitude towards Maxwell's frauds was succinctly explained by the Governor of the Bank of England, Robin Leigh-Pemberton. Commenting on the Maxwell case, he told the Institute of Directors that excessive regulation would stifle business and that the risk of occasional frauds must be accepted because all-embracing protection is impossible. In other words, some dishonesty must be expected and accepted. Perhaps Leigh-Pemberton's judgement was not surprising since he bears a heavy responsibility for failing to halt the biggest banking fraud in history, the development of the Bank of Credit and Commerce International.[4] Those who should impose punishment are occa-

4 The Bank of Commerce and Credit International (BCCI) was perhaps the greatest and the least exposed financial scandal of the past half-century. Founded by Agha Hasan Abedi in Bombay in the late 1940s and later based in Pakistan, the company developed into a vast and largely clandestine international banking operation, heavily involved in money laundering and the financing of terrorism. Its network of influence reached into the highest places, not only in the Indian subcontinent and the

sionally themselves tainted. So professional neglect in Britain still remains unpunished and the Governor's robust homily in praise of inactivity provoked no noteworthy objections.

A second professional group to be targeted for blame are the lawyers. Individual lawyers provided assurances to innocent third parties which were wrong, even dishonest, and which permitted Maxwell's frauds to occur. Has anyone heard about the Law Society, or Parliament, or Whitehall, investigating the role of those lawyers? It is the same cultural inactivity that restrains any investigation into the behaviour of the legal profession with regard to the miscarriages of justice in the so-called IRA trials.[5]

The accountancy profession is the third group whose behaviour with regard to Maxwell should be investigated. Again, there has

Gulf but also in Europe and the USA. The Bank of England, which had been watching the BCCI since the 1970s, became seriously concerned for its financial stability in the UK during 1989 and 1990, and allowed it to remove itself offshore without proper questions being asked. An astonishingly revealing account of the history of the BCCI and of the failure of the American, British and other regulatory authorities to deal with it is contained in the December 1992 Report to the Committee on Foreign Relations of the US Senate by Senators John Kerry and Hank Brown.

5   In 1974 IRA bombs exploded in pubs in Birmingham and Guildford, resulting in the conviction the following year of six and four Irishmen respectively. Fifteen years later the Court of Appeal finally overturned these verdicts on the basis that the evidence originally presented was either fabricated or inadequate.

been no inquiry. Suffice it to say that Price Waterhouse, who now preen themselves on their investigation of Maxwell's frauds and have so far collected £3 million in fees, are the same firm of accountants which authenticated as 'true and fair' the accounts of the BCCI bank, which operated as a vehicle for fraud. Again, it is 'politics as usual' and those advocating change have been silenced by the culture of inactivity until the next major fraud surfaces. To discover the reasons for this extraordinary state of affairs, let us, for brevity's sake, start in 1971.

The Board of Trade inspectors' famous condemnation of Maxwell's management of Pergamon Press, seemingly merciless, in reality held back – quite deliberately – from the complete truth. They did not explicitly accuse him of seeking to perpetuate a fraud. The inspectors were less than brave. The police were little better. Though the evidence was there, no one actually accused Maxwell of conspiring to defraud.

Seven years of investigation by the Fraud Squad failed to produce a prosecution and, in the interim, Maxwell had not only won back control of Pergamon but had also started his successful campaign to rewrite his past. Significantly, among his accomplices was the Labour left, who swallowed his protests that he was the victim of political enemies.

It is a mistake simply to blame Britain's laws for allowing the pariah to return. The real causes were Britain's structural weaknesses and those identifiable individuals who should have known better. Maxwell's resurrection after 1980 was achieved because he exploited the very British qualities which ten years later permitted his frauds: a certain laziness, short-sightedness and lack of principle. And, if this judgement about British society seems too harsh, I would challenge critics to name an equivalent to the Maxwell saga in another European country. It is against this background that we should look at the media's role towards Maxwell's life and crimes.

Maxwell's death immediately sparked a critical, introspective review by the media of their own record. In the first four weeks, before the frauds were revealed, the media's focus of attention was on Britain's defamation laws, which were blamed for protecting Maxwell from successful investigation and exposure. I believe that the blame heaped upon our libel laws is exaggerated and diverts attention from the real culprits.

It is certainly true that, in my own case, the immediate consequence of Robert Maxwell's untimely death was the disappearance of my first defamation trial, which was due nine weeks later. Just days before Maxwell's death, the barrister who was to argue my case in the three libel actions which I had brought against Maxwell had asked for a down payment of £100,000. That was just to prepare for a trial which was expected to cost the loser, in expenses alone, at least £1 million.

It is arguable that, had I not enjoyed the backing of a multimillionaire who, for a variety of reasons, had continued to support my book on Maxwell, I might have been finished. For Maxwell's threat to cause my financial ruin was certainly real and his weapon was the libel law.

In the aftermath of Maxwell's death it was argued that, if Britain's libel laws were amended to allow the media to plead the defences available in America (both of public interest and that any mistake not motivated by malice should not be actionable), Maxwell would have been exposed and the frauds prevented. I do not entirely share that view. First, I believe that the American media have abused those defences and have injured innocent people. Second, it was not just Maxwell's *use* but more critically his *abuse* of the libel laws which suffocated his critics. That abuse was only possible because it was permitted by the judges and the legal profession. Third, I disagree because many newspapers who complained about his abuse themselves abuse the same laws and procedures.

Take the role of the lawyers and judges first. My experience suggested that the procedures and rules that have to be followed to bring a libel case to court are unnecessarily and even deliberately complicated. They allow unreasonable possibilities of appeal and they provide scant protection for either plaintiff or defendant. Significantly, it was the judges who were unwilling to halt the costly procedural wrangles that were obviously a part of

Maxwell's deliberate weapon to cause financial hardship. The only beneficiary was the legal profession's income. My complaint here is that, to a significant extent, it is the lawyers' self-interest that makes libel cases so expensive. Just as in the case of the accountants and City practitioners, there is no pressure from outsiders, campaigning for change with authority and expertise.

So we come to the position of our newspapers and television. How contaminated are the media by this culture of inactivity, which too often shies away from assigning blame and protects those who should be shamed – the precise conditions that protected Maxwell?

I do not believe that libel laws prevented Maxwell's exposure, since the most prominent users and abusers of those laws are some of our own newspapers. There is no doubt that, when launching uncertain attacks, some newspapers and journalists console themselves with the thought that their target will not have the money to sue. If libel trials were swifter and cheaper, the average aggrieved citizen would more easily be able to sue newspapers. Hence the media's reluctance to press seriously for reform of the libel laws.

But the counter-cry will arise: newspapers are constantly being sued for libel and record damages are being awarded. My reply is: look at the majority of those cases! They are not cases of principle. They often involve pop stars, actors and actresses, whose complaints, with respect, are comparatively worthless: an actor is accused of being a bore, another of being a homosexual, and Sarah Keays[6] is accused of being a bimbo. These are the cases where newspapers, in defence of their sanctity and freedoms, are prepared to risk fortunes. Look how Richard Stott, editor of the *Daily Mirror*, continued, after Maxwell's death, the defence of a libel action brought by television personality Esther Rantzen, which he then soundly lost. What principle was Stott pursuing which was worth wasting some of the newspaper's precious funds? Truth? Honesty? Public interest? Surely not. It seemed to be a vendetta against someone he did not think would pursue her challenge to the end, or who would be ruined by the embarrassment.

The issue is this: why were the same newspapers who were prepared to risk fortunes attacking powerless or inconsequential personalities not prepared to risk the same huge sums of money to attack Maxwell? The only conclusion that one can draw is that it was not the costs that deterred some newspapers from publishing investigations. The deterrent was more fundamental: namely, the compromised status of the media in Britain today, which results from the same conditions – the culture of inactivity – which allowed Maxwell to flourish in the first place.

---

6 The jilted mistress of Cecil Parkinson, Secretary of State for Trade and Industry, who was forced to resign from Margaret Thatcher's government in 1983 after she had made a statement about their affair to *The Times*.

In its defence, it must be said that the Fourth Estate can only operate within the rules permitted by the other three Estates. The media cannot act in a vacuum. Since the others were unprepared to challenge Maxwell, the media's own possibilities were severely limited. Several individual journalists, I know, wanted to expose Maxwell and wrote, within the constraints operating on them, brave and revelatory stories. But, in the overall scheme, they were obstructed and hindered in the pursuit of their quarry to the bitter end by newspaper proprietors and television executives. The reason was that too many media executives in television and the press were and remain part of the culture of cosiness. Either they were unwilling to expose the man whom they often met socially; or, since they eagerly seek to identify themselves with the interests, luxuries and sinecures of government and power-broking, they ignore one of the fundamental principles of journalism, so wonderfully portrayed by Ben Bradlee of the *Washington Post* during the Watergate saga: the ambition and even the pleasure of causing discomfort to a wrongdoer, the more powerful the better. One eternal lesson is always ignored: power-brokers do not respect cowards.

Vis-à-vis the media, Maxwell succeeded because journalists who chose to work for him and even some of his media competitors had abandoned this high ground. The culture of inactivity has cast disdain on whistle-blowers who cause concern to the professionals, the regulators and the power-brokers, because too many of those involved in journalism seek equal status with the potential targets of the investigators. Since some in the professions, as I have indicated in the Maxwell case, are by their very inactivity themselves compromised, the media turned upon the libel laws as the reason for their failure to expose Maxwell.

That is the self-destructive mistake. Maxwell is not history, but a vital source from which to study the inadequacies of our society. His life and his death exposed terrible flaws, not in the laws and regulations, but in the essential nature of the people who administered and observed the execution of those laws. Maxwell exploited and exposed a uniquely British condition. He could not have prospered without the aid and comfort of many. His accomplices in this should be properly identified and asked to account for their deeds. That is the lesson that should be Maxwell's legacy.

Michael Grade

Violence and responsibility

1993

The early 1990s saw evidence of 'moral panic', with loud cries about a rising tide of sex and violence and assertions that television was to blame. The television establishment felt that it was being held accountable for the excesses of satellite, cable and video nasties. Michael Grade delivered the 1993 lecture as Chief Executive of Channel Four Television, a position he held from 1988 until 1997; in 1998 he became Chief Executive of First Leisure Corporation, and in October 2001 it was announced that he was to become chief of Camelot, the company which stages the National Lottery.

MY SUBJECT IS violence and responsibility. The context, of course, is the latest debate about violence on television, a subject which comes around regularly. I am enjoying my twentieth year in broadcasting and this is the umpteenth time that the debate has raged. It is an important subject and I shall try to put the issues into some kind of order and to remove some of the prejudice and emotion that have taken the place of reason in the hysterics which pass for debate on the subject.

James Cameron, with his impatience of hypocrisy and double-think, would have carved like a scalpel through the moral fog recently generated by the commentators and leader writers, pontificating about violence on television. Politicians, too, are quick to join in the general clamour. The Prime Minister, Virginia Bottomley and Kenneth Clarke have all recently condemned the amount of violence on TV and linked it to real-life crime. Timothy Renton, addressing a symposium on broadcasting at Manchester University just over a month ago, declared himself greatly worried by 'the growing incidence of sex and violence on the television screen, which follows on from what takes place in the cinema and video industry'.[1]

Here is a classic example of guilt by association. All the surveys show that the amount of violence on terrestrial television has declined steadily over the past twenty years. Yet we are thrown into the dock indiscriminately with the cinema and video, which

1 The Prime Minister was John Major. Virginia Bottomley was Secretary of State for Health and Kenneth Clarke was Home Secretary. Timothy Renton had been a junior minister until the previous year: he was Minister of State in the Home Office in Margaret Thatcher's government from 1987 to 1989 with responsibility for broadcasting policy.

beyond question are sometimes unacceptably violent. Note, too, that Mr Renton in his speech referred throughout to TV 'sex and violence' as though they were two halves of one indivisible whole like Marks & Spencer, or French and Saunders. This is not helpful. Sex and violence have their roots in diverse emotions, evoke different reactions from viewers and do not march together in the schedules. Bonking and bashing incidents do not increase or decrease at the same rate. In fact, this tendency of moralists to lump together in a single phrase all television's spicier causes of offence – sex, violence, language and taste – casts a kind of gener-alised moral fog over the area which does not make for clarity, let alone rational debate.

What is worse, we – the four public service terrestrial channels – find ourselves shackled to Rupert Murdoch's evangelical outlet, Sky's Movie Plus channel, one of whose recent offerings, *Death Warrant*, provides such delectable fare as prison inmates being smashed across the face with dumb-bells, speared with poles, having eyes sliced like salami with a circular saw and their faces gouged with crushed light bulbs. Mr Murdoch has recently publicly warned his senior executives that in his company 'there are limits'. Who draws them? The Yorkshire Ripper? I am sure that Mr Renton, a former broadcasting minister at the Home Office, reads his *Daily Mail* religiously. He must have noticed an article of 20 May this year, which claimed that 401 killings were seen in one week on eight British television channels. Of these killings, 289 – 72 per cent – were on the two Sky movie channels. Hence, I take strong exception to public service television being consigned to such company.

Sky's Movie Plus is the quintessence of this government's market philosophy translated to the small screen. In the course of the 1990 Broadcasting Act debate, the government said they would blow away the stuffy élitism of the old BBC/ITV duopoly in bracing gusts of consumer choice and unfettered competition. They said that, in a free market, what the public wants is sovereign. Presumably, if that means an endless succession of violent and sexually exploitative films such as *Rambo*, *Straw Dogs*, or any of the recycled *Death Wishes*, then so be it. To protect the consumer from such excesses, the government put in place the fig leaf known as the Broadcasting Standards Council. There was much talk from the government of consumer protection for viewers, as if television programmes are defective toasters. Clearly the government knew the risks involved, but in their determination to introduce the market doctrine into broadcasting, they overlooked them. Or, rather, they allowed themselves to be persuaded by Sky that, since their encrypted signal offered a greater degree of protection, they could therefore apply different standards to violent and/or sexually explicit material. The 'smart card' that unlocks the picture was better protection for children than the off switch.

It is an argument. But it is only persuasive if you believe that technology is childproof. I, personally, believe that videos and other TV gismos are actually adult-proof and that only children can beat those boxes of chips. But, above all, the Sky argument is only valid if you believe that violence as exploitation, violence just for the sake of profit, is something this government wants to be seen to be encouraging. There is a well-known dictum of finance and economics known as Gresham's Law, which states that bad money drives out good. Though first formulated in Elizabethan times, I believe it is relevant to the television age. It is not necessarily the most interesting ideas or most valuable artistic endeavours that will survive in an atmosphere of cut-throat commercial competition. They need some degree of protection, because they often begin as the passions of a tiny minority and, unless nurtured and guarded, will get no further because they offer no immediate commercial pay-off.

Having connived at creating a television environment which wars against moral discrimination, these same political champions of ethical standards then mount their pulpits and start wagging an admonitory finger at public service broadcasting about the tidal waves of unacceptable sex and violence flooding into their sitting rooms. Though most politicians admit they themselves do not have time to watch much TV, so the programmes they do catch are more likely to feature their own shining faces on *Newsnight* than Patrick

Malahide's shining bottom in *The Singing Detective*. Great cultural institutions, like the BBC and independent television, which have between them eighty years' experience in drawing the boundaries of taste and practising public accountability, whose policies have been shaped by some of the most fastidious and creative minds of our time, cannot be trusted to show social responsibility; they need the smack of firm regulation. Sky, on the other hand, having the advantage of inheriting the Murdoch empire's experience in running such morally elevating journals as the *Sun* and the *News of the World*, can do what the hell it likes.

Abraham Lincoln once told the story of a lynch mob who hanged a man for cattle stealing. The next morning the leader of the mob visited the grieving widow and said: 'The joke's on us; he didn't do it.' Some day the government, surveying the fall-out from their 1990 Broadcasting Act, not least the ITV franchise débâcle and its appalling permissiveness towards Sky, may be forced to admit the joke was on them. Terrestrial television was not guilty of the offences charged against it. But will they have battered or starved public service broadcasting to death in the meantime?

So what is going on here? Do senior politicians seriously believe that television is a major catalyst of real-life violence in society? Even the more conservative police chiefs link rising crime rates to a whole host of underlying causes: economic and social deprivation, mass unemployment and growing homelessness (especially among young people), the breakdown of the conventional family unit and moral uncertainty created by the decline of religious and other traditional institutions. You can add truancy, declining standards of education, alcohol abuse and violence in the home to this list of contributory factors. Are the politicians solemnly suggesting that violence on television is a factor to be mentioned in the same breath? The public does not think so. Gallup did a survey a few months ago asking the general adult population to classify a list of factors having 'very', 'fair' or 'little' importance as causes of crime. Five times since 1981 Gallup has asked these same questions. Over the years, social factors such as the breakdown in law and order, levels of unemployment, lack of discipline in schools, poverty and poor housing have remained in the very important category. Since the mid-1980s, drugs have also been high on the list. Violence on television, which was thought to have little importance in 1981, still remains so twelve years later.

It is, of course, an old tradition to blame communications technology for social disruption. A clear historical line joins the beheading of the bearers of bad news in ancient Greece and the government's ban on the direct speech of Sinn Fein politicians on television. A famous *Times* leader ran: 'Before the children's greedy eyes, with heartless indiscrimination, are presented every night terrific massacres, horrible catastrophes. All who care for the moral well-being and education of children will set their faces like flint against this form of excitement.' 'This form of excitement' was not the video nasty nor even *Grange Hill*, but the invention of cinematography. The leader was dated 1913. And, according to Marshall McLuhan, the arrival of the first comic books on the American scene was blamed for rising crime statistics. As he put it: 'The dimmest-witted convict learned to plead from the dock, "It wuz comic books wot made me do it, m'lud!"'

One can sympathise with the politicians to this extent. Many of the problems they face are intractable and have little pay-off in public relations terms. So any issue that interests the public, has a high profile and isn't too technical lends itself to heated rhetoric and is good. For a tabloid headline it is a godsend. The politicians haven't the foggiest notion what to do about rising crime rates, prisons heaving at the sides, the disintegration of the family, the collapse of public morality – and who can blame them? But, to add to their discomfiture, television confronts them with a vivid picture of the society they have done much to shape and they don't like what they see. So, like exasperated parents, they turn on us and cry: 'Whatever you're doing, stop it!'

The problem is that their smear sticks. The cry 'there is too much violence on TV' has now become as much a part of contemporary folk wisdom as 'Britain is swamped by immigrants' or 'the BBC is run by trendy left-wingers'. The lack of evidence for such opinions has no effect on the tenacity with which they are held. In the case of television violence, mountains of research reports warning against simplistic conclusions are blown away in gusts of fury by those appalled by the state of our society and casting around for the source of the depravity. Lo and behold, they discern its glassy eye staring at them from the corner of their living rooms. The Prime Minister himself, warning about violence on television, has declared: 'What we watch is the single biggest influence on many people's thinking.' Despite Mr Major's humble origins, that is an essentially middle-class, leafy-suburbs-of-Huntingdon view. The residents of one of those crumbling tower blocks in our inner cities, over-crowded and under-policed, have no problem in identifying the real causes of the daily violence they endure – and television is nowhere on the list. A much bigger influence on their thinking than the two-dimensional image of a villain on the TV screen is the three-dimensional thug hanging about at the bottom of the ill-lit lift shaft. The nearer you get to the sewer of social decay, the more accurately you can pinpoint the source of the bad smell. Indeed, I have heard it argued that the most disturbing TV images for the socially and economically deprived are not to be found not in violent movies, but in glossy commercials whose glittering prizes jarringly remind the have-nots of the things others can afford but they are denied.

When used by the general public, I suspect that the phrase 'there's too much violence on TV' has become a form of shorthand for a whole welter of anxieties felt by some viewers about the very presence and importance of television in their lives and the lives of their families. They may be greatly overestimating television's influence, but this is how they feel. One way of expressing this anxiety and resentment is by focusing on television's more disturbing images.

I am in no way suggesting that public concern about television's impact on society ought not to be taken with the utmost seriousness by broadcasters. There clearly is a problem here, but it is much more complex than some of our critics will allow. I should have thought, for instance, that common sense rather than any social theory suggests society is such an infinitely elaborate system of interlocking forces, pressures and relationships that there is no single cause of any social ill. Television will inevitably attract a disproportionate amount of attention, not simply because it is all-pervasive but because it is a mystery medium. Mass television is, after all, only half a century old and, in spite of thousands of research reports, relatively little is known about its effects on human behaviour. This is an issue that needs to be subjected to cool and careful analysis. We shall get nowhere by moralistic knee-jerk reactions.

Much of the heated public argument about violence on television is like a fireworks display in a fog. The causes of confusion are endless. In the first place, it is difficult to get an agreed definition of precisely what we are talking about. For instance, what have the following in common: a Tom and Jerry cartoon, news footage of the Mexico City earthquake, Carmen stabbed in Bizet's opera, the space shuttle tragedy, an African lion bringing down a gazelle, and Terry Wogan kicking a teddy bear in his chat show? Answer: they all figured in a catalogue of 'unacceptably violent' incidents on television compiled by the *Daily Express* some years ago from readers' letters.

Problems of definition are inevitable because no two human beings respond identically to the same stimulus; what gives one pleasure frightens another. If all the images reported to have shocked susceptible viewers were banished from our screens, the schedules would contain little other than the epilogue, the weather forecast on a calm day and gardening programmes, purged of distressing footage of vicious caterpillars savaging harmless plants. Nor is it possible to reach an acceptable definition by relying on some kind of public consensus, for the 'public' does not exist. There are as many publics as there are interests and passions in human nature. There is the public represented by the National Viewers' and Listeners' Association, which finds *EastEnders* offensive, and that other public, twenty-odd million of them, who watch it avidly every week. There is the public who protest at the gratuitous violence in some late-night films and the much larger counter-public who complain that, in cutting out the most violent bits, we programme schedulers are failing to treat them as responsible adults.

Viewers' memories, too, can be suspect. They often cannot recall on which channel they saw an offensive programme. So the BBC, ITV and Channel Four regularly receive wrongly directed complaints about programmes one of the others has transmitted. Worse, we are sometimes attacked about material none of us transmitted, stuff that was seen on hired videos. Still more confusing is not so much the fallible memory of some viewers as their overactive imagination. They will insist they have seen things in a programme that careful re-playing reveals no trace of. Two recent examples from my own channel. There was an alleged rape scene in *Lipstick On Your Collar*, where an admittedly aggressive husband, clumsily trying to comfort his distressed wife, inveigles her into bed for unenthusiastic, but certainly not forced, sex. A number of viewers not only complained of an unacceptably brutal rape, but went into explicit details that only their imaginations could have furnished, for none was actually broadcast. Then a recent episode of *Brookside* had a husband grabbing his wife and making as if to kick her, though no physical contact was shown and the sound effects were carefully muted. This scene provoked a sharp response from a number of viewers, many of whom claimed to have seen the actual kick and much more. These two incidents suggest that many viewers are particularly disturbed by acts of violence against women, whether actually shown or merely hinted at. That is a sensitivity we must always recognise. More difficult to answer is the philosophical question: since television at its best, like all the arts, is meant to appeal to and stimulate the human imagination, ought we to be held responsible if someone's imagination goes into over-gear and supplies the explicit detail we have deliberately kept off the screen, or never intended to imply in the first place? That is a conundrum for the Broadcasting Standards Council or the schools of media studies. The broadcasters can only make an infinite number of carefully weighed individual editorial decisions and hope they are right.

Let us be honest: though it is politically and culturally correct to deplore TV violence, the generality of the public are fascinated by it. They do not regard it as a regrettable reality which in an ideal world would vanish from our TV screens. Violence in its manifold forms has always been a central theme of our culture: classical culture, obviously – eliminate violence from Greek tragedy or the Bible or Shakespeare and they would be in tatters; but popular culture too. It is true that people's taste fluctuates. According to a recent survey, the public seems to be moving away from the more violent films towards family entertainment. This is a most welcome trend, but it is no use pretending it indicates a structural change in the human psyche, a return to the innocence of the Garden of Eden. Genres like the war film, the crime mystery, the western, the supernatural thriller will never lose their hold on the human imagination, nor should they.

Then there are the conflicting claims about the effect television violence has on those who watch it. Take the copycat argument. It is said that viewers, particularly young people, will be incited by what they see on TV to repeat the same behaviour on the streets. Implied here is a correlation that a hundred research reports have failed to establish. No one seems able to distinguish the chicken from the egg. Does watching violent television produce real-life aggression, or is it that aggressive personalities are particularly drawn to watch violent television? What about that other factor which seems to come from the depths of human nature rather than the television screen? If someone watches on TV a husband murder his wife by dropping an electric fire in her bath and the next morning disposes of his wife by the same method, it could be argued that television showed him how to vent his homicidal tendencies. But there is no evidence that television instilled those homicidal tendencies into him in the first place. Before the days of television, Agatha Christie offered her millions of readers a hundred ingenious ways of getting rid of an unwanted relative. But no one has suggested that Agatha Christie murder mysteries had any effect on the crime rate.

An offshoot of copycat syndrome is television's much overvalued powers of persuasion: TV must affect human behaviour, otherwise advertisers would not spend millions on TV commercials. That argument is nonsense. There are too many failed advertising campaigns to support this piece of glib logic. The public use television to select the brand that suits them, to help them make sense of the enormous choice of goods available. If TV is as powerful a persuader as the politicians would have us believe, how come the fall of the Soviet empire? There, the state had total control of TV, radio and all printed media for decades, but the people still resisted the message. The evidence for the copycat effect just does not stack up. TV is powerful, but as a communication medium, not a persuader.

In all this talk about the copycat effect of television, precisely which cat is being copied? What about the good cat; it never gets a mention. If television encourages imitation at all, then for most of the time it must be encouraging behaviour that is wholesome rather than antisocial. *EastEnders* has been attacked from time to time for setting a bad example, because drug trafficking, blackmail, homosexuality and illegitimacy have featured in its plots. But much more of its running time has been taken up with the themes of family solidarity, racial tolerance, care for the elderly, battles to save a stormy marriage and a host of virtues earthed in a totally believable community. Indeed, Dr Danielle Mercey, a consultant physician at the Middlesex Hospital, recently told a conference that an episode of *EastEnders*, transmitted in January 1991, encouraged more young people to have an HIV test than all the millions spent on government advertising, much of it (I might add) using frightening images aimed at instilling fear of AIDS.

It is possible to argue that images of violence on television have the opposite effect. For instance, the films *Threads* and *The War Game* spared viewers nothing of the horrors of a nuclear explosion, but it is doubtful that many who watched were spurred on to join the society for the propagation of nuclear bombs. Or consider some of the gruesome archive footage of First World War trench battles, often transmitted around Remembrance Sunday. To my knowledge, there has never been a single complaint about unacceptable violence in such programmes. It is as though the elegiac context in which the violence is shown transforms it from a brutalising to a piteous experience.

My predecessor at Channel Four must claim responsibility for producing the most violent series in the history of television. I refer of course to Jeremy Isaacs's epic twenty-six part series, *The World at War*. Every permutation and combination of man's inhumanity to man was shown in all its horror, but it is safe to say that the overall impression left on most viewers by the harrowing footage was an uplifting one to do with the triumph of the human spirit over organised evil. There is also the drip-drip argument, which charges that the sheer volume and frequency of violence on television de-sensitises viewers to the point where they take brutality for granted, breaking down a barrier of abhorrence which acts as a deterrent to real-life violence. Of course, it is beyond argument that sustained doses of any stimulus will have a numbing effect on the human system, so that it takes a greater quantity to produce the same effect. But, because viewers may become de-sensitised to violence on the screen, which is certainly a problem for the writer and producer, it does not follow that they will become equally blasé about violence in real life. Anyone who has been in wartime combat will confirm that a regular diet of John Wayne or Errol Flynn death-or-glory movies in no way prepared them for what they were about to experience on the battlefield. We may see innumerable car crashes on the television screen, but the horror is in no way mitigated when we first encounter those mangled bodies in a real-life car wreck. Recent horrific pictures from Bosnia have caused a worldwide public reaction of horror and pity for the victims. No evidence here of de-sensitisation.

The point is that television engages only two of our senses, sight and hearing. We can see and hear a violent act but not feel the pain of it. If we ever got around to marketing the 'feelies' of Aldous Huxley's *Brave New World*, where television viewers experienced the full sensuous impact of what they saw – the smell and taste and feel as well as the sight and sound of it – the chances are that nine-tenths of the violence would vanish from the TV screen overnight. Who would want to pay that price for realism? There is a paradox here. One danger in controlling too rigorously the depiction of violence on television is that what remains may not be violent enough. It may mislead viewers about the true horror of violence and seduce them into believing that people can be shot, slashed and beaten neatly, painlessly, almost forensically. Far from the shock of the real thing being lessened by its televisual representation, it may be all the more traumatic because the violence they have seen on the small screen has been distorted and sanitised.

At this point, there are some distinctions to be made between types of programmes which contain violent footage. One conclusive piece of research showed that viewers, including children, have a complex awareness of the distinction between the real and the fantastic. They take in their stride the stylised patterns of violent action found in cartoons and adventure films. Far from more violence being worse than less, a large number of deaths in, say, a James Bond film contributes to the air of unreality. Put differently, the more the violent scenes on television approximate to real-life situations viewers might find themselves in, the greater their degree of anxiety. The bloody extermination of a whole town by a green monster from Mars is perceived as harmless entertainment, whereas a realistic reconstruction on *Crimestoppers* of a masked intruder breaking into an old lady's home might fill some elderly viewers with fear.

We broadcasters need to keep a particularly close eye on that genre of programming known as 'faction', which uses a combination of fiction and documentary footage to cover a real-life event, precisely because it obscures the clear-cut boundary between fact and fantasy. Anything that weakens a television viewer's hold on reality is potentially dangerous. We have a duty not to play games with the public, nor wilfully to deceive them in such a way as to induce trauma. At the very least, this means adequate signposting and informative trailing of programmes so that the public does not contract for one experience and get another; expect family viewing and find itself confronted with a nightmare.

There is the further distinction between fictional violence and violent footage in news and current affairs programmes. Whether or not the world is a more violent place than it used to be is arguable. I read somewhere that historians claim that the thirteenth and fourteenth centuries were the most violent periods in our history. (I wonder whom the politicians of the time blamed? Probably media persons such as Geoffrey Chaucer, who produced parchment nasties, like the *Canterbury Tales*.) What is beyond doubt is that, because of the virtuosity of modern news-gathering technology, it is possible to give a much more comprehensive and often instantaneous account of what is happening in the world. Sadly, violence in one form or another figures largely in such an account and television journalists have a positive duty to report unpleasant realities so that viewers can understand and judge for themselves what is going on.

The very speed at which video footage of a violent incident can be sent to a TV newsroom means that often video packages arrive with only minutes to spare before a news bulletin deadline. There is no time for leisurely editing or measured debates about what ought to be shown. To me the miracle is just how often news editors get it right. When they do overstep the mark, the resulting public outcry is a backhanded compliment to their usual sure-footedness in showing just enough of a violent incident to enable viewers to understand its scale and significance without sliding into voyeurism. The knock-on effect of fact on TV fiction is obvious. Factual television's account of the passing scene is a major framework of reference for the fiction writer. Of course, some dramatic work will deal with positive, happy and peaceful themes in the teeth of harsh realities, much as one genre of films between 1939 and 1945 aimed to take people's minds off the war. But television would forfeit its right to be treated as a responsible cultural medium if its serious fiction lost touch with the texture of a world in turmoil as witnessed on TV news every day. God forfend we should turn our TV into an indigenous version of station KRML, which used to serve the coastal resort of Carmel-by-the-Sea in California. The station's policy was to broadcast only what it called sunshine programmes, news bulletins from which every mention of war, tragedy, disaster and death had been excluded; endless comedies but no dramas; soap operas purged of disease, divorce and misery; a diet of unremitting cheerfulness which the sceptics said resulted in a suicide rate in the town that was higher than the national average.

What are we to make of this mass of confusing and conflicting evidence? It is clear that violence on television can have a number of different effects on viewers. It may cause trauma or evoke pity, buoy the human spirit or plunge it into deep despair. Everything depends upon the social and moral context of what is depicted. Gratuitous violence is deplorable because it has no moral context; it is brutal imagery for its own sake. In fiction, it is without purpose, either in plot or character development; in factual programmes, it is not concerned to illuminate the human condition. It is raw sensation; explicit in the crude sense that pornography is often advertised as 'explicit', leaving nothing to the imagination, hinting at no truth that might explain or justify the otherwise inexplicable, a living being doing hurt to other living beings.

The way the moral context determines the nature of violence on television was neatly demonstrated by a survey of American men done in 1972, called 'Justifying Violence: attitudes of American men'. The researchers discovered that over a third of the sample did not regard footage of police beating up students as violent at all, in spite of the blood and screams and the meaty thwack of batons striking flesh. A majority of the sample also said that they would not classify archive film of US aircraft dropping napalm on Vietnamese villagers as violent. Apparently, violence is what they perpetrate against us; we merely apply legitimate force to them. So the moral ethos of a society at a given time influences the general acceptability of the violent act on television.

If we are talking about raw sensation without any context, I suppose that in terms of blood spilt and flesh mutilated one of the most violent programmes on TV has been the long-running BBC medical series, *Your Life In Their Hands*, which showed surgical operations in glorious Technicolor. The blood-letting was on an epic scale; flesh was cut and burnt, bones were sawn through, patients were torn limb from limb. Yet an average of twelve million viewers watched every week, probably with their fingers over their eyes. There was never a single complaint about unacceptably violent imagery. Why? Presumably because the moral context was positive; the aim of the blood and gore was to heal; the surgeons were rightly depicted as heroes in the battle against disease.

This surely brings us near to the nub of the issue about television violence. If the distinction between acceptable and unacceptable TV violence is set by the moral context, what happens when there is no consensus in our society about moral values? Programme standards are not worked out in a vacuum; they evolve as a result of a complex interplay between the broadcasters and the society they are addressing. Professor Bernard Williams, who chaired a

Home Office committee on obscenity, wrote: 'Every believer in some set of moral certainties has to share the world with other believers in some different set of moral certainties, and their only common interest may be in not accepting principles which allow someone else's certainties to persecute their own.' Hence a social milieu in which different ethical standards diverge from, or actually collide with, each other is one which presents great difficulties for broadcasters. Ought we to adopt a particular moral code and try to persuade everyone else to follow it? Or should we settle for offering a forum in which different moralities can encounter each other in a spirit of tolerance?

These are deep questions and broadcasters are not philosopher-kings, even though the politicians seem to be looking to us to demonstrate a moral clarity that most of them conspicuously lack. Contemporary broadcasters are denied the moral certitudes of a John Reith, who robustly insisted that the Bible was the final source of the BBC's ethics. Or there was Sir Arthur fforde, chairman of the governors of the BBC in the 1960s, who was once asked by an outraged viewer: 'Where does the BBC stand on bosoms?' He referred the enquirer to Milton's *Areopagitica*, adding: 'On second thoughts I ought to have drawn his attention to a passage in Dante's *Divine Comedy*.' Sir Arthur then helpfully quotes the passage in the original Italian. In 1993, the notion of the more contentious sequences in *Lethal Weapon 2* or *Rab C. Nesbitt* being judged by the standards of fourteenth-century Florentine literature taxes the imagination to the limit.

But you see the problem. Society has by default allowed television to assume a role in our society which the broadcasters neither want nor deserve. When family and community ties weaken, there are no protective barriers between viewers and television as a national source of image-making. So its power is magnified in much the same way as sound is amplified in a room empty of furniture. The violent images on the screen to which some take exception are magnified in impact, because they are filling a psychic vacuum left by the withering of other sources of authority. All this suggests, as many commentators have noted, that we face a major cultural crisis of which television violence is only one minor element. However great the general moral confusion, there must be some values, however few, binding a liberal democracy together, otherwise it would come apart at the seams. And one of these values is a concern for the vulnerable, for those who are in no position to defend themselves against a powerful medium invading their lives and imagination. I am thinking particularly of children. At present, both the BBC and ITV operate a watershed policy, which decrees that the hours before 9 p.m. are family viewing time, whereas programmes screened later may be more appropriate for adults and any children watching then ought to do so under parental guidance. This policy, now thirty years old, rests on two assumptions, neither of which is entirely justified: that popular programmes divide neatly into family and adult categories; and that there are grown-ups around in most households to supervise children's viewing habits.

A more fundamental question which broadcasters and society both need to address is: what precisely are we trying to protect children from? The standard answer is from knowledge for which their life experience has not yet prepared them. But this is very much the conventional wisdom of the print age, when adults occupied separate knowledge worlds, symbolised by public libraries with their junior and adult sections. As children matured, the idea was that the language and ideas they absorbed began to approximate more and more to those of adults, until the gap was finally closed and all knowledge was available to them. But television does not work like that; it encompasses everyone who watches it, adult or child, within the same information world. Also, television is a sequential medium. Programmes on very different subjects, making varying demands on viewers, flow past in no particular order. Thus *Blue Peter* used to be followed by the *Six o'Clock News* – plasticine by plastic explosive; chubby-cheeked British children by their skeletal African counterparts.

Now that violent video games and easily rented video nasties are universally available, mainline television is often likely to be written off as bland and boring by children. Understandably, therefore, the effectiveness of the watershed is being widely questioned, with proposals for change ranging from outright abolition to a second watershed being established at around 10.30 p.m., after which only the most adult programmes would be shown. My own view is that the watershed should be retained and in its present nine o'clock position. It has taken us thirty years to establish this compact or covenant between parents and broadcasters. To begin moving it around would increase the cultural confusion. At least parents and broadcasters know where they are. For all its weaknesses, the watershed is practical proof that public service broadcasting is held under ethical constraint; broadcasters are responsible to the wider community for a fair share of the consequences of their work. It also reminds programme-makers constantly of the special vulnerabilities of certain sections of their audience.

One of the most graphic examples of the divergence in standards between terrestrial and satellite television at the moment is in this matter of the watershed. At a time when public service broadcasters are resisting proposals from some that the watershed should be abolished altogether and from others that it should be pushed back to 10.30 p.m., the Independent Television Commission, which has so effectively regulated the boundaries of taste, permits satellite television to operate a more permissive eight o'clock watershed and an *even more* permissive ten p.m. watershed. There can be little justification for creating such confusion for parents. Three watersheds is two too many. Something has got to be done to establish equitable and comparable standards throughout the industry. However the picture gets into the home, parents have the same decisions to make. If we believe in maintaining standards, the encryption argument falls. Behind those who peddle this line is the notion of selling explicit violence for profit. That offends everything that public service broadcasting in Britain stands for. I do not really believe that the government wants it, even in the name of consumer sovereignty and the greater success of News International.

We need to keep a sense of proportion about all this. On the one hand, the broadcasters cannot create schedules which take account of the fact that some children might stay up way beyond nine o'clock until close-down. Adults, too, have their rights. To render all television suitable for viewing by five-year-olds not only restricts those rights but also ignores the statistical fact that less than a third of British households have any children at all in them. On the other hand, the broadcasters have neither the mandate, nor the authority, nor the means, to take responsibility for the education and nurture of children. That remains squarely where our society has placed it for centuries: with parents.

In fact, there is, if not a moral consensus, at least much common ground about ethical values within public service broadcasting itself. The tens of thousands of people involved at every level in the television programme-making process are not beings from outer space. The notion that the terrestrial broadcasters happily unleash upon the airwaves a flood tide of violence and sexual explicitness just for the hell of it is a gross slander. They do not spend all their lives walled up in concrete and glass dream factories. They live at the heart of the community as citizens, husbands, wives, partners, parents, neighbours. All the currents of sentiment and opinion swirling around in society flow through them. They, too, worry about the state of things in general and the impact of what they are doing in particular. Only those on the inside know the hours of agonised debate that go on in TV offices and viewing theatres and cutting rooms about what ought to be shown. The public would be able to appreciate just how seriously broadcasters take that task if they could see some of the material which ends up on the cutting-room floor and which does not get transmitted. Sky, of course, has its own set of values.

The late Sir Charles Curran, a former Director-General of the BBC, in his classic work on broadcasting philosophy and practice, 'A Seamless Robe', after analysing the role of broadcasting executives and the BBC governors on programme policy, concluded that the final defence against the gratuitously shocking or unacceptably traumatic lay not in government controls or managerial guidelines, but in the conscience of the individual programme-maker, tested against yardsticks established over the years through public service broadcasting's collective wisdom and experience. This tradition of moral and artistic integrity, which the BBC carefully nurtured and independent television has inherited, is a priceless asset which I fear may be dissipated if the balance-sheet mentality finally determines programme policy on any of the channels.

In the midst of all the clamour and controversy about this issue, I often remind myself that, in the end, television is just an art form; it is not a substitute for real life. Therefore the notion that everything relating to the human condition should be explicitly represented on television is at war with such central artistic virtues as reticence, the willingness to communicate experience without spelling it out, to coax the imagination without battering it into submission. There will always be true artists in the industry, who can use understatement, the oblique and metaphorical to emphasise what is not made manifest, thus allowing the imagination to flourish.

But, because television is an art form, programme-makers have both the duty and desire to extend the range of the viewer's worthwhile experience, to provide a platform for ideas and images that cast new and even disturbing light on what it means to be human. Yes, we broadcasters have a duty to Mrs Whitehouse and those who think like her. They are genuinely, if sometimes mistakenly, trying to conserve what they think is wholesome in our cultural life. But we also have a duty to Dennis Potter and all the serious creative minds who make British broadcasting a cultural force, not just a commercial commodity.

Speaking for Channel Four, its board and its staff, I believe we have a particular responsibility to those creative talents working in the most contentious areas of human experience: those, that is, with serious intention, not the exploiters. The vast majority of television output is perfectly congenial to viewers such as Mrs Whitehouse. Those parts which are not need to be both examined closely and protected and defended most fiercely, always provided they meet the traditional high standards of public service broadcasting. If we do not take responsible risks, our culture will wither and decay. Artists march to a different drummer from the rest of us. We must be prepared to offer them the freedom to create what we do not necessarily enjoy, agree with or approve.

In conclusion, let me briefly summarise my main points. Because we still do not know enough about the impact of television on the human psyche, I believe in intelligent regulation; but not just of terrestrial television. If satellite TV is allowed to do as it likes, it will inevitably drag the rest of the system down through the gravitational pull of material that establishes new low standards of permissiveness. Such coarsening of public taste must undermine what public service broadcasting has sought to establish over decades.

In this regard, I found somewhat risible the spectacle of this government huffing and puffing in righteous indignation at the horrid prospect of *Red Hot Dutch* (and other soft and hard porn) polluting our airwaves while apparently not noticing the delectable fare being served up on the Sky movie channels, such as *Emmanuelle, the monk*, 'a tale of forbidden passion, set in eighteenth-century Madrid, between a young monk and a seductress in league with the devil'; and *RSVP*, an 'erotic adult comedy about a film-maker who sets out to "audition" beautiful women'. I ought to resist the cynical conclusion that the proprietors of *Red Hot Dutch* own no newspapers and are, therefore, in no position of electoral support. But I cannot. Rupert Murdoch is the only proprietor of British national newspapers who is allowed to own more than 20 per cent of a licensed television service.

Public service broadcasters *can* be trusted. We are not infallible; we do get it horribly wrong occasionally. But, given that out of literally tens of thousands of hours of programmes on the four terrestrial channels each year only a handful cause legitimate public concern, the standards which have evolved out of the collective wisdom and experience of generations of greater broadcasters are holding; they are realistic and responsible. The great need is for yet more careful research, reflection and self-examination on the part of broadcasters. Knee-jerk moralising by politicians and others is not helpful. Public service broadcasting has a positive duty to enlarge the viewers' store of worthwhile experience and this means taking responsible risks. It means offering a platform for those who have new, more penetrating, and perhaps disturbing, light to cast on the human condition. We must defend their right to expression and their right to be distinguished from the 'anything goes if it makes a buck' merchants.

In a liberal democracy, there must always be a bias towards freedom of expression, in art as well as politics or any other area of human endeavour. John Milton's conclusion in *Areopagitica* is as relevant today as when it was first uttered: 'Give me the liberty to know, to utter, to argue freely, according to conscience, above all liberties.' Yet liberty without limits is meaningless. And the central problem of broadcasting is how to strike a balance between creative freedom and the susceptibilities of the audience. That is what the Annan Committee on the future of broadcasting said in 1974, and our dilemma could hardly be spelled out more succinctly. When the broadcasters fail to get that balance right, they face either public outrage or artistic frustration. It is a balance that can be stuck only programme by programme; it cannot be codified in a general principle or spelled out in a managerial directive. Even then, the boundary between the permissible and the forbidden in these contentious areas is not a clean-cut line, like an electrified fence. It is more like one of those disputed frontiers in unknown terrain: you only know you have crossed when someone starts shooting at you. So we shall occasionally wander astray and pay the inevitable price, a hide full of grapeshot.

James Cameron crossed many frontiers in his time, both geograph-
ically and in the human mind. I like to think he would cheer on the
broadcasters as they seek to give on television an account of the
human condition which is both honest and responsible.

John Tusa

Programmes or products?: the management ethos and creative values

1994

John Birt, who joined the BBC as Deputy Director-General in 1987 and became Director-General in 1992, was determined to secure the future of the BBC by persuading first Margaret Thatcher and then John Major that it could be run more efficiently. John Tusa's scarcely coded attack on Birt's management consultant approach to his mission reflected widespread internal distrust at what Birt was doing. John Tusa was Managing Director of the BBC World Service from 1986 to 1992, and has been Managing Director of the Barbican Centre since 1995.

E LECTRONIC AND PRINT media are now girdling the world instantaneously, rather than in the laggardly forty minutes of that Shakespearean slowcoach, Puck. The volume of processed information about the world grows by the nano-second and information is precision-targeted at, and micro-packaged for, particular interest and economic sub-groups. An inverse square law operates, whereby the more available the information, the less concentrated the attention it appears to get. At such a time, the memory and example of a great practitioner such as James Cameron properly acts as a reminder that journalism at its best is a simple human exchange, a person-to-person act of communication; that great events are best described and great personalities best caught by individual eyes; that understanding comes from the single mind; that theoretical systems of journalism are always less interesting than the personal response of the journalist; and that the only ultimate guarantee of journalistic integrity comes from the values of the individuals who operate them in practice.

Cameron was always aware of the transitory nature of the business of journalism. He was not – as the Psalmist warns us against being – puffed up. He looks back at the piles of old journalistic files, yellowing and fading into premature mortality, and muses in the foreword to his 1981 anthology, *The Best of Cameron*: 'Did I do this? Could it have been I who had this or that preposterous notion of history, could it have been this brash young reporter who stumbled on the fortunate phrase that somehow or other turned into prophecy?' And sometimes it was. As he put it candidly in an article for his trade magazine, *The Journalist*, in

1963: 'A few strong prejudices help. If you want to be solemn about it, you can call them values or beliefs, or what you will; something, anyway, that permits one occasionally to get pretty angry, or even the reverse. I have never been too good at the basic principle of reporting, which is total objectivity. I imagine I have been a bit subjective about everything I've ever done; I get no pleasure out of facts I dislike and a great deal from those I do, and I am told it creeps into the copy. Somehow I feel it's a bit late in the day for regrets. One survives.'

You cannot, of course, staff a modern media newsroom with an army of Cameronians. Think of the insubordination: resources do not permit such a luxury. Yet any management theory and practice that does not adequately take into account the human resource becomes a sterile exercise, undervaluing what should be most precious. Furthermore, the contemporary pressures of servicing outlets, of different programmes, of various editions, of conflicting deadlines are simply too great. As Charles Wheeler warned memorably, when asked of his opinion of a proposed rolling news network: 'When is the reporter ever going to get his work done, if he is on the air the whole time?'

It is, of course, not a problem that has crept up on us suddenly. Recently, a senior BBC correspondent said to me: 'We're not correspondents any more. We're scarcely even reporters. We have become reprocessors. There is no time for digging up the news.' Is this the condition of modern journalism? The BBC is, after all, solidly staffed and well resourced by comparison with its competitors. If such are the conditions for the BBC, what must they be like for its competitors?

What I have described so far are all recognisable editorial pressures. To the extent that editorial pressures deliver a better news and information service to their audiences, no journalist or broadcaster would want to halt the trend, even though many would want to monitor it and would want to be alert to the problems of journalistic overstretch. There are only a certain number of things that an observer of events has to say, only a certain number of thoughts to expound. Staleness and repetition can only be avoided if the journalist has the time to see, the opportunity to be present, the chance to think before rejoining the broadcasting treadmill driven by the remorseless demands of news gathering and programme delivery. Once, the journalist's anxiety was to get on the air. Today, the problem, the dread, is to get off it.

Further pressure comes from another direction, driven by other interests, answering to other values. The direction is managerial. The pressure is for efficiency. The demands are for measurable economy. Combined with the intensified editorial pressures, the two together lead to stringent re-examination of how the journalism is actually carried out. Let me make it clear that the issue is not whether some kind of management-driven change is or is not desirable; that ceased to be an issue once Whitehall itself took the 'First Steps' down that road and once institutions such as the BBC began to follow.[1] Nor is it an issue for those, like myself, who ask questions and express anxieties about it. What is at issue is the suitability of the methods chosen for the activities and institutions to which they are being applied. That is a proper, legitimate question.

It is this tension between the subjective, instinctive activity of journalism and broadcasting and the purportedly objective methods of some schools of modern management that I want to explore. I want also to look at the impact that management reform of one institution – the civil service – had when it spilled beyond the borders of the civil service into the entire public sector, including the BBC. My basic propositions are as follows. The new work practices that emerge from the twin pressures of extra editorial demand and novel management theory may certainly fit some criteria of efficiency. They undoubtedly fit the management jargon and assumptions of the day. They may well demonstrate that they use some scarce resources economically. But can they really demonstrate true effectiveness in all its complexity?

1 The 1979–90 Thatcher government set out to change the culture and management style of the Whitehall civil service. The most radical steps came with the launch of the 'Next Steps' programme in 1988, aimed at decentralising administration and achieving competition by moving functions from sponsoring departments to contracted agencies.

Journalistic effectiveness is one thing, management efficiency may well not be the same. For where, in all this reductive numericalism, is the room for creative insights. Where is the space for understanding. Where is the scope for richness of language, boldness of image, the shaft of emotion? We know the price of a programme; but, in the process of determining it, in our zeal to cost, to manage, to define, to pin down, are we in danger of losing sight of the true nature of the activity in which we are engaged, and of the people for whom it exists, our audiences?

The audience certainly wants to perceive that an institution for which it pays is not profligate with its money. It does not follow that the audience is primarily concerned that each individual production and programme should be absolutely economical with its costs. Yet what are the consequences of devising systems whose principal intention appears to be to ensure such detailed efficiencies at the micro level, perhaps at the cost of real damage to the fundamental purposes of the programmes themselves? In hunting down the merely quantifiable with remorseless zeal, are we not in real danger of losing the unquantifiable, of squeezing out the imponderables such as quality, of marginalising the inconveniently unmeasurable? Is the tidy driving out the inspirational? You cannot, after all, set a production quota for inspiration, a performance indicator for genius. But, if all the time is spent on measuring the routine, where is the intellectual space for fostering the remarkable? You can only hope to create an atmosphere in which it may occur. You can never guarantee that it will. Where in our lean, hard, spartan unsentimental world do we make room for those qualities, those activities that do not fit in with today's management-consultant-driven categories? Are we not in danger of falling into Oscar Wilde's trap? The cynic, he observed, is a person who 'knows the price of everything but the value of nothing'. Have we all become practising cynics, so obsessed with the price that we no longer attempt to consider value; so obsessed with what we can measure that we ignore what we cannot? Is even the attempt to set a price on value undermined by the very processes which now undertake the actual costing? To stay with the great Oscar, is not the entire world of number-driven management like his definition of fox-hunting – a case of the Unspeakable in pursuit of the Uncountable? Organisations are instructed to determine and live by their 'core businesses'; how often are they required to define and live by their 'core values'?

What is at stake is not whether an old institution is capable of learning new tricks. It must in order to survive. Nor is it a question of claiming that everything was fine in the past. It is a question of asking how much is controlled, what is controlled, at what level and, crucially, in what way. Such questions can only be answered against some historical background. We are where we are in this new managerial world not by accident, not by malign act of

divinity, but as the result of a defined and clearly traceable historical process. The new managerial techniques (and the pressures
and disciplines that flow from them) blow coldly and indifferently
on all parts of Whitehall and the public sector. Of those sectors of
which I have some personal experience, broadcasting moved into
the era of change rather earlier than most; the arts are following
fast, while the academic world is still in parts deeply unaware of
what exactly lies in store for it.

These new disciplines are only those that the private sector had
used for years. That in no way diminished the sense of shock when
they were first introduced into the public sector. For the BBC, they
started with a series of Performance Management courses in
country-house conference centres. These early courses had more of
theatrical performance in them than of management. A prototype
version had generated real and understandable hostility among
BBC participants, with its emphasis on games-playing, mask-
wearing and picture-painting as ways of releasing the supposedly
unbearable internal repression of the typical BBC middle manager.
They rebelled. They chose to stay repressed. They were ready to
rethink management, but they were damned if they were going to
reshape their personalities just because the Corporation wanted it.
More practically, these serious and competent people needed
persuasion that the new and wholly untried and untested vocabu-
lary of Objectives, Performance, Goals, Mission Statements and so

on was, first, something they could understand; second, something they might respect; and third, something they could usefully apply to the work they were already doing rather well, but might do better as a result.

My own attitude to this new activity was somewhat blunt and utilitarian. I suggested to the doubters that there were three reasons for taking it seriously. First, hard pragmatism. If Whitehall was moving in this direction, then it was wise not to ignore it. Second, it was not that difficult to understand and apply: the hoop was not a hard one to jump through. Third, it was already clear that the process was one that could be turned to our own advantage. We could learn from it. Only a fool would reject an activity from which something good could result. The impulse had indeed come from Whitehall; but the art was to turn it into something that we first mastered, then made our own.

But how did that managerial change come to Whitehall itself? Two names above all are associated with this revolution – Sir Derek Rayner, Margaret Thatcher's Efficiency Adviser from 1979 to 1983, and his successor, Sir Robin Ibbs, from ICI and the Downing Street Think Tank, from 1983 to 1988. While their primary task was to turn the civil service into a managerial machine that worked more like the private sector, it was inevitable that the changes introduced into Whitehall itself would end up well beyond it. Rayner set up a body called the Financial Management Unit, a small task force whose responsibility was to stimulate the introduction of new methods throughout Whitehall. I shall not attempt to summarise a large and complex process, but merely highlight some of the thinking that ultimately lapped over into the public sector world beyond. The Financial Management Initiative of 17 May 1982 recommended three instructions to allow all civil servants to do their jobs more efficiently: they should have clear objectives and ways of measuring whether they had been achieved; clear responsibilities for the use of resources; and suitable information, training and access to expert advice to exercise these responsibilities effectively.

Yet, even in 1982, the authors of the Financial Management Initiative noted that there were conceptual problems in applying these essentially private sector principles to the public service: 'The yardstick of profitability is lacking. Many government objectives are generalised, and the test of their success is often acceptability rather than a quantified measure of output. In some areas, final measures of output are elusive and only partial indicators of performance can be devised.' In other words, the Rayner team was well aware of the dangers of comparing apples with pears. Of course, both are fruit and both grow on trees, but there the differences begin. While the civil service might be like private enterprise in some respects, and while there appeared to be no other managerial model to which to turn, Rayner and his colleagues were sufficiently sensitive to realise that they were working by rough analogy, not with a rigid template.

They knew that civil service policies were not exactly the same as private sector products. A departmental policy or a government programme might be the final output of a public sector department or institution, but that did not make it the same as a material final output in the private sector. In the private sector, that material final output shows up inexorably in the financial bottom line. In the civil service, or more broadly in the public sector, the final output can only be measured in terms of the public good. The understanding of that crucial difference was flagged up from the earliest stages. The authors of the FMI did not believe that unwilling institutions could or should be forced to lie on a Procrustean bed of reform just in case it might be good for them. They were not of the sado-masochistic school of management.

There were other, now overlooked, elements in the Rayner formula. He insisted that the process of departmental scrutiny, of internal self-discovery, should be an internal one: 'Ministers and their officials are better equipped than anyone else to examine the use of the resources for which they are responsible. The scrutinies, therefore, rely heavily on self-examination.' Yet, a decade later in April 1994, a report from the Prime Minister's Efficiency Unit revealed that the government had spent £565 million on 6,800 external management consultancy projects, as a result of which a total of a mere £10 million had been saved in government expenditure. The report noted, too, that during the same period the £78 million spent on internal departmental consultancies had yielded £18 million of savings, almost double the level of savings achieved by the external scrutineers at a seventh of the cost.

Naturally, this report attracted some attention. Martin Kettle in the *Guardian* commented on 'the extraordinarily unmeasured power of management theory in any large contemporary organisation, whether in the private or public sector'. He went on to address the glaring disparity between the effectiveness of insiders examining their own organisation by contrast with outsiders: 'Today's dominant ideology despises in-house management in the public sector. It is treated as second-rate. It is constantly compared unfavourably with management that has learned "the disciplines of the private sector". The figures make one ask: what disciplines?' The paper that broke the story, the *Financial Times*, reported the views of the implicitly criticised management consultants that the civil service did not know how to use these reviews properly. One said that the excessive emphasis on controlling costs meant that the customers of these consultancy services were less effective at improving their processes than they should be. Another observed wisely: 'The best consultancy delivers benefits to the stakeholders in an organisation by creating partnership between the consultants and the clients.' How many other organisations have tried to create such a partnership between insiders and outsiders? How many organisations have asked themselves the question about the costs and benefits of external advice, or the more profound question raised by Martin Kettle about the 'unmeasured power of management theory'?

There is a deeper question applying to civil servants and broadcasters. What are those at the receiving end of fundamental and imposed external scrutiny supposed to think? First, that they are judged incapable of initiating and managing change themselves. Second, that they are excluded from an autonomous role in the transformation of their own work. Third, that they are destined to be permanently de-skilled from these activities. Fourth, that they are not partners in the process, but perpetual victims. The use of management consultancy may be an important management tool, but it can feel like a punitive raid by management rather than a liberating one, if deployed ham-fistedly and with the unspoken implication that such a superior activity cannot be trusted to insiders. This may also mask an unspoken fear by some managements: that, even if they did ask their staff what they thought, they would not get a constructive answer, or perhaps not the answer they want. Yet the experience of some consultants is that the best answers to an institution's problems always lie within that institution. Outsiders may be needed to frame the right question. But as one consultant said to me: 'If you ask people the right questions, the answer from inside will always be better.'

In a conversation with Peter Hennessy, Rayner mused on the process of introducing cultural change into an institution: 'Cultural changes are not brought about even by good desires. They're brought about by acquiring new habits and being able to observe that those new habits are effective and enjoyable to perform.' How typical of Rayner that he insisted on the need for enjoyment in the new tasks. He seemed quite untroubled by the fact that 'enjoyment' in cultural change cannot be measured. If the new tasks were imposed, dragooned, rigidly implemented, how could anybody from within the existing culture be expected to accept them, if they were imposed in a mood of glum conformism? Once again, the voice from the early years of the Whitehall revolution should draw all of us still involved in the process back to some of its fundamental assumptions.

It was shortly after Robin Ibbs took over the Efficiency Unit from Derek Rayner that a refined set of definitions emerged from the Financial Management Unit. These questions were simple, unavoidable and unobjectionable, yet the demands expressed by them were inexorable. As quoted by Peter Hennessy in his book *Whitehall*, ministers agreed that, once it was decided that a new policy or policy review was to be undertaken, 'the departments should state what is going to be achieved, by when, at what cost and how that achievement is going to be measured subsequently'.

Four questions that shook the public sector. Casually spoken, those pointed queries rolled off a thousand civil servant tongues to a thousand agencies or funded bodies as the new mantra. They were the new catechism of value for money, and those who could not answer its questions were definitely not of the body of the faithful in principle; and were very unlikely to be saved in practice. True, their invocation, like a cry to the High Priest of Baal, could become a substitute for thought. Certainly, it could be used as a new toy for civil service or bureaucratic delay, obstruction and obfuscation. Yet, though sometimes misused, nothing could diminish the potency of this simple agenda for scrutiny. And there was, of course, a civil service longstop, the catch-22, the fine print; just because you can answer all the questions satisfactorily does not mean that your pet project will be approved; but you will certainly not get it approved unless the answers are right.

Robin Ibbs's great achievement was the formulation of 'Next Steps', a plan, as its name suggests, to build on the Rayner reforms. By then the process of internal Whitehall reform was already seven years old. In publicly and directly funded bodies, such as the BBC World Service, we were very much aware of the way that the Whitehall game had changed between 1986 and 1993. It was more rigorous, more potentially intrusive, more time-consuming, but also offered opportunities for strategies of our own which could give us an advantage in the Whitehall contest. The process of interaction between ourselves and civil servants was guided, as far as we were concerned at least, by the reflection that we would not merely react to outside pressures, however novel they might seem at first. 'Yes', we insisted, 'any changes must be appropriate to the nature of our broadcasting activity, must not negate our managerial freedom and must not derogate from our position as an integral part of the BBC. We are not part of the civil service. We are broadcasters and journalists. We are not making policy. We are producing programmes to satisfy the listeners. We must always maintain that sense of difference and insist that the Whitehall changes are applied in a way that is appropriate and suitable to our activity. We will not curry favour with our Whitehall masters in the hope of appeasing them. We will actually become better at their newly devised game than they are. Above all, our own staff must accept that they are being asked to do something that enhances their skills, respects their knowledge and experience, and benefits their work in a perceptible way.' That was the fundamental stance from which we in the BBC World Service approached the new managerial demands being made of us.

But, while we were devising our appropriate responses to the new demands, Whitehall itself was taking stock. What was truly revelatory in the 1988 report to the Prime Minister from the Ibbs Efficiency Unit was not so much the headline conclusions about the need to transfer as much civil service activity to self-administering agencies as the self-scrutiny of the entire process of civil service change, revealed in the appendix. The Inquiry Team had canvassed working civil servants about their responses to managerial reform and how it was affecting them. The results contained strong warnings – to any management inclined to listen – about the pitfalls of radical change poorly handled, roughly introduced and crudely imposed. The comments did not make comfortable reading, not because they were critical, but because they were serious and relevant. As you read them, you thought: 'Any management which disregards this does so at its peril.'

What did those 'inside the whale' say? Many complained of the 'weight of paper surrounding the systems and the numbers of forms to be filled in'. As one person said, 'typical civil service; management has been bureaucratised'. Another queried whether the activities they were having to undertake were intended to last. 'Was it an integral part of the work of policy divisions, rather than a one-off, form-filling exercise?' The implication was that, if it represented a true change of working, then it might be justified. If it was a one-shot process to give its instigators a sense of personal achievement, then they were much less impressed. Another lamented the absence of feedback from management and added that top management failed to face up to the decisions with which their own new systems confronted them. Another observed perceptively that, while everybody was now more 'cost conscious' in general, what had been lost in the process was 'consciousness about results'. (The process was cheaper, you might say, but what was the programme like?)

The process concentrated attention on to inputs and their costs, 'not on outputs and value for money'. Others complained that, despite the talk of devolution of responsibility, the centre clung on to its power and dictated the way departments organised and managed themselves – this was 'totally at odds with the principles of good delegated management as set out in the FMI'. Robin Ibbs's 'Next Steps' paper candidly listed these criticisms as examples of the damaging side effects to be avoided by anybody introducing institutional change in the name of management efficiency and effectiveness. As a checklist to be set against the introduction of any new management system, it could hardly be bettered. As a process of management self-scrutiny, it can only be respected. By publishing such critical comments in such a prominent way, those responsible for change were signalling that they respected the views of existing staff, that they acknowledged failures in the process and that such critical self-awareness was a vital part in the process of reinvigoration of the institution. Can every institution say as much? The purpose of such critical self-review was and is to make sure that errors are not creeping into the processes and systems.

Now the conclusions that I draw from this review of the sources of the new management drive in the public sector are that those involved were properly sensitive to the difficulty and subtlety of what they were doing. They realised that there was not an exact fit between their chosen methodology of change and the civil service and public sector to which it was about to be applied. They understood that the imprecision of the fit had to be handled sensitively, but that it did not matter if the civil service did not become exactly like the private sector, indeed it was impossible that it should. They knew, in other words, in the shorthand of journalism, that 'programmes are not products'.

Just because something is like something else does not make it identical with it. That is a vulgar fallacy. If a programme is treated as a product, then those aspects of a programme which are will be magnified to the point of distortion. At the same time, those very immeasurable qualities that give a programme its essential difference from a mere product will be squeezed out. A programme is not like a widget, endlessly replicable and endlessly performing a pre-specified and limited function. A programme, let alone a good programme, defies definition, performs a multiplicity of functions and delivers a variety of unpredictable satisfactions. Systems of management control that tend to treat programmes like products can only end up defeating the very activity they claim to protect.

Of course, the fact that a programme is not like a widget is not a reason for avoiding the attempt at some analysis. Some programmes – particularly series programmes – are replicable. That is part of their function. In this they may resemble public sector services – the audience receives a programme as its final output. But the analysis appropriate to such programme series must be softer, more intuitive, more in tune with the nature of the activity, if it is to be useful and ultimately effective. None of this is to say that systems of management scrutiny and control are unnecessary or should not be used. That is yesterday's world. As Rayner recognised long ago, it may be the best system available. But, so long as the difference is not respected and a readiness to acknowledge the difference is not built into the system somewhere, the result will be a needless rigidity that the founding fathers of Whitehall reform showed themselves keen to avoid.

Have those warnings been taken to heart even in the civil service? Judging by a recent article in the *Observer*, they have not, and certainly the huge reliance on external consultancy to the exclusion of internal departmental self-scrutiny suggests not. The *Observer* article, headed 'Civil Service on Its Last Legs', noted: 'This month, an accountant's report revealed that the majority of agency chief executives are obsessed with meeting financial targets and drawing up business plans.' Does this have a familiar ring? The report added an – of course, anonymous – comment from a civil servant with two decades' standing: 'All the very naive management theories that have been chucked at us in the last ten to fifteen years have had a corrosive effect. They have not been thought through, they have not been applied by people who believe in them, and because the civil service is not used to this sort of thing, it has probably accepted fads and fashions too easily.' My only observation is that having fashionable fads applied by those who do not believe in them is marginally better than having them applied by those who do.

A certain kind of over-prescriptive managerial revolution runs into real difficulties as soon as it becomes inappropriate to the activity it is trying to manage. Bent as it is on quantification, based as it is on measurement, driven as it is by a belief that accurate measurement, promise of delivery and fulfilment of targets are not only sufficient in themselves but will draw approval from the audience, how does it deal with the unquantifiable, with quality, with inspiration? It is no answer to say that these imponderables are deliberately left outside and that the act of measurement applies only to those characteristics that lend themselves to quantification. The very authority of the system of measurement, the insistence on 'programme as product' is so intense that anything omitted from its compass is seen as having less or no legitimacy. In any case, the very rigour of the accountability system does not allow for such 'coned off' areas where the unquantifiable can flourish. In a management culture where only numbers count, the uncountable is not only illegitimate, it is insignificant as well. Professional judgement is dismissed as subjective hunch; professional experience is written off as disabling prejudice; those who have it are dismissed as tainted with experience; professional claims are rejected as mere special pleading or self-serving protectionism.

But management culture goes beyond counting and the digitalisation of the creative activity. It has given a set of new instruments to those – whether internal managers or civil servants – who do not wish to delegate responsibility, but seek to find ways of retaining it still more effectively. Think of the fun you can have with 'performance indicators'. Any manager worth his or her salt can think up so many required indicators of successful performance that the people responsible for delivering them are tied hand and foot. Like Gulliver, they have thousands of tiny strings attached to their limbs, all in the name of accountability and the need to prove beyond a numerical peradventure that the programme is doing its job. How could Gulliver prove that he was a giant? Because it took millions of ropes to tie him down. What is needed is not a cat's cradle of indicators but a handful of key ones that spring from the nature of the activity – programme-making – and give guidance as to whether or not it is being properly carried out.

It is not a question of crying, 'Stop the managerial bus, I want to get off.' That is not and never has been the issue. The issue is: 'Where is this bus going and have the passengers any choice in the matter?' It is a question of adapting the new systems when, where and how it is relevant to do so, always bearing in mind the nature of the institution to which they are being introduced. So long as the suitability of the systems to the institution is either ignored or put to one side, so long will the systems fail to deliver what it is hoped, and no doubt intended, that they should.

As long ago as 1989, an internal Bush House Report (not one written by a management consultant) identified the difference between two sides of an institution's nature – its ethos (that is to say its permanent disposition, its true underlying characteristics) and its pathos (that is to say the overt, often transitory, usually volatile expressions of feelings of the organisation). The report warned that the spirit of the ethos and its pathos needed to be kept carefully aligned; that sounds of distress from the pathos might give warnings that the institution's fundamental ethos was feeling violated. The ethos did not reject the process of change; but the pathos was uttering warning signals that the way change was being introduced was not felt to be congruent with the underlying ethos.

These were wise words. The external adviser may all too easily be seen as the intruder, the violator of the institutional ethos. The sounds of distress from the organisation's pathos at this sense of intrusion and violation cannot be dismissed as shallow, negative and superficial. Most importantly, the report implicitly stated that an institution's ethos is not owned by its management; it is owned by the staff. Any management that ignores this, that undervalues the basic ethos, or that tries even to reconstruct it without reference to staff, who know in their hearts of hearts that they embody that ethos in all daily actions, risks an internal psychological schism that will not easily be repaired. After all, most of those in the BBC are deeply loyal to the institution and the idea behind it. Who ever heard of anyone being loyal to a business unit or a cost centre?

I am consoled in these reflections by a number of thoughts. One of them came to mind recently when I was reading Kenneth Clark's autobiography. He tells of how he and the team making the series *Civilisation* had finished shooting in the Sistine Chapel and were about to wrap for the day when K. suddenly spotted the possibility of an extraordinary tracking shot down in the length of the Vatican Gallery corridors. They decided to have a go in the time available. He and they pulled off a piece to camera that was one of the wonders of the series. The shocking thing about this story is that it never crossed K'.s mind, throughout the series, that he should know what it cost. He concentrated on giving the viewer the best possible understanding of civilisation, the greatest possible access to objects and places we might never have seen, connected by the thought processes of a person whose lifetime love had been in seeing them, learning about them and understanding them.

Why did they make the series? Not because research told them to do so; not because it was demanded by a performance indicator; not because it fitted a predetermined genre of programme that the department was instructed to meet. They made it out of love and commitment, dedication to the subject, respect for themselves and responsibility to the audience – in a word, because they knew the difference between a programme and a product.

Jeremy Isaacs

The reporter's victories

1995

James Cameron was many things, but above all he was a reporter. Increasingly, the world in which journalists work is subjected to commercial and technological pressures, and Jeremy Isaacs – founding Chief Executive of Channel Four Television 1981–7, General Director of the Royal Opera House 1988–97, Chief Executive of Jeremy Isaacs Productions since 1998 and knighted in 1996 – used his lecture to celebrate 'great reporting'. Extracts in this lecture were read lightly and exactly by the actor John Bett.

A HORSE, A BUGGY and several sets of harness, valued in all at about $2.50, were stolen last night from the stable of Howard Quinlan, near Kingsville. The county police are at work on the case, but so far no trace of either thieves or booty has been found.

These words appeared in the *Baltimore Morning Herald* in 1899. They were written – his first appearance in print – by H. L.

Mencken, whom Alistair Cooke judges to have been 'the master craftsman of daily journalism in the twentieth century'. Here he is again, eighteen years later in 1917, describing a minor revolution in Cuba. A friend briefs him as soon as he arrives by sea in Havana. He is eating a plate of bean soup and smoking a cigar.

> 'The issues in the revolution,' he said, tackling the business in hand at once, 'are simple. Menocal, who calls himself a Conservative, is president, and José Miguel Gómez, who used to be president and calls himself a Liberal, wants to make a come-back. That is the whole story. José Miguel says that when Menocal was re-elected last year the so-called Liberals were chased away from the so-called polls by the so-called army. On the other hand, Menocal says that José Miguel is a porch-climber and ought to be chased out of the island. Both are right.'
>
> (*Gore in the Caribbees*)

Now to interview both parties: Menocal first.

> I found His Excellency calm and amiable. He spoke English fluently, and was far from reticent. José Miguel, he said, was a fiend in human form who hoped by his treasons to provoke American intervention, and so upset the current

freely chosen and impeccably virtuous government. This
foul plot would fail.

The gallant Cuban army, which had never lost either a
battle or a war, had the traitor cornered, and within a few
days he would be chained up among the lizards in the
fortress of La Cabaña, waiting for the firing-squad and
trying in vain to make his peace with God.

(*Gore in the Caribbees*)

The rebels are up-country, Mencken thinks, and inaccessible. But
no, says his guide, we'll take a hack. They stop outside a bank. In an
apartment above are the rebel offices, a doctor presiding.

The doctor, like *el presidente*, spoke excellent English, and
appeared to be in ebullient spirits. He had trustworthy
agents, he gave me to understand, in the palace, some of
them in high office. He knew what was going on in the
American embassy. He got carbons of all official telegrams
from the front. The progress of events there, he said, was
extremely favorable to the cause of reform.

As for Menocal, he was a fiend in human form who
hoped to provoke American intervention, and thereby
make his corrupt and abominable régime secure. All this
naturally struck me as somewhat unusual, though as a

newspaper reporter I was supposed to be incapable of surprise. Here, in the very heart and gizzard of Havana, within sight and hearing of thousands, the revolutionists were maintaining what amounted to open headquarters, and their boss wizard was talking freely and indeed in a loud voice, to a stranger whose only introduction had been, so to speak, to ask for Joe.

(*Gore in the Caribbees*)

I love that 'heart and gizzard' of Havana. Happy, and deservedly fortunate, the reporter who takes the trouble always to ask for Joe. You don't find Joe, by the way, in the press hotel.

Taking Mencken as my starting point and pillaging what others have written, I want to look at 'good reporting'. I shall be prompted by the winners of the Cameron Prize and their work. The roll-call is a remarkable one. They are reporters all. To their eyes and ears and voices and minds and microphones and typewriters, we owe something of what we have learned of the world in the past decades. We can be grateful to them for that. We can also be grateful for the simple literary pleasure – the right words in the right order – that their work gives us, even if (too often) it is also a set of grim reminders, telling instance after instance of man's inhumanity to man.

Mencken wrote a column. He wrote criticism. He was a lexicographer. Bernard Levin is said to have modelled his rhetorical style on Mencken the essayist in full flood. And that is wonderful stuff. But, like Alistair Cooke, I prefer Mencken the reporter. Here he is in Dayton, Tennessee, reporting the Scopes trial. Scopes was the schoolteacher charged with blasphemy for introducing evolution into the classroom in Christian fundamentalist country. The truths of Genesis, folks there maintained, were God-given. Man did not descend from monkeys. Scopes stood trial.

Mencken sent this despatch, in its first form, to the *Baltimore Evening Sun* in July 1925. He wrote it, he tells us, on a roaring hot Sunday afternoon in a Chattanooga hotel room, naked above the waist, and with only a pair of BVDs below. He found real religion out of town, up in the hills.

> The preacher stopped at last, and there arose out of the darkness a woman with her hair pulled back into a little tight knot. She began so quietly that we couldn't hear what she said, but soon her voice rose resonantly and we could follow her. She was denouncing the reading of books. Some wandering book agent, it appeared, had come to her cabin and tried to sell her a specimen of his wares. She refused to touch it. Why, indeed, read a book? If what was in it was true, then everything in it was already in the Bible. If it was false, then reading it would imperil the soul.
>
> Suddenly a change of mood began to make itself felt. The

last hymn ran longer than the others, and dropped gradually into a monotonous, unintelligible chant. The leader beat time with his book. The faithful broke out with exultations. Then a half-grown girl emerged from the darkness and threw herself upon it. We noticed with astonishment that she had bobbed hair. 'This sister,' said the leader, 'has asked for prayers.' We moved a bit closer. We could now see faces plainly, and hear every word. At a signal all the faithful crowded up to the bench and began to pray – not in unison, but each for himself. At another they all fell on their knees, their arms over the penitent. The leader kneeled facing us, his head alternately thrown back dramatically or buried in his hands. Words spouted from his lips like bullets from a machine-gun – appeals to God to pull the penitent back out of Hell, defiances of the demons of the air, a vast impassioned jargon of apocalyptic texts. Suddenly he rose to his feet, threw back his head and began to speak in the tongues – blub-blub-blub, gurgle-gurgle-gurgle. His voice rose to a higher register. The climax was a shrill, inarticulate squawk, like that of a man throttled. He fell headlong across the pyramid of supplicants.

(The Hills of Zion)

Newspaper reporters work fast. They never have the luxury of time. But they can use space, and, if they have space, the details stay in.

And it is the detail of it, the particularity, that makes that last report worth preserving. It brings the scene before us still.

At about the same time, I guess, that Mencken was re-editing that piece, James Cameron was learning the journalist's trade in Scotland. He worked for D. C. Thomson in Dundee, home of the *Dandy, Beano*, the *Hotspur* and *Red Star Weekly*. He commissioned illustrations to accompany lurid text; for example, a piece on a serial killer, 'The Man With the Glaring Eyes', had to have a picture of his latest victim beside it.

> It was a highly successful realisation; the draughtsman had clearly put his heart into his work, and he had delin-eated the character of the lady's injury with an almost clinical fidelity; hardly was a torn tendon or a severed blood-vessel out of place, and the blood that streamed into the rain-swept gutter had been limned by an enthu-siast. It did complete justice, I felt, to 'The Man With the Glaring Eyes'.
>
> I took this along for Mr Donald's approval with a quiet and calm confidence. When he saw it he blenched. He tore it from my hand and studied it aghast, and in speechless outrage. Finally he said: 'You must be mad.' Accepting that I might possibly on this occasion have overdone it, I murmured: 'It is a bit strong, maybe.'

> 'Strong, strong,' cried Mr Donald. 'It's no' a question o'
> strong; it's no' a bad scene. But for God's sake, boy – look
> at the lassie's skirt; it's awa' above her knees!'
>
> (*Points of Departure*)

After a couple of years the Thomson papers shifted him from
Dundee to Glasgow, just below the Cowcaddens (where my own
father had his shop) and he worked there on the *Sunday Post*. There
was no demarcation; he did everything: writing 'a nice wee middle';
ghosting 'Secrets of the Mayfair Vice Rings'; or, after a murder trial,
guiding a mother's hand through 'Why My Boy Should Not be
Hanged'. And subbing. Saturday night was press night. Sitting at
the subs' table, James would find himself listening to a colleague
wheedling the *Post*'s stringers into sending in something, anything,
juicy enough to merit inclusion in the next day's paper.

> 'Ay, Jock boy, good, good; to the effusion o' blood, eh; that's
> no' bad at all. Four fellas to this one lassie up the close-
> mouth; fine, fine. Fish-shop afire up by Bridgton; good,
> good – no fatal casualties, eh; pity, never mind, there's time
> enough; we can take fatalities up to around midnight; do
> your best, lad; try and get me a wee slashing in the Gorbals;
> it's a thin night for the town edition.'
>
> (*Points of Departure*)

It soon became apparent to Cameron, and to others, that his abilities could be put to better use than by the *Sunday Post*. He left for points south, joined the *Daily Express*, and became an itinerant foreign correspondent.

My own lifelong love affair with newsprint began young. We took several papers daily: the *Bulletin*, a sort of genteel tabloid, a spinster sister to the *Glasgow Herald*, run on the basis that the more names it printed, the more readers it would have. My brother and I were photographed for it once, on a spring day in the Botanical Gardens on our tricycles. With luck, I would find my name on the back page on a Monday: Glasgow Academy 2nd XI 83 for 7 (J Isaacs 22). The *Glasgow Herald* was a solid, businessman's paper, nurturer of many good journalists; and we took the *Manchester Guardian*. On Sundays, we took the *Sunday Express* (with Crossbencher, Nathaniel Gubbins and John Gordon) and Kemsley's staid *Sunday Times*; and the *Observer*. There was a weekly squabble for first crack at the *Observer*, bursting with writing talent. A wise friend of the family surprised me by telling me he never bought the same daily paper two days running; there was advantage in seeing what different newspapers had to say and making up your own mind. This precept I was happily able to follow, and even preach, when I went to work. My first employers, Granada, entrusted to me *What the Papers Say*, a weekly critique of the press, modelled on 'The Wayward Press', A. J. Liebling's perceptive jottings in the *New Yorker*.

What the Papers Say was forbidden by the Broadcasting Act of those days – the Television Act – from expressing an editorial opinion on any issue of the day. We confined ourselves for the most part, therefore, to contrasting and comparing the differing editorial slants newspapers imparted to their stories and to pointing to discrepancies in the facts reported. This could rebound. On Easter Monday, in 1960, the Aldermaston March for nuclear disarmament reached Trafalgar Square. (James Cameron marched on it.) The numbers reported as being there in Tuesday's papers varied from 250,000 in the *News Chronicle* to 30,000 in the *Daily Express*, with every variant in between. Grist to the mill, you might think, to *What the Papers Say*. But the programme that week was presented by a newly arrived South African exile, Ronald Segal, editor and publisher of *Africa South*, who had reached Britain that very day. He took the opposite point. What the discrepancies in the estimated numbers meant to him was democracy. In South Africa, if any report had appeared at all, only one estimate of numbers, issued by SAPA, the official South African Press Agency, would have seen its way into print.

Sometimes the programme slipped up. Kemsley's *Sunday Times*, a pillar of Conservativism, changed hands. Roy Thomson bought it. One Sunday, the masthead proclaimed: 'The *Sunday Times* is an Independent Newspaper of the Centre.' The presenter that week, Brian Inglis, commented: 'Lord Kemsley must be turning in his grave.' Lord Kemsley was alive and well and watching television, somewhere on the south coast. Sackcloth and ashes. Sometimes we caught the papers out. I remember the goings-on as the world's press covered the Dalai Lama's escape from Tibet, through the Himalayan mountain passes, to safety in Nepal. The *Daily Mail* scooped the world. 'I FLY OVER THE DALAI LAMA' screamed its banner over the byline of Noel Barber. Naturally, the other correspondents caught it from their news desks: 'MAIL FLIES OVER LAMA STOP WHY YOU NOT FLY QUERY FILE SOONEST STOP' etc, etc.

After the event, Robert Manning, who had been there for *Time*, revealed all in the *Atlantic Monthly*. Impatient for the Dalai Lama's long trek to reach them, the press corps hired an aeroplane to fly north over the holy caravan. As they buckled themselves into their seats for take-off, Noel Barber called out: 'Well, I don't know about you fellows, but I've filed.' The plane, for some reason – weather, mechanical failure – never took off. The *Mail*'s scoop led the world.

When I rang Barber's editor at the *Daily Mail*, Bill Hardcastle, to check this out, he begged me not to give the story wider currency. 'Noel is a very brave man, you know,' he said. 'He's never been quite the same since he got that bullet in the head in Hungary.'

Here is Nicholas Tomalin, a great reporter of our generation, reflecting on what it takes to be a journalist.

> The only qualities essential for real success in journalism
> are rat-like cunning, a plausible manner, and a little literary

ability. If you look at the jewels of the profession, you will see that this must be so. James Cameron, Cyril Connolly, Arthur Helliwell, Patience Strong, Alistair Cooke and John Gordon have nothing else in common, yet are all successful journalists.

Some are more literary and less cunning than others; some certainly are more plausible; but it is these three shared qualifications that make all of them recognisably of the same breed.

The rat-like cunning is needed to ferret out and publish things that people don't want to be known (which is – and always will be – the best definition of News). The plausible manner is useful for surviving while this is going on, helpful with the entertaining presentation of it, and even more useful in later life when the successful journalist may have to become a successful executive on his newspaper. The literary ability is of obvious use.

(Reporting)

And here is Tomalin in action – literary ability and all – in Vietnam. This is from the *Sunday Times*: 'The General Goes Zapping Charlie Cong'. The task is to kill VCs. The General leads by example. Tomalin interrupts his machine-gun fire with a question.

'How do you know for sure that Viet Cong snipers were in that strip you burned?'

'We don't. The smoke position was a guess. That's why we zap the whole forest.'

'But what if there was someone, a civilian, walking through there?'

''Aw come, son, you think there's folks just sniffing flowers in tropical vegetation like that? With a big operation on hereabouts? Anyone left down there, he's Charlie Cong all right.'

I point at a paddy field full of peasants less than half a mile away.

'That's different, son. We know they're genuine.'

The pilot shouts: 'General, half-right, two running for that bush.'

'I see them. Down, down, goddam you.'

In one movement he yanks his M16 off the hanger, slams in a clip of cartridges and leans right out of the door, hanging on his seatbelt to fire one long burst in the general direction of the bush.

'General, there's a hole, maybe a bunker, down there.'

'Smokebomb, circle, shift it.'

'But General, how do you know those aren't just frightened peasants?'

'Running? Like that? Don't give me a pain. The clips, the clips, where in hell are the cartridges in this ship?'

The aide drops a smoke canister, the General finds his ammunition and the starboard machine-gunner fires rapid bursts into the bush, his tracers bouncing up off the ground round it.

We turn clockwise in ever tighter, lower circles, everyone firing. A shower of spent cartridge cases leaps from the General's carbine to drop, lukewarm, on my arm.

'I ... WANT ... YOU ... TO ... SHOOT ... RIGHT ... UP ... THE ... ASS ... OF ... THAT ... HOLE ... GUNNER.'

(*Reporting*)

They took some prisoners and the prisoners, Tomalin reported, were, indeed, armed.

The General is magnanimous in victory over my squeamish civilian worries.

'You see, son, I saw rifles on that first pair of running men. Didn't tell you that at the time. And, by the way, you mustn't imagine there could have been ordinary farm folk in that house; when you're as old a veteran as I am you get to know about these things by instinct. There's no better

way to fight than goin' out to shoot VCs. An' there's
nothing I love better than killin' Cong. No sir.'

(Reporting)

What is extraordinary still in that writing is Tomalin's ability to get
it all down. You know he got it right. Here, in quieter vein, is James
Cameron in the north-east of Brazil. The piece appeared in the
Daily Herald. I have chosen it because I sent James on this trip
myself. For Rediffusion's *This Week* he covered Brazil, Bolivia and
Chile in six weeks. No one went much to South America in those
days. I am grateful James did.

> In Recife one begins to realise what an enormous country
> Brazil is – far bigger than the United States; four-fifths the
> size of Europe. The gigantic North-East is known as the
> land of *miseria morte*: the sorrows of death. It is one of the
> poorest places on earth. Here 24 million people – a third of
> the population – live, or half-live, on the permanent edge
> of famine in economic conditions pretty well indistin-
> guishable from those in the England of the 15th century,
> existing as feudal serfs on the gigantic estates of a few
> absentee landlords. When drought makes conditions intol-
> erable, villagers put their belongings on their backs and
> walk perhaps 200 miles to Recife or Bahia to find work.

There is no work and soon they find themselves in the alagados, the dreadful foetid slum towns of the refugees, and they very quickly die.

Into this melancholy region appeared the memorable figure of Francisco Juliao, the 'Marxist Messiah' who founded the Peasant Leagues. The generals called Juliao a Communist, though the Party itself rejected him because of his insistence on the religious dimension of man. He said: 'Christianity is the religion whose Founder sided with the poor.'

Miles out of Recife in the state of Pernambuco, down the drenched quagmire roads among the canefields, I found a very small and wretched place dominated by a very small and far from wretched man who also considers that he owes the Church a few respectful lessons in Christianity. The place is, by definition, not a one-horse town since it is called Dos Carvalhos, which means two horses. It is in the parish of a young priest, not yet 30, called Father Antonio de Melo Costa.

(The Defiant Priest of Brazil)

I can still hear that clear cultured voice, delivering the commentary. Father de Melo Costa, incidentally, came to a certain prominence in that programme and for years later was interviewed by every television crew sent to Brazil to report on poverty. You could see his girth thicken down the years. Journalists, sometimes, are a lazy lot.

In Chile, by the way, we got it wrong, or anyway out of sync with history. 'Allende, Allende, the voices are crying,' James introduced the film. 'Next month, this country could become the first democratic state ever freely to elect a Communist government.' But Frei's Christian Democrats won. Allende did not reach power till several years later.

James Cameron went straight from Santiago di Chile to San Francisco. We were to see Barry Goldwater nominated as Republican candidate for the presidency. It was in his hotel room, where some of us were chatting, that I saw and heard James answer the urgent telephone call from the *Daily Herald* copydesk in London. Glancing at a notepad marked in his elegant hand, he started speaking not 'copy', but prose, down the line. The text came out of his mouth, fully formed. He worked for popular newspapers. He wrote short paragraphs, but clean, long-limbered sentences. Just to read again or to hear that report from Brazil is to be made aware of standards slipped and gone, of a cool intelligence, an unsensational tone, totally vanished from today's tabloid so-called newspapers. The great feature of my time on *What the Papers Say* was Hugh Cudlipp's *Daily Mirror*'s attempt to extend the clear, lively excellence of its writing and presentation to coverage of foreign affairs. They tried, but it did not last. The *Sun* succeeded the *Daily Herald*. Murdoch bought it and that was the end of any attempt at an intelligent interaction with the world. And for the *Mirror* also.

Here is my favourite press guru, A. J. (Joe) Liebling (also my favourite writer on food and wine, and on boxing) in authoritative vein.

> There are three kinds of writers of news in our generation.
> In inverse order of worldly consideration, they are:
> 1. The reporter, who writes what he sees.
> 2. The interpretive reporter, who writes what he sees and what he construes to be its meaning.
> 3. The expert, who writes what he construes to be the meaning of what he hasn't seen.
>
> (*The Press: Experts*)

Liebling has it in for 'experts'.

> To combat an old human prejudice in favour of eyewitness testimony, which is losing ground even in our courts of law, the expert must intimate that he has access to some occult source or science not available to either reporter or reader.
>
> He is the Priest of Eleusis, the man with the big picture. Once his position is conceded, the expert can put on a

better show than the reporter. All is manifest to him, since his conclusions are not limited by his powers of observation. Logistics, to borrow a word from the military species of the genus, favour him, since it is possible to not see many things at the same time. For example, a correspondent cannot cover a front and the Pentagon simultaneously. An expert can, and from an office in New York, at that.

(*The Press: Experts*)

Liebling's point is not just that a real reporter can tell you more than an expert can, but that it helps to have more than one to hand. He found much news reporting pretty superficial.

I felt, after Suez and Gaza in 1956-7, and Earl Long's Louisiana in 1959, for example, that I might just as well not have read about them before going, because what I found was different. My point here is not that what I see is always exact, and that the harried press-association men are always wrong, but that different reporters see different things, or the same things differently, and that the reader at home has a right to a diversity of reports. A one-man account of a crisis in a foreign country is like a Gallup poll with one straw. The same goes for national news.

(*Elijah and Sinbad*)

Liebling knows how difficult good reporting is.

> I am a chronic, incurable, recidivist reporter. When I am working at it, I have no time to think about the shortcomings of the American or world press; I must look sharp not to come too short myself. Sinbad, clinging to a spar, had no time to think of systematic geography. To understand perfectly a new country, new situation, the new characters you confront on an assignment, is impossible. To understand more than half, so that your report will have significant correlation with what is happening, is hard. To transmit more than half of what you understand is a hard trick, too, far beyond the task of the so-called creative artist, who if he finds a character in his story awkward can simply change its characteristics. (Even to sex, vide Proust and Albertine. Let him try it with General de Gaulle.) It is possible, occasionally, to get something completely right – a scene, or a pattern of larceny, or a man's mind. These are the reporter's victories, as rare as a pitcher's home runs.
>
> (*Elijah and Sinbad*)

'It is possible, occasionally, to get something completely right, but the reporter's victories are as rare as a pitcher's home runs', or, let's say, a goalkeeper's hat trick. It is those rare victories that I want to celebrate.

My favourite Liebling reporting, with much to choose from, is his account of Governor Earl Long of Louisiana's attempt to hang on to power after various domestic upsets and imbroglios, including being confined, on his wife's say-so, to a mental hospital. Earl Long gets out of his hospital prison and runs for another term.

> It was after the 'reasonable and sensible' bit that he went into his general declaration of tolerance. 'I'm not against anybody for reasons of race, creed, or any ism he might believe in except nuttism, skingameism or communism,' he said.
>
> 'I'm glad to see so many of my fine Catholic friends here – they have been so kind to me. I sometimes say I consider myself forty per cent Catholic and sixty per cent Baptist.' (This is a fairly accurate reflection of the composition of the electorate.)
>
> 'But I'm in favor of every religion with the possible exception of snake-chunking. Anybody that so presumes on how he stands with providence that he will let a snake bite him, I say he deserves what he's got coming to him.' (The snake-chunkers, a small, fanatic cult ,do not believe in voting.)
>
> (*Nothing But a Little Pissant*)

Next day, to the Governor's press conference. Liebling is accompanied by Margaret Dixon, editor of the Baton Rouge *Morning Advocate*.

'Earl is the funniest man in the world,' she said over her shoulder as she drove. 'Life in the Capitol would be dull without him. Did you hear what he said to Leander Perez, the States' rights man, the other day? "What are you going to do now, Leander? Da Feds have got da atom bomb." And when Blanche went to live in the new house, he said she had "dis-domiciled" him. He has a style of his own – he's a poet. He said he was so groggy when he got off the plane that took him to Houston that he felt "like a muley bull coming out of a dipping vat". I don't know why it should, but the "muley" makes that line sound a hundred times funnier. It just means without horns.'

'It particularises the image,' I suggested. 'Bull is a word so general that it blurs: the dumb bulls in Spain, the tight bulls in flytime. "Muley" makes you see a bull of a peculiarly ineffectual kind.'

(*Blam-Blam-Blam*)

Earl Long had it in for the press, in a genial kind of way, particularly for the *New Orleans Times-Picayune*. (I like newspaper titles – the Cleveland *Plain Dealer*, the Bury *Free Press*, the Skibbereen *Eagle*. As an aside, Picayune means the small change in your pocket, as does Il Resto in *Il Resto del Carlino*.) Anyway, at the press

conference, the Governor is explaining that he got rid of the man
in charge of Louisiana's voting machines.

'And where is he now?' the woman asked, expecting,
perhaps, to hear that he was confined in a cachot beneath
the Mansion. 'He's hypnotising people and telling fortunes;
and locating oil wells,' the Governor said, 'and he got
himself a fine blonde and built her a big house and quit
home.' Outside of the *Lives of the Troubadours*, which was
compiled in the thirteenth century, I had never known a
better-compressed biography. I felt that I knew the
denuded hypnotist well. I remembered the comparable
beauty of the Governor's account of the last day of a
beloved uncle in Winnfield: 'He got drunk and pulled a
man out of bed and got into bed with the man's wife, and
the man got mad and shot my poor uncle, and he died.'

I asked him what he thought of Governor Faubus of
north-neighbouring Arkansas, who had won a third term
by closing the schools, and he said Faubus was a fine man,
but nobody had told him about the Civil War. 'Fellas like
Faubus and Rainach and Leander Perez and da rest of da
White Citizens and Southern Gentlemen in dis state want
to go back behind Lincoln,' he said. 'And between us,
gentlemen, as we sit here among ourselves,' he said,

arresting a chunk of fried steak in mid air and leaning forward to give his statement more impetus, 'we got to admit dat Lincoln was a fine man and dat he was right.' Then he caught my look of astonishment and cried, too late, 'But don't quote me on dat!'

Since he has won his last primary, I disregard his instructions. It was a brave thing for a Governor of Louisiana to say and would have made a lethal headline in his enemies' hands: LONG ENDORSES LINCOLN; HINTS WAR BETWEEN STATES ENDED.

Perhaps the most remarkable reportage of our recent times has been written by a Pole, Ryszard Kapucinski. Even in English, his accounts of the end of Haile Selassie, of Lumumba, and of the 'Soccer War' between Honduras and El Salvador stand out on the page as writing that deserves to last. Kapucinski's work is, as the blurb claims, reportage and autobiography and history. I regret that, for reasons of space, I have had to leave him out.

I cannot resist including, though, something of James Fenton, poet and journalist, who contrived to be there when Saigon fell, and was there again, though with less premeditation, when President Marcos of the Philippines was toppled.

Fenton's reports from the East were some of the very best things in the early *Independent*. I shall not forget his account of the Duke of Edinburgh's visit to China and the gaffe that lit it up. In Manila, he is in and out of the Palace during Marcos's last hours and immediately after.

And now, for a short while, I was away from the crowd with just one other person, a shy and absolutely thunderstruck Filipino. We had found our way, we realized, into the Marcoses' private rooms. There was the library, and my companion gazed in wonder at the leather-bound volumes while I admired the collection of art books all carefully catalogued and with their numbers on the spines. This was the reference library for Imelda's worldwide collection of treasures. She must have thumbed through them thinking: 'I'd like one of them' or 'I've got a couple of them, in New York' or 'That's in our London house'. And then there was the Blue Drawing Room with its twin portraits of the Marcoses, where I simply remember standing with my companion and saying, 'It's beautiful, isn't it.' It wasn't that it was beautiful. It looked as if it had been purchased at Harrods. It was just that, after all the crowds and the riots, we had landed up in this peaceful, luxurious den. My companion had never seen anything like it. He didn't take anything. He hardly dared touch the furnishings and trinkets. We both simply could not believe that we were there and the Marcoses weren't. I wish I could remember it all better. For instance, it seemed to me that in every room I saw, practically on every available surface, there was a signed photograph of Nancy Reagan. But this can hardly be true literally. It just felt as if there was a lot of Nancy in evidence.

Another of the rooms had a grand piano. I sat down. 'Can you play?' said my companion. 'A little,' I exaggerated. I can play Bach's Prelude in C, and this is what I proceeded to do, but my companion had obviously hoped for something more racy.

A soldier came in, carrying a rifle. 'Please co-operate,' he said. The soldier looked just as overawed by the place as we were. We co-operated. When I returned down the service stairs, I noticed that the green jade plates were gone, but there was still some Evian water to be had. I was very thirsty, as it happened. But the revolution had asked me to co-operate. So I did.

Outside, the awe had communicated itself to several members of the crowd. They stood by the fountain looking down at the coloured lights beneath the water, not saying anything. I went to the parapet and looked across the river. I thought: somebody's still fighting; there are still some loyal troops. Then I thought: that's crazy – they can't have

started fighting now. I realised that I was back in Saigon yet
again. There indeed there had been fighting on the other
side of the river. But here it was fireworks. The whole city
was celebrating.

That piece, part of a lengthy account published in *Granta*, is
anthologised by John Carey in his *Faber Book of Reportage*.

If I think of the reporting of our time, of the writing that has
stopped me in my breakfast tracks (and sometimes brought bile to
the mouth and a smart to the eyes), I think of Clare Hollingworth,
years ago, in the *Telegraph* from Algiers. And I think of Max
Hastings in the Falklands, and John Lloyd during the miners'
strike, and Neal Ascherson in Poland. I think of Ed Vulliamy and
Maggie O'Kane in Bosnia. I think of a remarkable piece by Chris
McGreal from Rwanda in yesterday's *Guardian*. I think of Robert
Fisk in the Middle East.

Fisk is the reporter of our day. The sequence of articles he
published in the *Independent* in March, 'Inside Algeria', were as
good as anything I have read in years. Fisk has eyes and ears, and a
nose for a story, and a fearless determination to hunt it out, and the
mind to grasp contradictions that marks all good reporting of
complex situations. And he has the gift of tongues. He speaks the
language. He has fluent Arabic, and in Lebanon or in Algeria, or in
Gaza or the West Bank, that gives him a head start. His stuff from

Algeria, diverse, multifaceted, was consistently interesting. I pick out this piece almost at random.

> High in the Kabyle mountains 200 miles south of Algiers,
> Ahmed Boutdra and his little army of peasants had quite a
> shock when they shot dead Si Mohamed Mustafa in the
> wadi behind their village last month. He had been leading
> a band of Islamists through the forest when he was cut
> down by a brace of old hunting guns; but what astonished
> Mr Boutdra was a note stuffed into the dead man's pocket.
> 'The following have been condemned to death,' it
> announced in ballpoint pen. 'Ahmed Boutdra, mayor of
> Igoujdal, his father Si Ahmed . . .' and it went on to list 28
> other men in the village. The grubby paper was signed
> 'GIA', for 'Islamic Armed Group'.
>
> Mr Boutdra seems undaunted by the discovery of his
> own death sentence. Tall and red-faced, dressed in a long,
> pale brown coat, the former supermarket manager has no
> intention of abandoning his Dad's Army of threadbare
> militiamen with their ragged trousers and tattered boots,
> their often toothless mouths, their calloused hands
> clutching engraved hunting guns from Brescia, old French
> service rifles – 'Made in Tulle, 1949' it says on most of
> them – and Second World War sub-machine-guns with

'Waffen SS' still visible on the stock. 'All our men are loyal,' Mr Boutdra says proudly. 'They will never betray our republic.'

Nor, on the face of it, is there any reason why they should. Up here in the Kabyle mountains, where the Mediterranean winks dark blue through the ravines and the hillsides are blackened by massive man-made fires which have burned through the forests that provided night-time cover for the GIA. Mr Boutdra's 230 militiamen are defending their homes. 'Over there, below Mount Tighrine, the GIA caught two of the men from Bounamane the other night,' Mr Boutdra says, pointing across the valley to an unburned hill. 'A taxi-driver and a shepherd were stopped on the road. The terrorists wanted the taxi and didn't want the shepherd to see them. So they slit their throats and left them beside the road. You see, we have to look after ourselves.'

I have simplified that, by the way, in cutting it. Fisk is at pains to tell us that, as always in Algeria, things are not quite what they seem. The hardest assignment Robert Fisk ever had was also the one by which he shall always be remembered. 'It was the Christians' tells what he found in the camp at Chatila, during Israel's 1982 invasion of Lebanon, just after the massacre.

The full story of what happened in Chatila on Friday night and Saturday morning may never be known, for most of the witnesses are either dead or would never wish to reveal their guilt. What is quite certain is that at six o'clock on Friday night, truckloads of gunmen in the uniform – and wearing the badges – of the right-wing Christian Phalange militia and Major Saad Haddad's renegade army from Southern Lebanon were seen by reporters entering the southern gate of the camp. There were bonfires inside and the sound of heavy gunfire. Israeli troops and armour were standing round the perimeter of the camp and made no attempt to stop the gunmen – who have been their allies since their invasion of Lebanon – going in.

What we found inside the camps at ten o'clock next morning did not quite beggar description, although it would perhaps be easier to retell in a work of fiction or in the cold prose of a medical report. But the details should be told for – this being Lebanon – the facts will change over the coming weeks as militias and armies and governments blame each other for the horrors committed upon the Palestinian civilians.

Just inside the southern gates of the camp, there used to be a number of single-storey concrete-walled houses. When we walked across the muddy entrance of Chatila, we found that these buildings had all been dynamited to the ground. There were cartridge cases across the main road and clouds of flies swarmed across the rubble. Down a laneway to our right, not more than fifty yards from the entrance, there lay a pile of corpses. There were more than a dozen of them, young men whose arms and legs had become entangled with each other in the agony of death. All had been shot at point-blank range through the right or left cheek, the bullet tearing away a line of flesh up to the ear and entering the brain. Some had vivid crimson scars down the left side of their throats. One had been castrated. Their eyes were open, and the flies had only begun to gather. The youngest was perhaps only twelve or thirteen years old.

On the other side of the main road, up a track through the rubble, we found the bodies of five women and several children. The women were middle-aged, and their corpses lay draped over a pile of rubble. One lay on her back, her dress torn open, and the head of a little girl emerging from behind her. The girl had short, dark curly hair and her eyes were staring at us and there was a frown on her face. She was dead. Another child lay on the roadway like a discarded flower, her white dress stained with mud and dust. She could have been no more than three years old. The back of her head had been blown away by a bullet fired into her brain. One of the women also held a tiny baby to her body. The bullet that had passed through her breast had killed the baby too.

James Cameron got into North Vietnam while the war was still on.

Through the daylight hours nothing moves on the roads of North Vietnam, not a car nor a truck. It must look from the air as though the country had no wheeled transport at all. That, of course, is the idea, it is the roads and bridges that are being bombed; it is no longer safe after sunrise to be anywhere near either.

In the paddies the farmers are reaping their third harvest of the year, which has been particularly abundant. They move among the rice with their sickles, bowed under a shawl of foliage, the camouflage that gives everyone a faintly carnival air, like so many Jacks-in-the-Green. At the corners of the paddies stand what look like sheaves of corn and are stacks of rifles. The roads stretch long and empty, leading from nowhere to nowhere.

Then the sun goes down and everything starts to move. At dusk the roads become alive. The engines are started and the convoys grind away through the darkness behind the pinpoints of masked headlamps. There are miles of them, heavy Russian-built trucks, anti-aircraft batteries, all deeply buried under piles of branches and leaves; processions of huge green haystacks. North Vietnam by day is abandoned; by night it thuds and grinds with movement. It is a fatiguing routine: working by day and moving by night.

The Americans fly raids overhead, as he moved about the country.

What supervened, I think, was not the emotion of fear (for I was in no particular danger) nor high-minded horror – there was somehow a sense of outrage against civility: what an impertinence, one felt, what arrogance, what an offence against manners. These people in North Vietnam are agreeable, shy people, and very poor. Will this sort of thing blow Communism out of their heads?

Is this reporting, or interpretative reporting? Is it too opinionated? I can only say that the question does not worry me. Some have argued that Cameron's evident sympathies vitiate his work.

I have never thought so. I would far rather know what a reporter's values and mind set were than have them flattened into a specious objectivity and fitted on to the proprietor's Procrustean bed of policy.

The piece that James Cameron is best known for, at least by students of journalism, is the one he wrote, while covering the Korean War, on Synghman Rhee's treatment of his own political prisoners. It was meant for *Picture Post*, but never appeared there. The proprietor, Edward Hulton, stopped it. The editor, Tom Hopkinson, who proposed to print it, was fired. Cameron resigned.

It is hard to find this piece today. In the introduction to a collection of his journalism, *What a Way to Run the Tribe*, Cameron says he has included it. But it is not there. I have had to rely on a later account of the matter in his autobiographical *Points of Departure*.

> This terrible crowd of men was worse than anything I had so far seen. I had come up against such groups and herds of prisoners before, of a condition and appearance that would have been startling anywhere but in the East; this was the first time that a lull in active work had given me a chance to enquire, and examine, and photograph.

This grisly mob of men projected the war in special terms of human abasement. There were about seven hundred of them, and they were political prisoners of the South Korean Government – they were not prisoners of war; their uniform was a filthy and indescribably ragged kimono. After so many weeks in which there had been so many distressing and troubling things to be seen this might have made little impression on me if the condition of these men had not been quite sensationally appalling. They were skeletons – they were puppets of skin with sinews for strings – their faces were a terrible, translucent grey, and they cringed like dogs. They were manacled with chains or bound to each other with ropes. They were compelled to crouch in the classic Oriental attitude of subjection, the squatting, foetal position, in heaps of garbage. Sometimes they moved enough to scoop a handful of water to drink from the black puddles around them. Any deviation from their attitude brought a gun butt on their skulls. Finally they were herded, the lowest common denominator of human degradation, into trucks, with the numb air of men going to their deaths. I was assured, by a willing attendant anxious to make a good impression, that most of them were. Sometimes, to save inconvenience, they were shot where they were.

The spectacle was utterly medieval. Around this gruesome market-place gathered a few knots of American soldiers, photographing the scene with casual industry. A matter of yards away stood the US headquarters; the officers wandered curiously around. Five minutes away stood the sequestered villa that housed the United Nations Commission in Korea. This had been going on for months.

Nobody had said a word.

The reporter's act is a hard one, the reporter's victories rare.

I have been fortunate in my life to work with good reporters: James Mossman, James Cameron, Robert Kee. Close up, you could see how difficult it always was for them to get it right, though they made it seem easy. James Cameron knew it was hard.

Today we journalists spend our time splashing in the shallows, reaching on occasions the rare heights of the applauded mediocre. It looks, perhaps, easier than it is. To the individual in this machine it brings its own dilemma: the agonising narrow line between sincerity and technique, between the imperative and the glib – so fine and delicate a boundary that one frequently misses it altogether, especially with a tight deadline, a ringing phone, a thirst, and an unquiet mind. Accept that, and the game is up.

(*Points of Departure*)

I salute all those reporters for whom 'the game is not up'.

Roy Hattersley

The unholy alliance:
the relationship between
Members of Parliament
and the press

1996

*Roy Hattersley was MP for the Sparkbrook Division of Birmingham
from 1964 to 1997 and Deputy Leader of the Labour Party from 1983
to 1992. He was made a life peer in 1997.*

I NITIALLY, I INTENDED to discuss the lobby system in the House
of Commons, a partnership between politicians and journalists, which – since it treats gossip as if it were fact and
invention as if it were truth – is profoundly damaging to the democratic process. But as I considered the consequences of that arcane
relationship – the personalisation and trivialisation of what should
be a battle of ideas – I realised the particular problem it caused for

a radical party. The temptation to say something on that subject was irresistible.

That does not diminish the constitutional argument for encouraging a return to serious debate. That argument is based on the admittedly unfashionable view that politics should be primarily concerned with principles, policies and programmes. A party's first democratic duty is to set out its manifesto. Its second is to oppose what it believes to be the shortcomings of its opponents' alternatives. Then, when the election is over, one of the manifestos becomes the mandate and its implementation the exercise of the popular will. Performance, the theatre of politics, is an essentially supplementary activity. It is not – or, at least, should not be – an end in itself. Yet, increasingly, journalists judge politicians, and politicians judge each other, according to what are euphemistically called 'communication skills'. When that happens, politics qualifies for the criticism that Stephen Sondheim makes of grand opera: 'What sort of a show is it that regards the singer as more important than the song?'

The emphasis on political performances is, in part, the inevitable product of our age – not simply the existence of television, which brings Prime Ministers into our living rooms, but a general impatience with anything which is thought to be tedious or boring. It is also intimately related to the drift away from ideology, which has characterised radical parties all over the world. Ironically the right (which once prided itself on its contempt for dogma) briefly redis-covered conviction politics and managed to encapsulate its philosophy in two or three brief, emotive and meaningless asser-tions. 'Competitive markets guarantee efficiency . . . Government is too powerful . . . Public expenditure is wasteful . . . Tax cuts benefit everyone.' The case for creating a new society cannot be made in such simple language. When radical parties attempt it, the result is often disastrous.

During the last two general election campaigns (in which I was constantly reminded of the 'buzzwords' which I should include in my speeches) I was asked if I would be kind enough to avoid ever using the word 'equality'. It was suggested that I should speak of 'fairness' instead. Nobody was particularly concerned that the two concepts have different meanings. Equality, I was told, was anathema to newspapers, who regarded it as the enemy of initiative and enterprise and the hope of acquiring more consumer durables – exactly the characteristics that they (and their advertisers) wanted to encourage. Three weeks before polling day was probably too late to convince the newspapers of their philosophical and soci-ological error. I now realise that the shortage of time was not the only problem. Being afraid of the language is only one step away from being afraid of the idea which it describes. Once we feel an obligation to use language that is acceptable to newspapers, we are not very far away from accepting their values.

The pressure to adopt those values has, during the last fifty years, been immensely increased by the emergence of the opinion poll – a major disincentive to ideological politics. I am anxious not to provoke an angry telephone call from Bob Worcester.[1] So I make clear that I want neither to prohibit opinion polling nor in any way to limit its use. I merely observe that its existence and increasing sophistication make politicians believe that they can choose between principle and popularity. Politicians always thought that they knew what the people wanted. Now the newspapers tell them with apparent certainty – tougher on crime, no quarter to the welfare scroungers, keep the blacks out. They can even identify the needs and demands of target voters – help with negative equity, tax cuts and action against incompetent teachers, real and imaginary. The newspapers, reflecting their readers' views for commercial as well as ideological reasons, reinforce the popular prejudices. There has never been a time in our history when it was more difficult for a politician to say, 'I will lead rather than follow'.

W. E. Gladstone, admittedly over-inclined to assume that Providence would come to his rescue, actually believed that the imperialists of Victorian England supported his decision to abandon General Gordon in the Sudan. Some of his Cabinet

---

1   Robert Worcester founded Market & Opinion Research International Ltd (MORI) in 1969.

warned him that he was facing electoral catastrophe. But they could not prove their point with graphs and diagrams. If the Liberal Party of 1885 had employed MORI, Gladstone would have faced a real test of courage and conscience. Imagine Gordon besieged in Khartoum today. The *Sun* would be demanding his rescue with headlines built around four words: Fuzzy, Wuzzy, Mad and Mhadi. Its article, entitled 'Twenty Things You Never Knew About The Grand Old Man', would be illustrated with pictures (taken secretly) of Gladstone's midnight excursions. There would be a telephone poll with one number for supporters of naked savages, the other for defenders of Britain's good name abroad.

On the day after the result was published, Michael Howard[2] would let it be known that he believed that General Wolseley should be sacked for making such slow progress along the Nile. I say 'let it be known', because that phrase typifies much that is wrong with political reporting in this country – a system, indeed a culture, which works on nods and winks and, therefore, discourages the careful analysis of great issues. It is also built on honour and, therefore, inevitably involves constant betrayal. And it is reporting that concerns me most. For it is in the 'reports' – I use the word in heavy inverted commas – that the distortion, the personalisation and the trivialisation are greatest.

2 Then Home Secretary.

Columnists distort too. But columnists are paid to be opinionated and didactic. You know where you are with columnists. On the rare occasions when I read something by Hugo Young with which I disagree, I know that he is suffering from vertigo, brought on by remaining too long on the high moral ground. When I read something by William Rees-Mogg with which I agree, I lie down until the feeling passes. And, when I read Janet Daley, I know that I am on a railway train and that they are giving away free copies of the *Daily Telegraph*. But all three of them, in their different ways, treat their subjects seriously. Unfortunately columnists, even in the better tabloids, are mostly read by people who are politically aware, and politically committed, already. It is reporters – or political correspondents, indeed political editors, as they are now called – who influence attitudes and elections. How many voters have changed their political allegiance after reading Boris Johnson?[3]

I do not see myself as the Gerald Ratner of the Members' lobby.[4] At the end of my political career and the beginning of my life as a

---

3 Hugo Young has been a political columnist on the *Guardian* since 1984. Lord Rees-Mogg has been a regular newspaper columnist since ceasing to be editor of *The Times* in 1981. Boris Johnson was a columnist on the *Daily Telegraph*; he became editor of the weekly *Spectator* in 1995, and a Conservative MP in 2001.

4 Gerald Ratner destroyed his successful costume jewellery business in 1991 with a throwaway joke in a speech to the Institute of Directors at the Albert Hall in which he described his products as 'total crap'.

tabloid journalist, I retain my admiration for members of both trades. I have always believed that politicians are better, both morally and intellectually, than is generally allowed. And I have come to realise that it takes great agility of mind to produce exciting, readable and accurate (well, more or less accurate) copy at high speed. I share the view of T. S. Eliot, whose literary standards (like his Anglican faith) were often thought to be too high. Journalists are distinguished from other, more generally exalted writers only by their motives. Eliot described what those motives are: the ability to work (perhaps work best) under pressure, an interest in the affairs of the day and the constant need for small sums of money. Unfortunately, journalists and politicians are not at their best when they work together, which in the House of Commons is, sadly, all the time.

The real importance of the House of Commons has diminished with the years. Only in entirely exceptional circumstances – weak government with small or non-existent majorities made up, in part, by suicidal backbenchers – are its ten o'clock votes of any interest. Its speeches, even its front-bench speeches, are rarely reported at length. Interest is concentrated on the essentially demeaning Prime Minister's Question Time. The rest of the week is left to sketch writers (not in my opinion an occupation for grown-ups), who are rarely as funny as they believe themselves to be. Real decisions are made elsewhere. The most important speeches are made 'in the country': not least because, these days, the Commons will not listen to a long and serious debate. Yet the hothouse atmosphere remains. The men and women who attend the morning press conferences at 10 Downing Street take senior politicians to lunch and then hang about the lobby, hoping to scavenge news of dissent or, better still, hint of rebellion. I am not sure if the relationship within the Members' lobby is best described as inbreeding or cross-breeding. But it makes the politicians simultaneously dependent on and intimately involved with the men and women who can make or break them. It is not a cosy arrangement, but it is certainly too close.

Nobody doubts that, in any system, politicians will speak in confidence to individual journalists whom they know well. But, by institutionalising the secrecy – encouraging MPs to sidle up to lobby correspondents and whisper in their ears – we promote the politics of rumour, innuendo and gossip. Why should a journalist work late into the night, mastering the intricacies of monetary union, when he or she can capture the front page by reporting that 'a source close to a Cabinet minister' has revealed that there will be resignations if the Prime Minister succumbs to pressure exerted by Eurosceptics and agrees to hold a referendum on the acceptance of a single currency? And the politician gains at least as much as the journalist. The source close to the Cabinet minister is usually the Cabinet minister himself. He is protected when the plans for a referendum are announced and he still fails to resign. When, he asks in bellicose innocence, did I ever say I would resign? The lobby correspondents know the answer, but the system protects their informants from exposure.

The trick works at the highest level. Thirty years ago, when I was a young parliamentary secretary, I made a habit of eating lunch each Thursday at the Reform Club, so that journalists could tell me what had happened at the morning's Cabinet meeting. One day, three most distinguished correspondents – Walter Terry then of the *Daily Mail*, Harold Hutchinson of the *Daily Herald* and James Margach of the *Sunday Times* – arrived very late. These three men were part of a group which had a special relationship with Harold Wilson and were, in consequence, known as The White Commonwealth. That day they had enjoyed a post-Cabinet drink with the Prime Minister, who had given them 'on lobby terms' an account of 'the public dressing-down' that he had given to one of his most senior colleagues. 'A public dressing-down?' I asked incredulously. 'Do you really believe him?' They looked at me with amused contempt. Of course they did not believe him. But he had given them the story, knowing that they would not identify the source and it was too good to question. It would make the front pages next day. What is more, as Walter Terry pointed out, 'Cabinet row' stories were very popular with his paper.

I thought of Terry's comment when newspapers apparently danced to a Labour politician's tune a couple of months ago. On 27

February, a member of the Shadow Cabinet made a speech to the Social Market Foundation entitled, 'Diversity within Comprehensive Education'. It would be wrong of me to identify him. It was reported in the national newspapers as an attack on the non-selective system. One of the more moderate reports was in *The Times*. It described the speech as presenting 'a damning picture of Britain's comprehensive schools'. I was so offended by what I read that I thought of mounting one of my mini-revolts. But, while I was still loading my popgun, my Shadow Cabinet colleague sent me a copy of his whole speech. Certainly it contained criticisms of some comprehensive schools – in my view, legitimate and reasonable. But it gave a balanced account of the system which emphasised its overwhelming advantages and committed Labour to its continuation. My wrath was therefore turned on the newspapers which had, I believed, reported the speech so prejudicially.

One of the editors for whom I work responded, out of either courtesy or malice, by sending the cover note which had accompanied the full seven-page speech. It contained not a good word about the comprehensive school principle, listed some specific failures and quoted the two sentences from the full text that were explicitly critical of non-selective schools. I do not know who the covering note was intended to fool: the education establishment, the floating voter or the leader of the Labour Party. Nor do I know whether whoever staged the coup should be congratulated for

ingenuity or criticised for contrivance. It is, however, worth speculating on why the newspapers were so easily led.

With some newspapers, the problem was undoubtedly simple
sloth. How often do we review a book after a superficial reading of
the text and a close study of the dust jacket? But sloth was only part
of the reason. Some newspapers wanted to write the story 'Labour
Attacks Comprehensive Schools'. They knew that the party cannot
be dissociated from the idea of non-selective education and they
realised that, whatever brief plaudits might be distributed on one
day in February, the apparent admission that comprehensive
schools had failed would do damage to the party. Radical politicians underestimate at their peril the thoroughness with which
right-wing newspapers pursue and promote their prejudices. I
speak as a journalist whose interview with the cleverest parrot in
the world was cut in order to remove a comment which might have
been construed as criticism of government immigration policy.
Labour politicians are inclined to think of conspiratorial phone
calls between editors and the Chairman of the Tory party.
Normally such discussions are unnecessary. Pursuing one political
line is a way of life – house style.

Nothing that happened in the flurry of last summer's brief, and
bogus, newspapers realignment changed that. Attacks on John
Major were attempts to rescue the Tory party. Expressions of admiration for Tony Blair were gestures made not in the direction of

Labour, but towards a general public that would have thought the Tory tabloids mad if they had accused him of mindless extremism. John Major is about to be sanctified again. Decisions are now being taken about which calumny should be spread about Tony Blair – secret socialist or closet Conservative.

Sophisticated politicians are required, during some time in every speech, to announce that they have never believed in the conspiracy theory. So, I admit, there are many reasons why journalists are disinclined to read long speeches. Chief amongst them is the certain knowledge that they will not be allowed to write long reports about them. A hundred years ago, William Ewart Gladstone made speeches that lasted for two, three and, on some occasions, four or five hours to meetings of several thousand people, who described its contents, by word of mouth, amongst a much smaller electorate than we have today. Then, even the newspapers that detested him and abhorred his politics devoted a whole page to a more or less objective report of what he said. Now, as much because of pressure on time and space as the product of prejudice, even Prime Ministers are lucky to command a couple of paragraphs. The extract is chosen on the basis of the journalist's judgement of what is newsworthy. And newsworthy is not necessarily the same as important. The reckless parenthesis or ad lib, particularly if it includes a name, is far more likely to get into the paper than the policy statement. The selection of extracts makes politicians peculiarly dependent on the goodwill of journalists, who reflect every speech through the distorting mirrors of their own judgement.

That is why so many friendships, bogus and genuine, are set up. Journalists, being human, like politicians who like (or appear to like) them. In every political system, it is possible to socialise your way to good headlines. But in Britain, because of the lobby system, it is easier than in most. Perhaps this is the moment to admit that *Private Eye* used to do me more than justice. It was not gluttony that carried me into all those restaurants. I was eating my way – through the columns of the national press – into the Cabinet. And mighty boring it often was. I am not sure that every generation of politicians should be required to endure the same initiation test.

That sort of camaraderie is certainly bad for democracy. The best journalists are likely to mention, in an aside, that from time to time they eat or drink with politicians. But they are unlikely to explain that recent socialising is the reason why they report his views or think of her as a candidate for promotion. Week after week, I read that half a dozen members of the Shadow Cabinet are not up to the job of running great departments of state. Most of them I know, from personal experience, are the sort of people who are crucial to the next Labour government's success. They will take a grip on their ministries and run them with great professional competence. They are interested in competence not visibility. Visibility is part of the politician's obligation. But, in the House of

Commons, visibility is often defined not as speeches made and policies proposed, but as a gregarious attitude towards lobby journalists. In my experience, politicians are promoted beyond their ability for three reasons: close association with the party leader, significant position on the party spectrum, and misguided exaltation by the press. Of the three, the misguided exaltation is the most dangerous and most likely to lead to the swift and terrible fall from grace, favour and office.

When a candidate is chosen by a journalist for preferment, he almost always becomes the nominee of almost every newspaper. I remember Harold Wilson once telling me that, if I wanted promotion, I should win the support of one Prime Minister, not ten newspapers. Fortunately, one thing led to another, not least because political correspondents hunt in a pack. When I contributed recently to the obituary of Gordon Greig, a man I both liked and admired, I was struck by how many of his colleagues said that he had been the political editor who always decided which was the big story of the day. 'He told us what the lead should be.' The herd instinct is one of the reasons why trivia is often turned into sensation.

You may recall that five years ago Neil Kinnock was alleged to have said something indiscreet about National Insurance contributions. Originally only one newspaper ran the story. Eventually others followed suit. When I complained to an admired friend at the BBC that broadcasters had given belated, but absurd, prominence to a basically unimportant event, he insisted that the Corporation had no choice. So many newspapers had pretended it was important that they had to pretend that it was important too. So do not tell me that television compensates for the shortcomings of newspapers by allowing politicians to speak directly to the people. I believed that once. But that was before I spent hours of my life on College Green, somewhere between the Henry Moore sculpture and a nervous breakdown.[5]

What happens on College Green? The television reporter asks the politician to describe the new policy as briefly as possible. The politician responds to the request and is told that his statement was admirable in every way, but slightly too long. He tries again, but still exceeds his ten seconds. Arguments about the problems of compression are met with the invincible but infuriating explanation that the news bulletin is barely twenty minutes long, only five minutes will be devoted to politics, two political subjects must be covered, other parties must have their say, and each participant has to be identified. 'So, when we've done the recording, will you walk toward the camera for an establishing shot?' Do not tell me that television makes up for the inadequacy of newspaper coverage of serious politics.

5   College Green is an open space on the north side of the Palace of Westminster.

Indeed, in this week when *Panorama* officially became a chat show, it is easy to argue that television accelerates, rather than holds back, the increasing inclination to confuse politics and Vaudeville.[6] Too many television and radio commentators see themselves as personalities in their own right: performers with their own following. This is not a criticism of the tough interview, about which only the feeblest of politicians complain. John Humphrys and James Naughtie actually encourage politicians to talk about serious issues.[7]

But some commentators think of themselves as partners in a double act, with the politicians as straight men feeding them the punch lines. My example of that syndrome comes from the work of Jeremy Paxman,[8] who (let me say in case vengeance is suspected) always treats me with a depressing courtesy that makes me fear I am too old and frail to bully. He was not so kind a month ago to Emma Nicholson.[9] The doctrine of the mandate and the manifesto, which I set out at the beginning of this lecture, is inconsistent with

---

6   *Panorama*, traditionally the BBC's flagship current affairs programme, gave itself over to an 'exclusive' interview with the Princess of Wales in which she revealed personal details of the breakdown of her marriage to Prince Charles.

7   John Humphrys and James Naughtie are the main political interviewers for BBC Radio 4's morning *Today* programme.

8   The often aggressive anchorman for BBC2's *Newsnight*.

9   A Conservative MP who in 1996 switched to the Liberal Democrat Party.

a Member of Parliament, who has been elected as the nominee of one party, changing allegiance without resigning and fighting a by-election. During the week that Emma Nicholson left the Tory party and joined the Liberals, she was interviewed on *Newsnight*. Indeed, she was interviewed on everything. But I foolishly hoped that *Newsnight* would be the programme that asked her to comment on the constitutional propriety of being elected on the promise to cut taxes and then voting to increase them. Instead, Mr Paxman quoted some of Ms Nicholson's criticism of Conservatism and then asked: 'Why don't you come clean and admit it for what it was, pure opportunism?'

Long ago, some of us were taught that the only questions that have any meaning are those which are susceptible to more than one answer. But I doubt if even Mr Paxman hoped for Ms Nicholson to answer: 'Fair cop, guv. You've got me bang to rights. I am a cynical opportunist.' He was performing. And, in her solemn rejection of the accusation, Ms Nicholson was performing too. The result was Vaudeville, with Paxman as star and Nicholson as full supporting cast. Showbiz is no alternative to sensible debate.

That is why I felt so strongly this week that Labour's local government campaign launch should not have begun with a recording of the Tory party Chairman losing his temper on the radio accompanied by staged laughter from some of the party's media advisers. In the long run, Labour is not going to win elections because of the inadequate personality of its opponents. It is going to win because of the superiority of its policies. And the more the party co-operates in the media game, the more the media game will reduce its chances of concentrating on the issues that matter.

I base that firm conclusion around the single word 'gaffe'. What both Clare Short and John Prescott said last week about taxation was of absolutely no political significance. Both comments were blown up into stories in part because of the instinctive malice of some newspapers. But Labour's reluctance to talk about tax provided them with the opportunity. Nobody in their right mind expects an announcement of tax rates. Indeed, one of my few parliamentary successes was when I asked Geoffrey Howe what the standard rate would be if his party won the election and he told me that it was the most stupid question he had ever heard. It was a question which Kenneth Baker had asked Labour to answer at five consecutive press conferences. That rule still holds good, but it is not the same as arguing against a bold statement of general principles. Where Labour leaves a vacuum, all the tricks and connivances of a basically arcane system are used to the party's disadvantage, including the last refuge of desperate sub-editors, a headline that proclaims another gaffe.

There are immense dangers for radical parties in becoming enmeshed in the devious game that characterises the relationship between politicians and political journalists. We can, in the short term, believe ourselves to be super-professional, contradicting their errors of fact, refuting their malicious allegations and making cutting off-the-record criticisms of colleagues who step out of line. But in the end, a radical party succeeds or fails according to the strength of its ideas, not the success with which, in the idiom, it puts a spin on the day's news.

Alan Rusbridger

The freedom of the press and other platitudes

1997

Alan Rusbridger has been editor of the Guardian *since 1995. Having been at the centre of a number of high-profile and very expensive legal actions, he looked again, but from the point of view of a working editor, at the issues of privacy and press freedom raised by Louis Blom-Cooper in his 1989 lecture.*

B ROWSING THE INTERNET the other night, as editors tend to do nowadays instead of drinking, I stumbled across a website entitled Baby Shark's Lawyer Joke Website – which, as it sounds, is a website inexplicably devoted to cruel humour about lawyers. Surfing further I discovered there were at least 35 other websites devoted to the same genre.

Encouraged, I explored further in search of Baby Hack's Journalist Joke Website, but found none. I will not speculate on why it is that lawyers should be the butt of so much – no doubt well-intentioned – mirth. But I will pass on one lawyer joke told by Baby Shark. It concerns a client who, for reasons which can only be guessed at, thinks it prudent to inquire of his new lawyer how much he charges:

> Lawyer: £100 to answer three questions.
> Client: That's a bit steep, isn't it?
> Lawyer: Yes. Now what's your third question?

I emphasise from the start that I like lawyers. Many of my best friends are, as they say, lawyers. One of my themes here is how many of the battles for press freedom in this country have been fought most effectively by lawyers, rather than journalists. I even play golf with a lawyer. So, if I begrudge the amount of time I have spent with lawyers in my first two years of editing the *Guardian*, it is only because I would rather have spent the time editing the *Guardian*. Let me run through a couple of the battles which have led to all this lawyering. My motive in doing so is not that of the General, pushing his salt cellars around the dinner table in a misty-eyed re-enactment of heroics in the field. It is rather to illustrate the ambivalent attitude we have in this country towards the press.

The way the laws of a land protect or hinder newspapers in their legitimate work is one measure of how a society regards its freedoms. My chosen title is 'The freedom of the press and other platitudes', because I sometimes think that the freedom of the press is one of those phrases so ritualistically incanted that it begins to lose its meaning. We pay lip service to Milton, Hazlitt, Wilkes, Junius, Delane, Barnes, Scott and others who, over three centuries, helped the press gain its comparative freedom in this country. However, in reiterating the importance of a free press, we usually manage to insinuate a qualifier. As in: 'I stand second to none in my belief in the freedom of the press, but . . .'

My complaint is that the very people who are in a position to do something positive to defend the principle they consider so important often do so little in practice. They give the impression of believing that freedoms, once won, can be taken for granted. One learned lawyer, with a genuine background in fighting for freedoms elsewhere, referred to a recent free speech cause in this country as being 'at the luxury end of the human rights spectrum'.

Well, possibly. But that sounds to my ears very much like the people who told the *Guardian* and the *Sunday Times* to shut up about the corruption of Parliament because we have the least corrupt Parliament in the world. If you don't police minor corruption, it soon becomes major corruption. If you start discounting luxury freedoms, the danger is that others will discount staple freedoms.

My time with the lawyers over the past two years has broadly been spent on just three cases. One, involving a former government minister, is due to come to trial, and so it would be improper to refer to it beyond saying that it is a case that has now dragged on for more than two years and in which the costs already easily exceed £1 million.[1] Another, involving the former minister Neil Hamilton, has lasted even longer and still awaits the verdict of Sir Gordon Downey, the Parliamentary Commissioner for Standards. But Sir Gordon has written his report, which sits ticking away in a government safe, so nothing can prejudice the outcome of that hearing. The third case involved allegations of police corruption amongst the police, a case that against all the odds we won, but which is now being appealed.

The case of Neil Hamilton is almost too familiar to dwell on. It has many remarkable elements: a government minister who had probably lied on numerous occasions, but who still had the full

---

1 In 1995 Jonathan Aitken, then Chief Secretary to the Treasury, brought a libel action against the *Guardian* and Granada TV for allegations that he had not declared free hotel accommodation at the Ritz in Paris, paid for by its owner, Mohammed Al Fayed, the controversial owner also of Harrods in London; that he must have known of illegal arms sales to Iran by a company of which he was a director; and that he procured prostitutes for Arab clients in London. At the last moment, Aitken's case collapsed when the *Guardian* discovered evidence that his wife and daughter were not, as alleged, at the Ritz in Paris with him at the time. Aitken was subsequently charged with perjury and perverting the course of justice and sentenced to eighteen months in jail.

support of his Prime Minister to fight an election; a man for whom the 1689 Bill of Rights was changed, with the full support of the then government, in order to allow him to fight a libel case; a man who threw in the towel at the court door and yet nevertheless protested that he must be presumed innocent until proved guilty. Neil Hamilton has now turned into a cross between Horatio Bottomley and the Vicar of Stiffkey and may, I hear, soon be the subject of a feature film, with Bob Hoskins and Al Pacino vying to play Peter Carter-Ruck. The articles that we ran over a period of more than three years had at least one beneficial effect: the establishment of the Nolan Committee to look into standards in public life. But, even though we won the action, we were still left with a bill for more than £300,000.

In a way, the story of Tim Smith, the other subject of our original articles, was even more remarkable. An MP is rumbled for taking up to £25,000 from a businessman under investigation by the Department of Trade and Industry to speak up for him in Parliament, an act which in many countries would be regarded as a criminal offence. He tells his Chief Whip. The Chief Whip does nothing, tells nobody, makes no note of the conversation, does not consult a law officer, or even refer the matter to the House of Commons Privileges Committee. Instead, Mr Smith is made Vice-Chairman and Treasurer of the Conservative Party.

When his behaviour is first exposed publicly by a newspaper,

Parliament shows its disapproval by voting him on to the Public Accounts Committee, the Commons body responsible for overseeing probity in public spending. As my distinguished colleague Richard Littlejohn is fond of saying: 'You couldn't make it up.'

Had we not published uncontested extracts of his admissions to Sir Gordon Downey, Mr Smith would have presented himself for re-election to the voters of Beaconsfield, who would have been forced to vote in the dark. Does that matter? I think it does.

A former Australian Chief Justice once said in an important libel judgment that the purpose of protecting the flow of information, ideas and debate was to equip the electors to make choices, the elected to make decisions and, thereby, to enhance the workings of representative government. By those standards, in the Tim Smith case, the press succeeded and Westminster itself utterly failed the citizens of this country. When MPs lecture the press about the feebleness of self-regulation in the newspaper business – as they frequently do – they might like to remember the name of Tim Smith. Indeed, a new government committed to a programme of radical constitutional reform might care to look at the whole edifice of privileges that Parliament now claims for itself.

Parliamentary privilege means that MPs in effect enjoy immunity from prosecution for dishonesty in relation to their work. Privilege means that they can set up their own tribunal to judge themselves. Privilege means that they can suspend that

251

tribunal, if the business of getting themselves re-elected intervenes. Privilege means that they can appoint to the tribunal MPs who have announced their verdict before considering the evidence. Privilege means that MPs can waive it when it suits them. Privilege also means that they can refuse to waive their privilege, even if it becomes an impediment to the courts getting at the truth. Privilege in effect means that a Prime Minister can decree that the tribunal cannot sit. And Privilege means that Parliament can dictate how and when, if at all, any of the tribunal's deliberations are reported.

The third case involved a police station in London where there was serious suspicion of widespread corruption. The Police Complaints Authority moved in and began to investigate allegations that officers were involved in planting and dealing in drugs and faking evidence against suspects. Sir Peter Imbert, the Metropolitan Police Commissioner, described them as 'the most serious allegations of police corruption for twenty years'.

Anyone who has lived through the Brixton and Toxteth riots and the recent litany of miscarriage of justice cases would know that a situation like this in an inner-London police station is potentially serious. Go back and read Lord Scarman's analysis of the causes of the Brixton riots, which is still a model of a fair and lucid report. By the time we published our article in January 1992, there was a full-scale inquiry into the station with six officers working on it. One Detective Constable had already been charged with theft and fraud. The culmination came when eight Stoke Newington officers were transferred to other stations, an act virtually unprecedented in the history of the Metropolitan Police.

We ran two pieces about the transfer of the officers, together with background material that we had accumulated during an investigation lasting some months, conducted with the full knowledge and co-operation of the officer in charge. Nowhere in either of the articles did we name a single officer who had been transferred. No officers complained about the articles at the time. The inquiry went on to become the biggest into police corruption ever undertaken by the Police Complaints Authority. Many officers were, in time, cleared, including some of the unnamed officers transferred. But, in time, no fewer than thirteen people convicted on the evidence of officers from the police station had their convictions overturned by the Court of Appeal. In a further twenty cases, the Crown Prosecution Service offered no evidence. In all, more than £500,000 was paid out by the Met in damages as a result of civil actions taken against officers from Stoke Newington. One of the unnamed policemen in the article was convicted of smuggling two tons of cannabis and sent to jail for ten years.

So far so uncontroversial. By that I mean that the police had quite properly acted on public concern. The courts had done their bit. And a serious newspaper had fulfilled its duty to keep people informed of what was going on in their community. Guess what happens next.

Writs from eight officers arrived nearly three years to the day after our articles had appeared. The officers were backed by the Police Federation, a trade union which had until then won ninety-five libel actions in a row against newspapers in just three years and lost none. If you are a small local paper and you get a writ from the Police Federation, you have no option but to give in. These are known as 'garage actions', because the officers involved can build a nice little extension as a result of these libel suits. In the last three years, libel actions have netted policemen more than £1.5 million in damages. That's a lot of garages.

On this occasion we thought that we would not give in, even though the combined costs by the start of the trial were knocking on £600,000. We thought that our reporter was a decent man who had behaved responsibly and should be defended. Two senior policemen, one of them a former Deputy Assistant Commissioner at Scotland Yard, were willing to testify on our behalf.

It is at this point that the peculiarities of the British law of libel begin to bite. The judge in the case disallowed any evidence of anything that had happened after the *Guardian* pieces appeared. No reference to damages, quashed convictions, prosecutions, policemen going to prison: nothing. I was not allowed to give evidence. We were not allowed to try to persuade a jury that we genuinely felt we had acted in the public interest. I do not think I am being unfair to the trial judge if I say that he could not have given us less help throughout. His summing-up managed to omit anything but a passing mention of the *Guardian*'s case. It was very nearly a travesty of natural justice. It was certainly a frightening and disillusioning experience. If we had lost the case, we would have forfeited a great deal of money, about £750,000. As it was, we won.

Like the publisher of the 'Letters From Junius', arraigned on a charge of seditious libel in 1770, we were saved by the sturdy refusal of a London jury to convict. After Henry Woodfall's acquittal, Junius wrote 'A Letter to the English Nation', in which he said:

> Let it be impressed upon your minds, let it be instilled into your children, that the liberty of the press is the palladium of all the civil, political and religious rights of an Englishman; and that the rights of juries to return a general verdict, in all cases whatsoever, is an essential part of our constitution, not to be controlled or limited by the judges, nor in any shape questionable by the Legislature.

My only observation on our forthcoming legal battle is that the trial judge, supported by the Lord Chief Justice, has ruled that a newspaper is not, after all, entitled to have a jury trial for libel cases. Juries can sit in complex fraud trials lasting many months, but can no longer be trusted with a libel trial lasting weeks. Juries could be trusted with eighteenth-century libels, but not twentieth-century ones.

Both the Hamilton and the police cases felt like slightly hollow victories. In one, the plaintiff was free to appear on every TV station in the land, protesting that he must be considered innocent until proved guilty, backed by everyone from the Prime Minister down. The implied corollary was that the *Guardian* was guilty. The logic of the situation should, of course, have been precisely the reverse, but have you noticed anyone arguing that the *Guardian* must be assumed innocent until proved otherwise?

With the police case we had changed nothing in terms of the law. We had scraped by. If it loses on appeal, the Police Federation will in all likelihood write the case off as an unlucky result and revert to its policy of shutting down reporting on police corruption. Communities will remain in the dark.

As a new editor, the last two years have been a bruising introduction to the way the law operates in regard to what we publish in this country. At the time of publication, an editor can have little confidence that an article he publishes in good faith and in the sincere belief that it is in the public interest will receive much, if any, protection from the courts. He cannot guess what sums the article could cost him, what defence he will be able to mount, what damages might be involved, nor now even whether he will be able to argue his case before a jury of his peers. Editors without supportive and well-resourced owners would be foolish to risk their papers on too much robust journalism under these circumstances.

Why have I spent so much time describing the two cases? Because the *Guardian*, as well as attracting a certain amount of praise from some quarters, also encountered opposition, ranging from a studied indifference to our concerns to outright hostility from people in authority: the sort of people who talk about the 'freedom of the press, but . . .'.

With Hamilton there was a scarcely concealed fury among many MPs – and, I'm afraid to say, even journalists – that a newspaper should vigorously attack corruption in Parliament. This attitude was startlingly at variance with the ordinary voters in Tatton, who on 2 May made their opinion resoundingly clear by throwing out Neil Hamilton.

Let me give you two examples of this attitude among senior MPs. Here is Roger Gale, talking on the radio about the *Guardian*'s work in exposing 'cash for questions':

> One of the problems is that the national press . . . has no interest whatsoever in the institutions of the United Kingdom . . . not only Parliament but also the Church and the Monarchy . . . institutions that the press is doing its damnedest to undermine.

Here is Sir Archie Hamilton on the same subject:

> What we're coming under is a tremendous amount of slur
> and innuendo being used by partisan members of the
> media to try and get rid of ministers. And somebody has to
> stand up and fight this.

Sir Archie went on to advocate

> a number of bits of legislation to restrict freedom of the
> press . . . it is going to be necessary because we cannot go
> on having politicians being picked on in this way, nor
> indeed our institutions undermined.

This is mystifying stuff. It is as if you reported someone for shoplifting
in Marks & Spencer, only to be ticked off by a store detective for
undermining a Great British Institution. What Mr Gale and Sir Archie
are really yearning for is a return to the 200-year-old concept of
seditious libel: an ingenious law whereby the state could punish
anyone for publishing anything that tended to lower the public's
esteem for the government or a public official or an institution. It was
a particularly effective law because truth was no defence. The criminal
harm lay in lowering esteem and the truth might do that most effectively – the greater the truth, the greater the libel, as the saying went.

But these throwbacks to the eighteenth century were not obscure rent-a-quote MPs, hired by Radio 4 producers for light relief. Roger Gale was at the time Chairman of the back-bench Media Committee and Chairman of the Conservative Parliamentary Media Committee. He was, in other words, the official spokesman for rank-and-file Conservative parliamentary opinion. Sir Archie Hamilton has just been elected Chairman of the 1922 Committee. He had already been rewarded for the wisdom of his radio intervention by being appointed to the House of Commons Standards and Privileges Committee, just in time to adjudicate between the *Guardian* and his traduced namesake, Neil.

A minor protest to Tony Newton, Chairman of the Standards and Privileges Committee, about Sir Archie's appointment was incidentally rejected on the grounds that it had been approved by a vote of the House. A protest to the Speaker was rejected on the grounds that it was a matter for the Leader of the House. The Leader of the House was, needless to say, Tony Newton. Could you make it up? I think you couldn't.

I do not know how the man on the Clapham omnibus now struggles in to work. Possibly in a Ford Galaxy. If you found Ford Galaxy Man and asked him if he would like to know whether his MP is corrupt or not, or whether there is a major investigation at his local police station – and, if so, what it's about – you would get a pretty definite answer. Not only would he like to know, he would probably think he had a right to know. Pressed further, he might well reply that, not only was it the right of his newspaper to tell him about it, it was its positive duty.

As it happens, there is a legal concept which would help Ford Galaxy Man: it is called Qualified Privilege. Qualified Privilege might colloquially be defined as the 'right to know'. More precisely, it is the doctrine that there is an equal and legitimate interest in a group in society being told something as there is in a newspaper telling it.

Most famously, this concept has been enshrined in the famous American Supreme Court judgment in the Sullivan v *New York Times* libel case, handed down in 1964 by a great Supreme Court justice William J. Brennan. Even those, like Sydney Kentridge, who disagree with it, acknowledge the judgment as magnificent. 'It is,' Kentridge has written, 'impossible to read it without a feeling of excitement.' Brennan's judgment was a ringing defence of the right – and duty – of a free press to be able freely to report on matters of public importance. It was written in terms and with a conviction that are, I'm afraid, hard to imagine coming from any British judge.

As with the *Guardian*, the Sullivan case concerned an unnamed police official. At the original trial the man, Police Commissioner L. B. Sullivan of Montgomery, Alabama, collected $500,000 in damages from the *New York Times* for publishing a pro-civil rights advertisement. In upholding the *New York Times*'s appeal, Justice

Brennan revolutionised American libel law, even allowing newspapers to publish false statements uttered in the heat of debate, providing that they were not maliciously made. It was a judgment which differentiated for the first time between reporting of people in public life and reporting of private individuals. It held that the press ought to be allowed more discretion in informing society about people who held public office.

Brennan said, among other things: 'Debate on public issues should be uninhibited, robust and wide-open and . . . it may well include vehement, caustic and sometimes unpleasantly sharp attacks on government and public officials.' Newspapers faced with the possibility of huge libel damages might well succumb to a 'pall of fear and timidity' and tone down any criticism of public officials. The threat of massive costs 'dampens the vigour and limits the variety of public debate'. Public officials would in future have to prove actual malice: i.e. the plaintiff would have to prove that the reporter had been reckless as to whether what he was writing was true or not.

In the thirty-three years since Brennan's judgment, the Americans have tussled with Sullivan, tugged it, poked it and developed it. There have been arguments over who qualifies as a public figure and how to define 'actual malice' or 'reckless disregard for the truth'. What qualifies as 'substantial' investigations before publication, as opposed to 'exhaustive' investigations? Some plaintiffs have used it as an excuse to turn newsrooms inside out on discovery to find evidence of malice or simple sloppiness in research.

But, fundamentally, Sullivan has stood the test of time. The fear that the judgment would be used by newspapers recklessly to destroy politicians has not come to pass. Litigation has demonstrated that the burden of proving 'actual malice' is not out of reach – indeed, research showed that plaintiffs have been able to meet the burden of proof in fifty per cent of cases. The Supreme Court has held to the line that matters of public concern deserve more First Amendment protection than speech on matters of private concern. I do not think anyone could look at the press in America since Sullivan and say it was less responsible than our own.

Of course, Brennan had a relatively easy job. He could refer back to the constitution for his inspiration: 'Congress shall make no law abridging the freedom of speech, or of the press.' He could quote James Madison, the author of much of the constitution, who even defended the right of the press to make honest mistakes:

> Erroneous statement is inevitable in free debate, and it
> must be protected if the freedoms of expression are to have
> the 'breathing space' that they need to survive.

The problem here is that we have no written constitution. There is no First Amendment, no guarantee of free speech or a free press.

We famously have liberties, but no rights. Even where, in Britain, there have been ringing declarations of free speech – Wilkes, Hazlitt, Milton, John Stuart Mill, Blackstone, Delane and the rest – they have invariably been defences of the right to an opinion rather than the right to report or reveal. Some academic lawyers believe the libel law in this country, which protects fair comment more than it protects straight reporting, has led to a tradition in the British press which is more polemical than factual. More than one person has remarked that a culture has grown up where comment is free but facts are secret.

That's Britain. Elsewhere in the world things have been changing. The thirty-odd years since Sullivan have seen its influence spread, as country after country has adopted some form of 'public figure' defence. It is enshrined in the way the European Convention on Human Rights has been interpreted by the European Court. Variations of it have taken root in Australia, Canada, India and South Africa. A recent case in South Africa, the Holomisa case, resulted in a ruling that a defamatory statement which relates to 'free and fair political activity' is constitutionally protected, even if false, unless the plaintiff can show that the publisher acted unreasonably. The judgment gets round the problem of defining a 'public figure' by focusing, instead, on the nature of the material. Any publication that can show it behaved with reasonable care while reporting matters in the public interest will be protected.

I do not argue that Sullivan is a perfect solution. Many journalists have reservations about it. But it does at least start from the right place. It is worth asking what the prospects are of getting something like Sullivan in Britain as some protection for serious newspapers genuinely trying to do their job.

Pretty gloomy, I would say. The judgment of Lord Keith in the Derbyshire case was a considerable step in the right direction.[2] It was a genuine breakthrough in establishing in common law a positive right to free expression and in recognising that the values underlying Sullivan apply in this country. But in the ordinary courts, where millions of pounds hang on the word of a judge, a different attitude prevails. Mr Justice French certainly had no truck with any notion of Qualified Privilege in the Police Federation case, or in the case between Albert Reynolds, the former Irish Prime Minister, and the *Sunday Times*. The Court of Appeal has generally rejected any applications on Qualified Privilege on the grounds that it is up to Parliament to introduce it. The Court notes that nothing of the sort was attempted in last year's modest – though not unhelpful – Defamation Act.

---

2   In 1989 Derbyshire County Council and its then leader, David Bookbinder, brought a libel action against the *Sunday Times* over allegations of misuse of pension fund money. In 1993 the House of Lords determined that a local government council as such cannot sue for defamation.

So, without a constitution, it would fall to Parliament to bring in a law which would make it easier for newspapers to criticise and expose politicians. You only have to utter that sentence to realise it is never going to happen. The words 'turkey' and 'Christmas' spring to mind. But it is worse than that. Not only did Parliament not step one inch down the road towards helping the press report matters in the genuine public interest in the recent Defamation Act, the very word 'Sullivan' was used as shorthand for something really rather repulsive and alien. The general attitude was not that the British press needed any help: rather, it needed punishing. Let me quote two, not unrepresentative, interventions in the debates. In the Commons, Sir Peter Tapsell demanded more protection for MPs, not less:

> Individual members can be subjected to persecution, not
> from the executive or from the Sovereign, but from what
> many people regard as an over-mighty press that is owned,
> for the most part, by foreigners.

In the Lords, Lord Ackner ridiculed the notion of lower damages against newspapers. He wanted higher damages:

> I am in favour of large awards not because they are intel-
> lectually satisfying but because it is one way of saying to

the press: 'Very well, if you invent facts' – as they
frequently do – 'or if you distort the truth' – as the better-
quality papers usually do – then it will be an extremely
expensive experience.

Imagine, incidentally, the reaction if the *Guardian* had claimed that
MPs were 'usually' corrupt. Yet a former law lord can assert that
broadsheet newspapers 'usually' distort the truth and no one blinks
an eye.

The official position was put by Lord Inglewood, a junior
minister at the Department of National Heritage, who said that the
government took the view that standards of care and accuracy in
the British press were not such to give confidence that it could be
trusted with anything like a Sullivan defence.

So we are at a crossroads. The courts are reluctant to do anything
without a nod from Parliament. And Parliament is hostile to the
press and unlikely to help. London, meanwhile, remains the libel
capital of the world. It is called 'forum shopping'. London is the
place Hollywood stars and Russian mafia crooks now choose to
fight powerful American media organisations, because they know
that here they have the best chance of winning. It is the place from
which US courts refuse to enforce libel judgments, because the law
is so draconian towards the press: they are appalled that English
libel law has no First Amendment protection and that, uniquely in

civil law, it places the burden of proving truth or fair comment on the defendant.

But I do not want this to be an unremitting whinge. It is foolish and unproductive of newspapers simply to sulk and protest. And the problem is much bigger than simply whether or not a public figure defence law is incorporated into English law. That is merely an illustration of attitudes to a free press and free speech. As journalists we should be concerned about the whole balance of laws relating to information.

We should be alarmed at the discreet hints being dropped about how the government might exploit Article 8 of the European Convention on Human Rights to insinuate a privacy law into this country by stealth. We should be frightened by the implications of the proposed Data Protection Bill, which could prohibit 'doorstepping' as well as allowing anyone access to information on them held by newspapers, and requiring journalists to divulge their sources.

We should also be alarmed that a government which for twenty years in Opposition had a manifesto commitment to a Freedom of Information Act can now promise only a White Paper and express a 'hope' that a full Bill would be introduced in the next parliamentary session.

We should be concerned that the new government should wake up to the wholesale areas of public life, now privatised or quangoed, where the press's once honourable role of informing the community it serves has been eroded. Will they notice the implications that flow from the withering away of local democracy's powers and functions; or that swathes of education, health, planning authorities and public utilities have replaced statutory rights of openness with non-statutory codes of conduct?

Confidentiality clauses have started to creep into contracts of employment. Newly privatised bodies have begun to use commercial confidentiality and the law of confidence as an excuse to withhold information from the press and public. I spent some of my life as a cub reporter covering Area and Regional Health Authorities. Now, out of all the NHS Trust federations, only half hold more than one public meeting a year, the statutory minimum.

No wonder local communities have found that the flow of information from local bodies is drying up. No wonder people begin to feel alienated and powerless to influence decision-making in crucial areas, such as health, education and planning. Is it any wonder that such alienation translates into apathy at the ballot box and that 30 to 40 per cent turnout in local elections in Britain is less than anywhere else in Europe?

Don't take my word for it. Read the evidence to the Nolan Committee. Read Simon Jenkins's important book, *Accountable to None*. This is not a left-right issue, if anything is these days. It is about the functioning of a free press in nurturing and sustaining democracy.

The challenge for journalists is to accept that the overwhelming majority of people do not generally associate newspapers in this country with such an honourable function. A MORI poll last month showed that 76 per cent of the population does not trust journalists to tell the truth. There are two crumbs of comfort in this figure. One is that politicians score worse (78 per cent) and government ministers still worse (80 per cent). The other is that the overall balance of trust in journalists has shown a net improvement of 13 per cent in the past four years. We do not aim or expect to be loved. But these figures are still a pretty dismal reflection of the public's regard for our trade, and one which ought to cause us pause for thought.

The problem is easily stated. It is best put by the character in a Tom Stoppard play who, in a variation of the 'Freedom, but . . .' speech, says: 'I'm with you on the freedom of the press. It's the newspapers I can't stand.'

There are, by and large, two classes of national newspaper in this country. One attempts mainly to inform: to provide reasoned and thoughtful coverage of politics, social policy, the arts, business and economics. The other aims mainly to entertain: with serious news increasingly an incidental accompaniment. That is a crude characterisation, and the words 'broadsheet' and 'tabloid' are too blunt to be meaningful distinctions; but most people, I suspect, would acknowledge its basic truth. It is a trend that has been long in the making: indeed, it was one of the themes that preoccupied James Cameron towards the end of his life.

The difficulty, then, is making sure that decent, serious journalism can flourish in a society, without also opening the door to
brutalist and intrusive journalism. Or, to put it the other way
round, the challenge is to see whether it is possible to restrict the
latter while enabling the former. James Madison had it easy, you
might say. Rupert Murdoch was not around in 1787.

At the moment, the tendency is nearly always to legislate for the
worst, rather than the best. It was not a dangerous radical, but the
venerable Bill Deedes,[3] who, in 1990, cautioned against this
approach when he said:

> It is when the antics of a minority provoke calls for new
> curbs on free expression, and when public indifference on
> the subject prevails, that the liberties of the majority are
> most at risk.

There are three main rights to be balanced in any attempt to resolve
this conflict: first, the right to privacy, dignity or reputation,
however you phrase it; second, the right to freedom of expression;
and, third, the right to know. Each right is in balance with the next

3 William Deedes began his career as a journalist in 1931 and covered the Italian
invasion of Abyssinia in 1935. He was editor of the *Daily Telegraph* from 1974 to 1986
and still writes regularly for the paper. An MP from 1950 to 1974 and a government
minister from 1954 to 1964, he was made a life peer in 1986.

and all three rights must be treated together. Parliament cannot do this alone, nor can the courts, nor can the newspapers. But there ought now to be an opportunity to do something to balance these three rights and mould them into a coherent approach to information to take us into the new millennium.

We have a new government, a new Prime Minister, a new Lord Chancellor, a relatively new Lord Chief Justice and plenty of new thinking in many areas of public life. If lawyers, editors, broadcasters and politicians could only get together in a spirit of openness, we could surely produce something – I was going to call it a New Deal until I heard Michael Howard use the phrase recently – something which is good and which is lasting.

Let me briefly suggest how this new coherent strategy on information could be forged and list some of the established assumptions and attitudes that such a partnership would have to challenge. Journalists first: let us confess that we are used to living in the bunker. We have, for as long as I have worked in this business, assumed – often with justification – that there was a conspiracy to make our working lives as difficult as possible. We have lived with ludicrous official secrecy laws, anachronistic D-Notice Committees, manipulated lobby systems and one of the most draconian libel laws in the civilised world.

We have lived with the threat of a privacy law, attempts to make us reveal our sources and, lately, the uncertain menace of data protection legislation. The result is that a generation of editors felt that they had to stand shoulder to shoulder, because it would have been fatal to concede the merits of, say, a privacy law, without a compensating bias towards easier libel laws or freedom of information.

The result is that we have, ineffect, been driven to defend the indefensible. We have stood by and watched a decade of intrusive stories published and meekly held our silence. Bit-part actresses, BBC weathermen, part-time newsreaders, little-known barristers, minor-league sportsmen, backroom arts administrators, inconsequential back-bench MPs – and even broadsheet newspaper columnists – have been dragged in front of us and what should have been private has been made remorselessly public. Hospital wards have been invaded, widows have been traduced, phones have been tapped, confidences betrayed, interviews invented and lives ruined in the name of precisely what public good?

Is it inconceivable that journalists ought to be able to admit that some of this is plain wrong? That there is a case for a privacy law, if drafted carefully and interpreted sensibly by a discerning judiciary? That self-regulation has frequently been a fig leaf behind which we have disguised our unease? And that, for perfectly understandable reasons, we have not been good at discussing these issues openly?

Let me give one example of the sort of issue rarely analysed by journalists, but which seems to be a fair question and one we should ask ourselves. It arose when I was tackled recently over dinner by the beady-eyed Chief Constable of Oxfordshire, Charles Pollard.

The Chief Constable said that he had been following with interest last year the widespread media campaign against Clause 89 of the Police Bill, during which a variety of voices from the *Guardian* to the *Telegraph* had insisted that a High Court judge should be required to sanction any bugging of premises by policemen investigating serious crimes. That was a proper concern to raise, he said, but all the same he was intrigued to note that the media's own code of conduct appeared to allow the use of clandestine listening devices and telephone intercepts, so long as we were satisfied that it was in the public interest. What special privileges did we claim that we had only to satisfy ourselves, whereas even a circuit court judge was not protection enough for the police? I thought it was a good question.

There are other areas that, in a less embattled climate, we might be prepared to consider as a quid pro quo for a more enlightened attitude from politicians and the courts. Why do no British papers carry a regular column, such as American newspapers have, for daily corrections and clarifications?[4] Why do we not give more

---

4 In 1997 the *Guardian* introduced a daily column with this title – Corrections and Clarifications – on its leader page and appointed a Readers' Editor. In the first three years he received some 19,000 communications from readers and the column published over 4,000 entries. By late 2001 the *Mirror*, the *Observer* and the *Independent on Sunday* had also appointed Readers' Editors.

serious consideration to the opportunity – or even right – to reply in contentious cases. French and German newspapers have them, and find them useful devices for keeping the lawyers at bay.

Why, when we are so tough – and rightly so – on the registration of MPs' interests, do we never discuss journalists' outside interests – particularly financial or political journalists? Lord Wakeham has done a splendid job at the Press Complaints Commission, but does that mean we never again debate the whole question of self-regulation? And whatever happened to ombudsmen?[5]

As I have said, it was difficult for British journalists to indulge in this kind of soul-searching in a climate in which we felt under threat. But there is another reason: as a profession, we do not take ourselves very seriously in this country. Indeed, we cannot really decide if we are a profession or a trade. Unlike our American colleagues, we are happy to call ourselves hacks. We do not have graduate schools of journalism looking in depth into the sorts of questions raised here. We do not have an effective lobbying group of British editors. Defamation Acts are passed with scarcely a whimper or representation from the press. We leave it to the lawyers. There is not a British journalism magazine tackling current ethical issues to compare with the *Columbia Journalism Review*.

---

5 In 1989, all national newspapers (except the *Financial Times*) agreed to appoint an ombudsman to rule on readers' complaints.

Our inability to take ourselves very seriously is, in many ways, the most attractive quality of British journalists and the journalism they produce. The danger is obvious: that others will not take us seriously, either.

Then there are the challenges for the lawyers. I have already said that there are enlightened solicitors, barristers and judges who have played an honourable part in fashioning a coherent philosophy of free expression. Often they have taken the lead. But they seem to me, and to many of my colleagues, to be in the minority.

Is it too much to ask that judges should develop a more sophisticated view of the press than Lord Ackner's: that there are only two types of newspapers, those which invent facts and those which distort them, and that both are deserving of punishment?

Many judges really do give the impression that they believe that the *Guardian* is indistinguishable from the *Daily Star*, or *The Times* from the *Sun*. Do senior judges ever get out and meet journalists? Do they ever visit newspaper offices and see the conditions in which newspapers are produced? The speed at which decisions have to be taken? The care with which most journalists on serious newspapers approach their work?

Is it, then, right to legislate for all newspapers as though they were the worst nightmares of Rupert Murdoch? Is it proper that in libel cases – uniquely in civil law – the burden of proof should be on the defendant? Is there no variation of the Sullivan rule which would make it easier for bona fide journalists to write carefully researched stories about legitimate areas of public concern? Would they take the trouble to read Anthony Lewis's brilliant account of Sullivan, which observes of the judgment that, without it, it is

> questionable whether the press could have done as much as it has to penetrate the power and secrecy of modern government, or to confront the public with the reality of policy issues . . . The ultimate beneficiary was not the press but the public, which was able to hear criticism and exercise its voice.[6]

They should read also the excellent research by Eric Barendt, Professor of Media Law at University College, London, and his team, who did bother to speak to journalists.[7] It proves beyond doubt that the libel laws do have a 'chilling effect' in inhibiting reporting of matters of public concern. Read Professor Barendt on the costs of libel, often much more of a threat and a factor in self-censorship than damages. He says:

6 *Make No Law: the Sullivan case and the First Amendment.* (Vintage Books, 1992). Anthony Lewis was Chief London Correspondent of the *New York Times* from 1965 to 1972, and now writes a column for the same paper.

7 *Libel and the Media: the chilling effect* by Eric Barendt, Laurence Lustgarten, Kenneth Norrie and Hugh Stephenson. (Oxford University Press, 1997).

> The level of legal costs in libel cases is more out of propor-
> tion to the money received by complainants . . . than in any
> other area of the law.

Might it be worth adapting the principle of slander, where damages
are awarded only if the plaintiff can prove actual damage? How will
judges interpret the European Convention on Human Rights now
that it is to be incorporated into our law. Will they regard it as
giving our courts a democratic mandate to weigh free speech
against other aspects of the public interest?

Could judges ask themselves whether trial by jury ought not to
be considered a fundamental right, especially when the plaintiff is
a public figure himself and truthfulness is the issue? Will they look
at the new reporting restrictions which continue to be introduced
at every level of the judicial system? If protection is given to newspapers to write about powerful public figures, should legal aid be
available for people who are not rich and not in public life?

Finally, we would ask of the politicians that they live up to their
promises on freedom of information. Only last year [1996] Tony
Blair described a Freedom of Information Act as

> Not some isolated constitutional reform, but a change that
> is absolutely fundamental to how we see politics devel-
> oping in this country.

Resist the temptation to use Article 8 of the European Convention on Human Rights as a back-door method of introducing a Privacy Bill. Resist a Privacy Bill altogether, unless it is accompanied by an enlightened reform of the defamation and information legislation. Look at the whole swathes of public life where the flow of information has dried up and local democracy has been driven into the shadows. Examine your own system of privileges. Be watchful about the implementation of data protection legislation and allow proper exemptions for responsible media organisations.

I shall no doubt be criticised by some of my colleagues for conceding the slightest grounds for privacy legislation. They will cite the name of Robert Maxwell and tell me that any privacy law is unworkable. I can only say that I would happily sacrifice the freedom to expose the love life of a BBC weather forecaster to eleven million prurient eyes, if it meant that the courts would give greater protection to papers or broadcasters reporting corruption or dishonesty in public life.

Privacy legislation works only in a context in which all aspects of information are reviewed calmly and openly: with the courts moving on defamation, the government moving on freedom of information, and the media moving on intrusive journalism. Then we could have a new set of rights: the right to privacy, the right to free expression and the right to know.

It has to be planned as a coherent information policy instead of what we have at present: a ragbag of laws and conventions based on privilege, precedent and prejudice. Freedom of the press is too important to be left to the press alone, or to the judges alone, or to politicians alone. But, together, we ought to be able to craft codes and laws that ensure a balance, so that it is a freedom in which we can all believe wholeheartedly, without feeling the need for weasel qualifications. We should be able to defend the freedom of the press: no ifs, no buts. And we should all think it our duty to nurture it.

I have quoted James Madison. Let me end by quoting Junius, his British contemporary whose identity has often been guessed at but never definitively revealed. In the same decade that Madison drafted the American First Amendment, Junius wrote an essay dedicated to his publisher, Woodfall, who stood trial on his behalf. One passage in particular was really the Sullivan defence, expressed nearly 200 years before Justice Brennan got round to writing it:

> A considerable latitude must be allowed in the discussion of public affairs, or the liberty of the press will be of no benefit to society. As the indulgence of private malice and personal slander should be checked and resisted by every legal means, so a constant examination into the characters and conduct of ministers and magistrates should be equally promoted and encouraged. They who conceive that our newspapers are no restraint upon bad men, or

279

> impediment to the execution of bad measure, know
> nothing of this country.

It is sad that we are forced to look so longingly to America, when once there were men here who understood these principles. We should be true to our own history, but at the same time we should wake up to the fact that freedoms wither unless they are defended.

I think that the climate is right to do that: to do something to ensure that the freedom of the press is more than another bit of Heritage Britain, another of those things that we used to do terribly well.

John Humphrys

Pandering to populism

1999

John Humphrys has been a presenter of BBC Radio 4's Today *programme since 1987 and of BBC TV's* On the Record *since 1993. With both commercial broadcasting and the BBC, for their different reasons, increasingly desperate to hold on to market share, his lecture took a practitioner's look at the debate about 'dumbing down'.*

A S A HUMBLE BROADCASTER it is impossible not to feel a bit of a fraud to be delivering the James Cameron lecture. Compare what we, as professional broadcasters, do now with what Cameron did in his prime.

We ask questions, sometimes even the right ones, and occasionally we get answers, sometimes intelligent ones, sometimes revealing ones and sometimes honest ones, even from politicians. We need to be reasonably quick-witted (in my case at a god-awful time in the morning), reasonably well-informed and moderately articulate. If we're doing it on the box, it helps if we

281

are not too hideous to look at. If you're a woman, it is a positive advantage to be blonde-haired and have large eyes. Short blond hair, you will notice. Long hair is out. It helps to develop a 'personality' – grumpy, irritable, charming, smooth. It does not much matter which, just so long as the audience can recognise us as 'personalities'. We must have a discernible brand. Some of us do not even have to think: just read from an autocue. We have a hundred and one ways of catching the attention of the audience. We can shout or bark or sneer or laugh or raise our eyebrows or look down our noses (metaphorically or literally) and, if we're doing it on the box, we can rely on any number of technical gee-gaws to grab the attention of a bored audience – fancy computerised graphics or space-age sets. We have a lot going for us.

What did Cameron have? He had a typewriter. Of course, he also had his own innate ability: an insatiable curiosity, for a start. He watched, he listened, he asked questions too – and then he wrote it down. But he didn't have the equivalent of clever graphics and fancy sets. Not so much as a still picture to force our eyes to the page and keep them there, just a column or two of black type asking to be read. He was born as broadcasting began and he grew old with it and I was curious to find out what he thought of broadcast journalism. Here is what he wrote for the *Guardian* in July 1984: 'We all have our addictions and mine, unfortunately, is the news. I say unfortunately because for an old-fashioned newsman accustomed to words, TV journalism is lamentably awful, and becoming worse by the week. I do not mean the pitiful *Sixty Minutes*, the amateurish badness of which was recognised even by its presenters and not a moment too soon, but the general offering of contemporary affairs to a public for millions of whom the telly is basically its only source.'

That is quite an indictment. Is the accused guilty as charged? First, let us ask whether it matters very much. If you had asked the young Cameron to define the most powerful forces in the land, I dare say he would have turned to the giants of manufacturing industry, the owners of the factories that produced the wealth without which no great trading nation could prosper, or even survive. When Cameron was a young man and Eisenhower talked of the power of the military-industrial complex in the United States, we all saw images of factory chimneys and endless production lines producing endless profits and we knew exactly what he meant. They were the wealth creators; thus they were the real powers in the land. You will search in vain for their modern equivalents in the top ten of the most powerful people in Britain today compiled by the *Sunday Times*, or even in the top one hundred. But at number four you will find Rupert Murdoch. He produces no wealth in the old-fashioned sense of the word, forges not a ton of steel, nor fashions that steel into cars or washing machines. He takes the nationality of the country that will best serve his business interests. But, by God, is he powerful.

One of our home-grown press barons, the late Lord Rothermere, revealed a lot about the pecking order when he told the *Daily Telegraph* about his contacts with Tony Blair, himself unsurprisingly number one in that same list. 'On average,' he said, 'I reckon to see Mr Blair two or three times a year, but not as often as Conrad Black who, in turn, sees less of him than Rupert does.' While Lord Thompson, an old press baron, bought a television station in the early days of ITV and described it with his usual subtlety as a 'licence to print money', Murdoch saw the real worth of television. Money, yes. But power too. And with that power the ability to make much, much more money and to influence us all in ways that a Thomson or even old Beaverbrook, with his campaigning *Express*, could only have dreamed of. Never, since Gutenberg ran off the first printed copy of the Bible, has there been as powerful an information machine, or indeed as powerful a cultural force, as television. Those who appear on it have become the icons of our age. Those who watch it are influenced in ways it would have been impossible to imagine only two generations ago. Those who choose not to watch it are influenced, whether they like it or not.

It is true that television has not brought about the death of newspapers, as many predicted. Instead they feed off each other. Nor has it yet killed reading, though it has influenced the books we buy a great deal. But picture a world without television and then try to deny its force. The more our lives have become dominated by television, the more our sense of reality, of how the world works, of what people are all about, becomes the one presented to us by television. So it does matter what picture of the world television gives us. If television presents the world in a way that panders to the worst sides of our nature, or turns everything into something we respond to as if it were all a form of light entertainment, then that is also how we shall start to respond to the world. At the extreme, we become insular, disengaged, passive voyeurs, not just of television but of the world.

So television does matter. A lot. And television news and current affairs matters, in my view, more than anything else on the box. I happen to believe that British television is the best in the world. You may quibble about that. You may argue, as some do, that British television is merely the best television for a British audience. I recognise the distinction, but I stick by my own definition. That may surprise those who have read some newspaper accounts of what I wrote in my book, *Devil's Advocate*; or not, if you accept that the basic law of journalism is 'first simplify, then exaggerate'. But I base my belief on many years of living abroad and many more of living in Britain. We all have our own experience of American television, of course; Lord knows, we see enough of it on our own boxes. What we do not see is American news, and praise the Lord for that! There are, or at least have been, some shining jewels in even that tarnished crown. *Sixty Minutes* probably remains the gold standard for current affairs broadcasting and there have been great American newsmen over the years: Walter Cronkite, of course, John Chancellor and Eric Sevareid. Ed Morrow's wartime dispatches have never been bettered. Nor has the definition of television that he produced in 1958: 'This instrument can teach; it can illuminate; yes it can even inspire. But it can only do so to the extent that humans (that means you) are determined to use it to those ends. Otherwise it is merely wires and lights in a box.' If that seems, forty years later, a somewhat grandiloquent statement, I suspect it says more about these cynical times than it does about Mr Morrow. Look at what has happened to American network news in the last ten or fifteen years. The typical nightly news is now so provincial, so narrow-mindedly insular that it makes a parish magazine look like the *International Herald Tribune*. And why? Ratings chasing. That's why. If they can get Dan Rather to wear a sweater while he's reading the news and pull in another million viewers as a result, then that is what they will do. If audience research suggests that foreign news is a bit of a turn-off, then out it goes. It is called populism. Let us not challenge the audience with anything that might be even a little demanding, in case they leave us and go to another channel. Anyway, it is a helluvva lot cheaper to buy a new sweater for Rather.

Fair enough. If every million extra viewers can be counted in tens of millions of dollars of advertising revenue and if the shareholders are screaming for results and the viewers have hundreds of other, brain-dead channels to point their zappers at, do we have a choice? Yes, we do. My concern (and the concern of many others both outside and inside the BBC) is that we should not follow the Americans down that bleak road.

Of course, we have ITV and Channel Four and Channel 5 and Sky and a burgeoning family of cable channels, but it is the BBC that matters most. As Michael Grade once put it, the BBC 'keeps the rest of us honest'. Whether that still applies is what most concerns me here. There are some worrying portents. Let me deal first with those whom the BBC is meant to 'keep honest'. Honesty is not the word that most readily springs to mind when you look at some of the shenanigans that some documentary makers have been getting involved in over the past few years. The most blatant of them, you will remember, was exposed by the *Guardian*. Just about everything was faked in *The Connection*, a Carlton documentary about drug-trafficking for ITV.[1] The man shown as a drug cartel boss was no more than a retired bank clerk with low level drug connections. The courier shown swallowing heroin and then described as a 'walking time bomb' had in fact swallowed nothing

1 Broadcast in 1996.

more harmful than a mint. The programme pretended to show a continuous journey from Colombia to London, but it did not. In all, sixteen instances of faking were discovered in the one programme. Carlton was fined £2 million. That may have hurt them, but the programme actually hurt every single one of us, whether we work for Carlton or the *Today* programme or the most humble local broadcaster. It sent out the message that our trade was not automatically to be trusted.

The point is not that faking is new. What is new over the past few years has been the conscious and deliberate fusing of journalism and entertainment in the pursuit of ratings, which inevitably makes faking more likely. As John Willis, former deputy director of Channel Four, put it: 'The line between fact and drama in documentary has grown increasingly blurred and, in the struggle between journalistic truth and dramatic excitement, drama is winning.' He is not alone in that view. The British Film Institute commissioned a survey earlier this year of more than 500 television executives, producers, researchers and camera crew to find out what they thought of the way television is going. Half of those working in documentaries and current affairs said they felt that they had been pressured to distort the truth and misrepresent the views of those interviewed to create 'exciting, controversial or entertaining programming'. Richard Patterson, who wrote the report for the BFI, said: 'It is worrying that both new entrants and established workers in the industry see a diminution in quality standards.'

That doesn't matter if you are concerned only with chasing the ratings, but it matters a great deal if you are concerned with the preservation of public service broadcasting. Rupert Murdoch, for one, does not believe in public service broadcasting. He once told the Television Festival in Edinburgh that he had never heard a convincing definition of public service television. He is suspicious of 'élites' who argue for special privileges and favours. 'Much of what is claimed to be quality television here is no more than the parading of the prejudices and interests of the like-minded people who currently control British television', he said. What does he believe in? He believes in the market. No more, no less. So, incidentally, did Margaret Thatcher. She once said to a BBC executive: 'You take public money. You spend public money. Where is your profit?' The Murdoch view is that anyone who provides a service that the public wants at a price it can afford is providing a public service. He is not, of course, alone in that view. Richard Eyre, ITV's chief executive, came close to that in his lecture at the Edinburgh Television Festival this summer. He told us that public service broadcasting would soon be dead.

Between those two speeches in Edinburgh the same audience heard from someone on the other side of the debate: Ray Fitzwalter. For years Fitzwalter edited Granada's *World in Action*, an example of television journalism at its best. His organisation, the Campaign for Quality Television, believes in public service broadcasting and he defined the essence of a purely market-led system: 'The market makes no pretence to universal appeal or universal availability, nor does it necessarily seek to educate or inform, nor does it recognise citizens. Only consumers. The market seeks – quite properly – to make a profit where it may. When driven by global corporations it will seek to produce to the lowest – not the highest – common denominator acceptable to the maximum number of markets.' Fitzwalter was one of those editors and producers who thrived under the rule of men such as Sidney Bernstein.[2] Under a 'purely market-led system', they are a vanishing breed. When Gerry Robinson became Chief Executive of Granada Television in 1991, he called the staff together and told them, in so many words, that anyone who did not put profit first, second and third had no place in the organisation. But Robinson operates in a different world from the one occupied by Bernstein and his contemporaries. Back in the 1960s, all they had to worry about was holding on to their licences. They knew they would do so, if they produced good, challenging television and served their regions with local programming. My old company, TWW, lost its licence

---

2 Founder of Granada Television and its chairman until 1979. He was made a life peer in 1969.

because it was more concerned with reaping higher profits than putting them to good use in making television programmes. What the old ITV companies did not have to worry about was where the profits were going to come from. Selling advertising time was about as difficult as persuading a page three model to take her top off. They were in commercial heaven: no competition. That is no longer the case. With all the competition from Channel Four and Channel 5, BSkyB and the cable operators, there is only one way to persuade the advertisers to buy your slots for large sums of money and that is to deliver big audiences. Most serious programmes do not deliver big audiences. It really is as simple as that. Anthony Smith, one of the most eminent producers from the heyday of the duopoly and one of the founders of Channel Four, is clear how he thinks things are going: 'The old view that broadcasters had wider responsibilities is rapidly fading. Principle comes a poor second to profit. You have only to look to the number of serious documentaries now broadcast on ITV.'

The Independent Television Commission has said: 'The strength of ITV's continuing commitment to regular, serious documentary and arts coverage, clearly set out in the licence applications, now appears to be in question.' That was in March 1997. Two years on, things had got no better. Indeed, they said that, without *We Can Work It Out*, ITV over the previous year would have had the lowest output of current affairs programmes on record. The Campaign for Quality Television, too, believes that things are getting worse. For more than twenty years, it points out, ITV earned a world-wide reputation for producing major documentary films on matters of public interest in a format which also interested viewers. Now that tradition – which simultaneously served viewers, advertisers, the network of ITV companies and the wider public interest – is under threat. In 1994 the main slot for serious documentaries (10.40 p.m. on Tuesday evenings) transmitted thirty-four hours of documentary programming. In 1997 the figure had dropped to eighteen. What the ITC describes as 'serious documentary coverage' has been cut back to the point where it is barely viable to produce. Having been allowed to wither by ITV itself, serious documentaries are now sown so thinly, so randomly, throughout the network schedules that it is all but impossible for the audience that used to watch them to know when they might appear.

Let me be clear what I mean by serious documentaries. They are well researched, original journalism offering, in the old phrase, a 'window on the world'. Some of the best are investigative, revealing corruption in high places or dangers to our health or way of life. They also cost a great deal of money. In the first year of *Network First* on ITV, thirty-four were transmitted, some of them drama documentaries, such as *Date Rape*, others international investigations, such as *Yugoslavia: Death of a Nation*. Most of them were first-rate and attracted very respectable audiences of almost four million, not at all bad for 10.40 p.m. But that did not last long. Gradually the budgets for the programmes were reduced, there were fewer of them and the audiences started to fall. From the middle of 1997, ITV stopped commissioning new *Network First* documentaries. The man who was in charge of factual programmes at the time told production companies that he was only interested in films or series that could successfully run at 9.00 p.m. What did he mean by 'successfully'? Answer: many more viewers. Welcome back to the ratings war, and the docusoaps and 'infotainment' – a hideous word for often pretty hideous programmes: a mongrel bred from the old world of serious television crossed with soaps from the new ratings-generating world of entertainment. In the words of Roger Graef, one of Britain's leading documentary makers, infotainment is 'the Dutch elm disease of quality television'. Quite simply, what they have done is to use the characteristics of soap operas – colourful characters, conflict, narrative – to turn material gathered by fly-on-the-wall cameras from real life into entertainment. They have the benefit of being cheap to make and mostly popular. They have the drawback of being a substitute for serious programmes and of turning us all into zombies. Peter Salmon, controller of BBC1,[3] says that docusoaps have now probably run their course. Well, Hallelujah to that, but I am not holding my breath.

3 The BBC's Director of Sport since September 2000.

What else has ITV been up to? They killed off *News at Ten* for a start and tried to con us into believing that moving it to make room for third-rate movies, or repeats of the old favourites, from nine until eleven in the evening was going to improve the news.[4] Rubbish. They told us that *Tonight With Trevor McDonald* was going to be the new benchmark for serious current affairs journalism. And what did we get? A few serious pieces and an awful lot of froth. Within a few weeks of it going on the air, it was clear that entertainment values were fighting news values and often winning. In the first month, we had a report which made the extraordinary revelation that, if you drink lots of alcohol, you get drunk and that, if you drink it on an aeroplane, you get drunk even more quickly and might behave badly. There was a group of volunteer students sitting and drinking – in a scientifically controlled experiment – just in case we did not believe that drinking a lot gets you drunk. We had the intrepid reporter joining in and telling us that she was feeling pretty squiffy too. The whole idea was to show what lies behind 'air rage'. I feel they missed a trick. They should, surely, have had the students beating each other up, with the reporter swinging a punch or two herself. Next time, perhaps.

4 ITV killed the nightly *News at Ten* slot in March 1999. Under political pressure it restored a truncated version for three nights a week at the start of 2001. By then, the BBC had responded by moving its main BBC1 evening news bulletin from 9 p.m. to 10 p.m.

None of this would matter if it were not presented as serious journalism. If the presenter said: 'Look, we know you folks at home have the attention span of a goldfish and can't be bothered trying to understand something that requires a bit of effort, so just sit back, open a beer and enjoy!', that would be one thing. Instead, we are shown the bloodied blouse of an air stewardess, who has been badly hurt in an attack by a drunken passenger and invited to believe that what we are about to see will offer some real insight into a serious matter. Then we watch a giggling reporter getting drunk on camera. Or we see the cameras poking around the Priory Clinic, pretending to take a serious look at how it deals with serious problems, which turns out to be a voyeuristic voyage around a few shop-worn celebrities that the clinic could package very nicely as promotional material.

So how did ITV respond to all the criticisms of *Tonight With Trevor McDonald*? It chopped fifteen minutes off the programme and stuck it on the air on a different day even later in the evening. We must wait to see how it turns out. Meanwhile, where in the ITV schedules is the sort of stuff that gave it its reputation in the days of the duopoly – *World in Action*, *This Week*, *News at Ten*, serious documentaries? And what of Channel 5? In the words of its own programme controller, Dawn Airey: films, fucking and football . . . and a lot else besides. Dawn and I had a bit of a ding-dong at the Edinburgh Television Festival this year. I suggested it was mostly the soft porn that gave the channel its viewers and she said that was rubbish. So what, I asked her, was her hot tip programme for the new schedules. 'Oh,' she said, 'no doubt about that: *The Female Orgasm*. I rest my case. As for *Channel 5 News*, it stunned the entire industry by proving that a news reader could walk around the set and read the news at the same time; and, no doubt, chew gum as well. Our masters in television are nothing if not suckers for new gimmicks and they were mightily impressed. Pretty soon it seemed obligatory for every presenter in the land to walk or stand or do a quick song-and-dance act at the same time as they were reading their links, interviewing the Prime Minister and performing a spot of open heart surgery. Frankly, I don't much care where the presenter is positioned – or how – so long as the stuff they read is well written and decent journalism. I worried more about Channel 5's attitude to news infecting others. It seemed to me that their approach to both presentation and emotional reporting had come together in a new idea of what journalism is about. Their aim was to appeal to a younger audience, which they believe is largely alienated from mainstream news programmes. The most obvious change, as I have suggested, is stylistic: Kirsty Young wandering around the studio and chatting with journalists from time to time. But it is in the content of the news that the real change has taken place.

Chris Shaw, its first editor, believed that the first responsibility of news is to make it relevant to the people who are watching it, to be more 'inclusive', that great buzzword of the late 1990s. He told Brendan O'Neill of *LM Magazine* that 'many people want news which feels relevant to them. They don't want us to rely on the language of authority, but on language that feels more "on side" and more in tune with their interests.' The result is reporting that concentrates on what might be thought to appeal to the audience rather than matter in any wider sense. O'Neill gave as an example an interview with Don King which spent as much time asking how he keeps his hair standing on end as about his legal battles as a boxing promoter. A victory of style over content? Not according to Shaw: 'I vigorously refute the notion that we are all style and no content. *Channel 5 News* is not a format, it's an approach; more than that, it's an attitude.' That attitude says journalism is primarily about identifying with an audience, not reporting authoritatively what is going on in the world. 'What we are arguing is that credibility can be achieved through empathy as much as it can through authority,' he said.

I think that is an extraordinary remark. Credibility through empathy means no more than reflecting the world back to an audience as they already see it. It also means talking down to them as if they were children, because it assumes they cannot take anything that does not square with the outlook and attitudes they already have. It is patronising but, from a journalistic point of view, worse than that. Getting 'on side' with your audience is just as much a distortion as getting on side with any interest group or powerful lobby. Serious journalism is about not being on side with anything except the facts. Once you let anything have priority over that, you have sold the pass. Shaw's approach to 'authority' is revealing. He contrasts the language of authority with the language that feels on side. He seems to think authority is in itself bad, presumably because he equates it with the old world of deference. Hence, in his eyes, the antidote to authority is chummy populism. But authority is not the same as unthinking deference. In journalism, authority does not flow from someone's position, but from building a reputation for dispassionate reporting of the facts as far as that is possible. The new journalism does not want to build a new authority for us to respect, but to chuck it away in favour of allowing us all to cling together feeling good.

Some people see in this new journalistic language that 'feels more on side' a new, shared vernacular, to replace the class-divided languages of the toffs and the mob. But, quite aside from the objections to this particular language and how it corrupts journalism, why should we want a shared vernacular? Society is richer and stronger when there are a lot of divergent voices having their say, opening our eyes to their view of what the world is like. And, if there has to be a new, shared vernacular, do we really want it to be this one? Do we really want to live in a world dominated by a media in which the battle for ratings pushes it into ever more extreme sensationalism and in which journalism and entertainment converge around the easy, comfortable, unchallenging values of infotainment? Add it all together and you might conclude that the BBC has not exactly succeeded in its challenge to keep the rest of them honest. So then the question must be asked: is it keeping itself honest? There are some worrying signs.

I am always being quoted as saying that I believe BBC television news is dumbing down. Not true. I have never used that expression, nor do I believe it. The BBC produces an enormous amount of intelligent material – more than ever before in terms of total output. Indeed that's part of the problem. When I joined the BBC a generation ago there was a short television bulletin at tea time and a fifteen-minute news at nine o'clock. That was it. No breakfast television, no one o'clock news, no *Newsnight*. When I became a foreign correspondent for television news I was one of just four. We were deemed to be such an élite little group that the Director-General would hold the occasional dinner for us. That stopped pretty soon. He was a rather remote, aloof figure and I think he was slightly taken aback by these coarse hacks who drank his best claret and argued very loudly. If the present DG wanted to do the same, he would need to hire the Albert Hall to fit them all in. It seems everyone is a correspondent these days. Specialise or die, seems to be the BBC's motto. If you specialise in more than one subject, your title changes from day to day depending on what you happen to be reporting. God knows what the viewer must make of it. What's wrong with being a reporter? Even reporters aren't reporters any longer. They are 'news correspondents'.

The standard of reporting is as high as it has ever been. If there is a problem, it is that there is so much air time to be filled now that even that great army of correspondents has difficulty satisfying all the editors all the time – not least because of the insatiable demands made by News 24 and Radio 5 Live. It can mean that, when a big story breaks, a correspondent has no time to think. He is bounced around from one live two-way to another, often struggling to read the latest wire copy in between, unable to get out there and see what is happening and talk to people.

Nevertheless, if you are one of those who do not want to wait for a scheduled programme at one, or six, or nine, and want to catch up with the headlines, then you are very well served indeed. But what if you want something more thoughtful and you rely on the One or the Six or the Nine? The first thing to note is that there are fewer of you. When I was presenting the Nine, its audiences were in the eight or nine million range. Now they are around five million. I wish I could say that is because I left television for radio, but the audience did not drop the moment I stopped reading the news on a regular basis. Nor had it risen when John Simpson and I started doing the Nine. I believe the presenter has virtually no affect on the size of the audience, in spite of what the marketing masters would have us believe. But there has been a steady decline over the years in the audiences for mainstream news programmes. It may have something to do with the fact that, as a nation, we no longer feel that we almost have a duty to sit down and watch the evening news. It may be a generational thing. It may be that we offer people too much news. It may simply be that there is now so much competition for the viewer. Whatever the reason we can no longer take the audience for granted.

So what have we done about that? Well, the Nine is more or less unchanged. If anything, it is more serious than it used to be, with a deliberately high ratio of foreign stories. *Newsnight* has been shortened to accommodate the needs of the Scots. That, I think, is a pity. It damages *Newsnight* and the signs are that the Scots do not much care for it either. The Six is an enormously important programme. It may not be watched much by the 'great and the good', who inhabit the home counties, because at 6 p.m. they are still doing their great and good things and have not got home. But it has the largest audience of all the television news programmes and its viewers are, by and large, less likely to seek serious news and current affairs anywhere else. It might not be accurate to say that BBC News should be judged by the direction taken by the Six, but it is a damned powerful pointer and it needs looking at carefully.

On the basis of the first few months it seemed clear to me that the re-launched Six had gone softer and opted for an agenda dominated by social issues with a consumerist angle. There is nothing wrong with that, if it is what the viewers want, so long as the harder-edged stuff is there too, and so long as we retain our critical approach to the stories. The first of the new programmes reported on Kosovan refugees in Scotland. The reporter had decided that the local people had taken them to their heart and would give them a warm welcome and everyone was really happy. Possibly, but it seemed for all the world as though we were being fed a cosy little story to make us feel good about ourselves. One series of 'special reports' included an account of what the RAF were getting up to in the Balkans. It was topped off with the obligatory live interview – this time with an RAF officer rather than a reporter – that would not have been out of place in an RAF recruitment film. It asked none of the awkward questions that were being raised at the time about the conduct of the air war. There have been endless other examples of the same kind: a 'live' interview with the boss of a water company being invited to say that they would have less money to spend on all their wonderful environmental programmes if they were forced to cut water prices (oddly enough, he agreed with that proposition); a 'live' interview in the City of London after the anarchist riots, when the reporter was so anxious to condemn the rioters that there was no reference to the short-comings of the policing tactics. All terribly comfortable, all of it appearing to support the establishment view, the status quo, the non-controversial. If there is enough of that sort of thing, ultimately we grow used to it. It creates a mood. It helps to condition the audience. It makes it more difficult for us to do our real job, which is constantly and endlessly to ask the awkward questions.

I have emphasised the 'live' aspect to all of those reports. It sounds good for a news programme to say: 'And now we go over, live, to our correspondent.' But why? It makes sense, if you are running News 24 or Radio 5 Live and have endless air time to carry live news coverage of events as they happen. We should obviously go 'live' if a story breaks while we're on the air, or there's a significant development in a running story. But in none of the cases I have mentioned was that the case. The reality now is that we 'go live' somewhere in every programme, often several times, whether there is a point to it or not. You may say that it does not matter. But it does. For a start, it costs money and most of us are having to trim our budgets. There comes a point when you have sliced off the fat and are cutting into the muscle. That is what is happening to many programmes now, including my own *Today*. But it is not only money that is wasted. It frequently wastes valuable air time, which means there is space for fewer stories to be covered or less time for analysis. 'Going live' also goes wrong a great deal. In one recent week, the 'live' reporter was knocked off the air night after night, on one occasion because it was chucking down with rain and on another because he was trying to broadcast from a boat. Both stories could better have been covered by well-crafted, edited reports.

Perhaps my bosses feel that having the presenter chat to reporters in the field makes for more friendly television. 'So what's going on, Bill?' . . . 'Well, Trevor . . .' I don't think it does make the viewer feel more welcome. If anything, I think it excludes the audience. The correspondent is not meant to be reporting for the sake of Trevor; he is meant to be talking to us. The same applies to the phony matiness of using first names. Some of us are now doing it with interviewees who are not colleagues, even with politicians. It is one thing if politicians do it to us; it is quite another for us to do it with them. The viewer, or listener, is entitled to ask: 'What kind of relationship is this?' These may seem pretty unimportant issues taken one by one, but their cumulative effect worries me. It links to the seductive appeal of entertainment values. There is no great mystery about what makes the most entertaining and populist journalism. You concentrate on human interest, anything to do with sex, jealousy, conflict, money, power, suffering: anything from which you can elicit an emotional response and make it accessible. Accessibility is good if it means telling a story that is clear and simple and free of jargon and assumed knowledge. It is bad if it means you deal only with material that people can relate to from experience in their own lives, the patronising assumption being that anything outside their experience will be a turn-off. Then out goes the difficult stuff and in comes the human interest story of the victim. Or the private lives of the famous. Or endless crime. Or endless consumerism. Any student of local television news knows that police stories about murders and robberies, human interest stories about traffic jams and old people waiting for hospital treatment, and light pieces about dogs that yodel and fish that sing are the staple of such programmes, often to the exclusion of anything else. The pressure is on to make events part of a never-ending narrative and for you to make it absolutely clear where you stand in relation to it: everybody in it is either a good guy or a bad guy. If you need a twist, you turn everything on its head and make the good guys bad guys and the bad guys good, but you always hold on to the formula that this is a story about heroes and villains. Famous people (mostly pop stars and sportsmen) are always complaining that the media 'build 'em up and then knock 'em down'.

Allison Pearson has provided a powerful and colourful analysis of what's been going on. 'The commercial imperative to deliver clear-cut fables starring creepy Iagos and ravished Desdemonas has smothered any lingering loyalty to journalism. All the world's a soap-set now, and men and women merely players on short-term contracts. Soap opera offers a crisis-crammed vision of life, with precious little breathing space for the unportentous or mundane.'

She made clear why this is worrying: 'The danger is that, in some weird way, we are starting to apply that template to real lives – our own as well as others.' The real danger, for us at the serious end of broadcasting, is that we may contribute to that danger.

Let me quote a man whom 1 believe sets the standard when it comes to serious reporting – my old friend John Simpson. 'Our duty is to make reporting as interesting and accessible as we can. If we don't bother, if we put aside serious things in favour of the silly or comfortable or merely local, then we are failing in our responsibilities.' He thinks that there is a simple rule of thumb by which viewers can judge for themselves whether the news they are watching has been dumbed down: how much information are we being given from the outside world, as opposed to the cute, the consumerised and the mental chewing gum with a social angle? If it falls consistently below a third, then we should worry. He is not worried yet, partly because the Nine is still such a serious programme and partly because big institutions such as the BBC have a general approach, an overall standard, which always seems to reassert itself after a time.

I hope he's right about that. It is more difficult for ITV. If they truly believe that the only way to survive is to chase the ratings and that the most effective way to do that is to take the most populist approach with the least demanding fare, then they may be justified. They have to sell their commercials or die and the advertisers can increasingly pick and choose where they display their wares. But it is different for the BBC. Our licence payers have no choice. They must pay their licence fees and they are entitled to the best we can offer. It is not good enough for the BBC to defend itself simply by trumpeting the excellence of a great costume drama or wildlife programme or even brilliance like *Walking with Dinosaurs*. Nor can the BBC rest on the 'something for everyone' approach. If 'something for everyone' means defending the bland or banal, the sensationalist or the scurrilous, the derivative or the down market, then we must simply accept that some people must be disappointed. They can find it elsewhere. Cater for minority tastes as well as the mass market by all means. That is part of our remit. But quality and integrity must be the hallmark of everything we do. The BBC must have the confidence to believe that, if it is doing its job properly, it is providing a civilising influence from which every single one of us ultimately benefits, however much or however little we watch or listen.

My main concern, though, is with our news service. The BBC is a public service body committed to acting in the national interest. In spite of everything, it can still build bridges between all people and all classes and bring us together in moments of great crisis or celebration. It must use its guaranteed income to deliver a news service that no commercial organisation would contemplate and, if the ratings for serious programme are 'disappointing', then so be it.

It must resist the temptation to push serious programmes to later and later slots in the schedules. *Panorama* was once on BBC1 before the *Nine o'Clock News*, then immediately after it; now it is on at 10.00 p.m. *Question Time* has been moved to 11.00 p.m. and *Omnibus* to 10.40 p.m. *Newsnight* has lost a chunk of air time as a sop to the Scots. My own *On the Record* has been moved twice, testing the patience of even the most enthusiastic viewer. If the schedules can be cleared for sporting events, they should also be cleared for big debates on some of the great political issues affecting the nation. In the long term the BBC's ratings will fall. That is not an admission of defeat; it is simply a recognition of the inevitable. The rate at which they fall will be determined by how well everyone in the BBC performs, but fall they will. And, the more they fall, the more the BBC must defend its intrinsic values: good, honest and accurate information, education and entertainment. If it chases the ratings at the expense of those values, it does not deserve to exist. The proliferation of new channels is a threat only if the BBC regards ratings as its justification. The only reason for the BBC is to offer public service broadcasting that none of the other channels can even approach.

Peter Hennessy

Open government, Whitehall and the press since 1945

2000

Professor of Contemporary History at Queen Mary, University of London 1992–2000 and Attlee Professor of Contemporary British History since 2001, Peter Hennessy was a journalist on the Times Higher Education Supplement, The Times, *the* Financial Times *and the* Economist *between 1972 and 1984. His many books include* Cabinet *(1986),* Whitehall *(1989),* Never Again *(1992),* The Hidden Wiring *(1995) and* The Prime Minister *(2000).*

I SHOULD LIKE TO THINK that James Cameron would approve of my theme in this lecture, because he could be very funny in his columns about what he memorably called the 'Defenders of the Face' among those set in authority above us. He knew very well that the highest unofficial classification level in the Whitehall lexicon was and remains 'Politically Embarrassing'.

When pondering a new piece, historians begin by reaching for the founding file in the archive; journalists start by hunting for the first good story from behind the scenes. I shall start with an episode that satisfies the joint cravings which flow from the streams of my professional life. Come with me to Mr Attlee's 10 Downing Street and the Cabinet Office in the spring of 1946 and let me try to reconstruct the first really serious Whitehall leak inquiry of the post-war years. What ghastly breach of security had triggered it?

Two related pieces in *The Times* of 25 March 1946 on the future of the iron and steel industry were the culprit. The paper's 'City Notes' of that day, rather than the news story filed by its Parliamentary Correspondent (anonymous as all *Times* people were until 1966), gives the flavour of the item and the special offence it caused within government circles.

The intro itself has a wonderful period flavour.

> The question whether the iron and steel industry is to be nationalised or not came up to the Cabinet for discussion for the first time on Thursday. It may thus be an appropriate moment to review the progress of this controversial question.

Quite so. John Wilmot, the Minister of Supply, had drawn up a paper on the pros and cons which, said *The Times*, 'reported generally in favour of nationalisation. This report came before the special Cabinet economic sub-committee presided over by Mr [Herbert] Morrison [Lord President of the Council] . . . Mr Morrison's committee, presumably finding itself in some uncertainty, neither endorsed nor rejected Mr Wilmot's report. The whole question was, it is understood, passed up to the Cabinet itself for decision without prejudice and without recommendation.'

The secret and sacred world of the Cabinet committee system had been breached. Sir Norman Brook, the formidable Secretary of the Cabinet, swung into action and set off from Whitehall to Printing House Square in Blackfriars to confront the editor of *The Times* personally with his offence against the interests of the state and good (i.e. private) government. As Brook reported later to the Prime Minister, Clem Attlee:

> Mr Barrington Ward was in Germany when the article was published and I went to see him on 1st April, the first day after his return to London. I told him that I had come on my own initiative and not at the suggestion of Ministers: that I had not come to ask from whom the information had been obtained; but I had thought it wrong to let this article pass without letting him know that we, as officials serving the Cabinet, thought that the publication in the press of such details of Cabinet organisation (the member-

> ship of particular committees, which Ministers had attended a particular meeting, etc.) were a hindrance to the efficient discharge of public business.

How did the editor of *The Times* react? Did he run through his head the words penned in 1852 by John Thaddeus Delane, his fabled predecessor in the editor's chair: 'The duty of the journalist is the same as that of the historian – to seek out the truth, above all things, and to present to his readers not such things as statecraft would wish them to know but the truth as near as he can attain it.' No, he did not. Far from politely telling the Cabinet Secretary to push off, Barrington Ward, as Brook put it,

> appreciated my point, and agreed that 'there were things which were necessary to the news and things that were not'. Would I leave it to him to look into the matter? I said that, having made my comment, I was quite content to leave it at that.

Days of innocence and deference.

Whitehall, however, did not leave the matter there. The Lord Chancellor, no less, conducted a leak inquiry at the Cabinet's request. Lord Jowett found 'strong grounds for believing that the *Times* article . . . was based on information derived, either directly or indirectly, from officials in the Ministry of Supply who were familiar with the course of the Ministerial discussions on the subject. But the relations between the Ministry of Supply and the Iron and Steel Federation are necessarily so close that it is not surprising that some information reached the press.' As a result, the Lord Chancellor advised the Prime Minister that there should be no recourse to a prosecution under the Official Secrets Act.

The file ends with a brisk, Attlee-style Cabinet paper on 'Leakage of Information', stating that the Lord Chancellor would investigate on his behalf 'all future cases on apparent leakage of official information regarding matters under discussion by the Cabinet or its Committees'.

Thanks to John Major's decision in 1992 to publish both the terms of reference and the membership of ministerial Cabinet committees and the ministerial rulebook, 'Questions of Procedure for Ministers', it is difficult to appreciate fully nowadays the lengths to which ministers and officials went to preserve their 'secret garden' of a Cabinet system in the early post-war years. Here is a passage from the first, Attleean consolidated version of 'Questions of Procedure':

> The underlying principle is, of course, that the method adopted by Ministers for discussion among themselves of questions of policy is essentially a domestic matter, and is of no concern to Parliament or the public.

Note that 'of course'. These truths were held to be self-evident and that form of words survived as late as the 1966 version of QPM. Even when I began operating as a Whitehall correspondent in the mid-1970s, the principle of complete privacy of process (let alone content) continued to be asserted. Jim Callaghan's 1976 edition of QPM, for example, declared that 'the method adopted by Ministers for discussing among themselves questions of policy is essentially a domestic matter and such discussion will be hampered if the process by which it is carried on are laid bare.'

Jim Callaghan, whom I always respected and came to like very much, authorised more than one leak inquiry into my activities when I blew a scattering of his Cabinet committees and ministerial groups. They were normally conducted by a very decent, old-fashioned chap, the late Basil Lock, the Cabinet Office's security man. He was a former airman who had run RAF Coastal Command. I had his photograph above my desk in *The Times* building in order, as it were, that he could keep an eye on what I was doing. He never caught one of my helpers. I would usually be leaked the result of his leak inquiries. I grew rather fond of him at a distance. If for some reason he was not assigned to one of my leak inquiries, I used to make discreet inquires after his health.

We have come a long way in twenty-five years. The January 2000 edition of the Cabinet Office's Guide to Departments on 'Cabinet Committee Business' is now a quite open document, which lists all of Mr Blair's Ministerial Cabinet committees and gives you the contact name and number of the Cabinet Office official who services them. In the late 1970s and early 1980s, Bruce Page and I used to work ourselves to the bone to extract and publish stuff like this.

It would be misleading to suggest that the British press, even its more investigative arms, had pushed hard or consistently throughout the post-war period against what Jimmy Margach of the *Sunday Times* once called 'the walls of Whitehall's forbidden city'. With a few brave exceptions, the late 1940s and the 1950s saw a depressing spread of the disease of lobbyitis, which took root in Westminster in the 1880s when political journalists first organised themselves into a group of lobby correspondents.

Francis Williams, the former Editor of the *Daily Herald* who went into Number Ten with Attlee as his Press Secretary, was eloquently and critically accurate about this in his long-forgotten book, *Parliament, Press and the Public*, published in 1946. Williams had worked in the Ministry of Information during the Second World War and watched with dismay as the lobby contagion spread to other groups of specialist journalists. By the end of the war, he wrote, it was

> normal practice for some of the big Departments to hold
> regular background and news conferences with the press.
> At these conferences information is sometimes given by the

> Minister, sometimes by the Public Relations Officer and sometimes by other senior officials of the Ministry. In a number of cases only correspondents belonging to a recognised group, with its own officials and rules, are now invited to these conferences . . . It is easy to see the advantages of such a system to a Department.

Williams touched on the ever-present temptation to collude and the price of such collusion:

> Such a system also means that the newspaper correspondents concerned give up much of their independence. Some of them tend to depend so largely on official sources for information and to develop such obligations to the officials with whom they work, that they become mouthpieces of authority, taking their 'line' from the Minister . . .

There is nothing new in 'spin'. There were, Williams concluded, people of ability and independent judgement among the press corps who took their own line. But 'their presence does not alter the general principle that anything which ties newspapers too closely to official sources of news, or sets up obligations which may conflict with a newspaper's primary responsibility to the public, is a bad system and ought not to exist'. Amen to all of that. The lobby

is now both a much diminished and a more transparent phenom-
enon, but the Williams critique still has bite in terms of the
turn-of-the-century version of a dependency culture in which the
spinners and the spun currently operate.

Number Ten press people in any generation rarely relish the
awkward squad who rub up against the cosy and the collusive. Here
is a brief provided for Attlee's successor in 10 Downing Street,
Winston Churchill, in the autumn of 1954. At issue was the
question of which Minister should be the regular briefer of the
lobby correspondents, Lord Swinton or the Chancellor of the
Exchequer, Rab Butler. Such things were way beneath the ken of the
Prime Minister, who preferred to deal with the Press Lords directly,
rather than dally with any jobbing journalist.

As a result, an idiot's brief on lobby practice had to be prepared
for the grand old man by Fife Clark, Director-General of the
Central Office of Information into which the Ministry of
Information had mutated at the end of the war. Swinton, Fife Clark
told Churchill, had been the lobby correspondents' 'friend and
advocate for 2½ years and the lobby are very grateful to him, just
as they have become very fond of him personally. Their gratitude
has been expressed not once but many times in the secrecy of the
lobby room'. This is more masonry than journalism. 'Three years
ago,' Clark continued, 'Ministers were not so sure that they could
"trust the lobby". Now they know they can.' There was, however, a

minority among the ranks of the lobby correspondents who sullied this cloying scene. It was, wrote Clark, 'headed by Derek Marks and Robert Carvel of the *Daily Express*, but it is fair to say that this group is dissident on most issues and it would not be easy for any Minister to provide them, week in week out, storm or calm, with all the news they think they ought to have.' There you have it: the expectation of a master/mendicant relationship which only the rough trade on the Beaverbrook press cut up about. Not the slightest trace of Delane's dictum there, let alone more modern notions of a 'right to know'.

It took another half-generation before Whitehall began to address the possibility that there might be a case for substantially greater press and public access to official information. The declassified records suggest that it needed the 1968 Fulton Report on the civil service and the glancing blow it struck in the twentieth of its twenty-two recommendations, suggesting that a further inquiry was needed into 'ways and means of getting rid of unnecessary secrecy both in policy-making and administration', to provide the momentum for an examination of the virtues and the perils of a deliberately created increase in openness.

The first post-Fulton stab at an openness policy has been generally overlooked during the thirty or so years since, partly because it resulted in a truly feeble White Paper, *Information and the Public Interest*, published in June 1969. This concluded lamely that: 'There would be the greatest difficulty in defining satisfactorily what categories of information should qualify for . . . special protection and what should not', adding the breathtakingly complacent gloss that the public and Parliament should not be worried about the Official Secrets Acts, as they did not 'inhibit the authorised release of information in any way'. 'Information and the Public Interest' swiftly became overshadowed by the intellectually robust and impressively coherent Franks Report on Section 2 of the Official Secrets Act, commissioned by the Heath government in 1971 and published in 1972, which eventually formed the basis of the narrower, more defensible Official Secrets Act of 1989.

Harold Wilson's Number Ten file, which traces the road from Fulton to the mouse of a White Paper a year later, was declassified this January. It turned out to be a revealing little gem on what, following Robinson and Gallagher's terminology, might be called the 'official mind' of official secrecy.[1] Wilson, to his credit, combined in a bizarre fashion an opener's temperament with a paranoia about leaks to which the Public Record Office files frequently and vividly attest. Yet, but for his personal insistence, it is most unlikely that the fifty year rule would have been reduced to thirty by the 1967 Public Records Act. In this sense, Wilson could be called the political patron of the boom in contemporary British history since the thirty

1 Ronald Robinson and John Gallagher, *Africa and the Victorians* (1965).

year rule came into force in 1972, thanks not least to the press attention that new batches of files now routinely attract when made available at the Public Record Office in Kew.

Initially, post-Fulton, Wilson 'had doubted whether there would be much of a demand for a review of the [Official Secrets] Acts', but he had been struck by a speech delivered by Ted Heath, then Leader of the Opposition, at the Granada press awards in January 1969. (Heath had pledged that, once elected, his government would review existing official secrets legislation as 'politicians should make it possible for the media to improve the level of political discussion by reducing and eliminating the obstacles that stand in their way'.) Never one to be outbid by the competition, Wilson declared in a speech a week or so later, at a dinner in the Savoy to celebrate the fiftieth anniversary of the *Sunday Express*, that following the Fulton recommendation 'the whole question of the release of official information, including the Official Secrets Act, should now be under consideration'.

All sorts of grand people were considered for the chairmanship of a committee of inquiry into secrecy. Wilson suggested the former Labour Minister Bert Bowden (by this stage ennobled as Lord Aylestone), but his Principal Private Secretary, Michael Halls, cautioned against this. Since Aylestone had left politics to run ITV, 'he might well come out with far too liberally minded a report – almost Swedish', declared Halls, as if such a thing was both inconceivable and deeply shocking in a British context.

The senior civil service, not just Halls, was, in fact, truly alarmed by the possibilities an inquiry might open up. The two great figures of the late 1960s Whitehall – the Cabinet Secretary, Sir Burke Trend, and the Head of the home civil service, Sir William Armstrong – weighed in with a beautifully crafted brief for the Prime Minister and the Cabinet, perfectly designed to make Ministerial flesh creep. It moved from one classic fallback position to the next:

> The Prime Minister may wish to draw the Cabinet's attention to the broad categories of information which are likely to be at issue in this enquiry. The first category consists of factual and statistical information; the chief limitations on the release of more information of this sort are how far there is a real public demand for it and how far civil service numbers can be increased to cope with the work of preparing it for publication.

Fallback number one: nobody really wants it and it will cost a lot of money if we do it. Then:

> There is likely to be much greater public interest in the second broad category of influence – the stuff of which policy decisions are made.

Tricky, this. There is evidence here of public demand. Don't worry. Fallback number two takes care of this one. We are satisfying that already. 'By the Green Paper approach, the government have [sic] extended the process of public consultation . . . and this process is likely to continue.

Now the *coup de grâce*. Fallback three is deployed. Go directly for Ministers' neuroses:

> Many policy decisions, however, are based not only on an assessment of measurable factors but also on a number of subjective judgements on questions such as the influence of other commitments and the reactions of various interests at home and abroad. The publication of a full analysis of the considerations involved in a policy decision may not be practicable or expedient in every case. For example, would Ministers wish to publish such analysis in advance of the decision to go ahead with the development of the Concorde project: or would they now wish to commit themselves to do so in advance of a decision whether to put Concorde into full production?

This cascade of fallbackery has a malign beauty. It is an art form.

As always with the best that Whitehall breeds, a way out is suggested. It turned on what James Cameron called the 'defence of the face':

An outside enquiry may well produce general recommendations which, if accepted, could restrict the government's freedom in the process of decision making. Since, however, it seems necessary to meet the public demand for such an enquiry, it is desirable to frame its terms of reference in such a way as to minimise, so far as is possible, the risk of embarrassment.

This is beyond parody. You could not make it up without risk of being accused of exaggeration. In the event, there was no enquiry, no embarrassing report. The Inner Cabinet ruled it out. That inside job – the puny White Paper – was its surrogate.

In 1969, the internal debate was all about the loss of control. It still is as, thirty-one years later, an emasculated and wrongly named Freedom of Information Bill goes through its last Parliamentary stages. Wrongly named? How can that be? Because FOI and open government are two different things. As Robert Hazell – Professor of Government and the Constitution at University College London – told the House of Commons Public Administration Committee in 1999:

The government still does not fully understand the difference between open government and freedom of information. Open government means the government

> publishing information largely for its own purposes: infor-
> mation that the government thinks we need to know or
> might like to know. Freedom of information requires the
> government to disclose information which we decide for
> ourselves we want to know.

The distinction has never been better put. The Prime Minister, Tony Blair, does not understand this distinction; but that is not altogether surprising, as he does not believe in open government for the Cabinet let alone for the public. But the Home Secretary, Jack Straw,[2] does understand the Hazell distinction. For he has admitted privately to the view that 'Freedom of information is for oppositions not for governments', adding that, 'open government is for governments'.

So, as a journalist-turned-historian, to which post-war premiers would I grant an openness, if not a freedom of information, prize?

Third place goes to Ted Heath for commissioning the Franks Report, which showed that the limits to official secrecy could be both narrowed and liberalised. Had he been re-elected in 1974, I am pretty confident he would have legislated in a reformist direction. I have always suspected Mrs Thatcher allowed the 1989 legislation to proceed because, with a streamlined secrets law, juries might, when faced with future Clive Pontings, be more readily persuaded to convict.

2 Home Secretary 1997–2001, Foreign Secretary 2001–.

Second place goes to Harold Wilson for the 1967 Public Records Act and the Thirty Year Rule. Think how diminished we historians would be if, last January, we had been eagerly awaiting the opening of the 1949 papers, rather than those for 1969.

First prize – by a clear margin – goes to John Major. We have already seen how in 1992 he declassified both the ministerial rulebook and the bone structure of the Cabinet committee system. In addition, in 1993–4 he placed the first properly institutionalised openness regime on a codified, if not a statutory, basis with (again for the first time) someone outside the Whitehall loop, the parliamentary ombudsman, having a say in disputed disclosure cases. Major also had a sense of delayed open government. He backed his public service minister, William Waldegrave, in his drive to re-review and release, if possible, once highly sensitive documents that had been retained beyond the thirty-year norm. As a result of the so-called 'Waldegrave Initiative', nearly 100,000 files have been released, many of them Cold War related, enabling contemporary historians to reconstruct for the first time the secret Cold War state, which was grafted on to the existing one for the late 1940s.

There is a symbiotic link between past, present and future here: a need for what the Chief Executive of BP, Sir John Browne,[3] has called 'accelerated history' – that is a proper freedom of informa-

---

3 Lord Browne of Madingley since 2001.

tion regime with ministers only able to keep policy advice and material under wraps within a carefully circumscribed inner ring of genuinely sensitive matters. Without such a regime, as Sir John Hoskyns, once head of Mrs Thatcher's Number Ten Policy Unit, pointed out nearly twenty years ago, 'there is no learning-curve' in the government, the press or the country at large.

Ted Heath put it splendidly at the Granada Awards lunch in 1969. 'An open society,' he said, 'is one in which the people, through the press and television, can have ready access to the information on which they can judge policies and policy makers . . . The result of unnecessary secrecy is that it exalts the "informed circle", the off-the-record comment and leak. The manipulation of news takes the place of news-gathering.'

How familiar that sounds a generation later. If you believe, as Philip Graham[4] did, and I do, that the prime function of quality newspapers is to provide 'the first rough draft of history', such matters as public records and freedom of information policies are central to the two professions in which I have spent my adult working life. Whether the current quality press in Britain even aspires to Philip Graham's gold standard is a different question.

4 Former proprietor of *Newsweek*.

Tony Benn

The media and the political process

2001

After a parliamentary career spanning half a century and including service as Postmaster General, Minister of Technology, Secretary of State for Industry and Secretary of State for Energy, Tony Benn retired from the House of Commons at the 2001 General Election – announcing with characteristically pointed wit he that he was leaving Parliament in order to spend more time in politics. His Cameron Lecture in 2001, a bravura performance from the lectern which can scarcely be done justice in written form, was delivered against the background of military action in Afghanistan following the terrorist attacks in the USA on 11 September.

I FIRST MET James Cameron nearly forty years ago. Earlier than that, in the early 1950s, he had been a member of the Fleet Street Socialist Journalists' Forum, which was very active in the early part of the Cold War – though some of the journalists who belonged to it were warned that it was a very risky being a member if you wanted to get on. After 1963, when Jimmy and I both spent time working on Harold Wilson's speeches, I saw him regularly, and continued to do so for the next twenty years or so. I read him in the *News Chronicle*, watched his television programmes, and admired his work for peace. On one occasion he wrote something about me in the *Guardian* which wasn't entirely accurate, so I rang him up about it, and the following day he wrote the most gracious apology (which has not always been the case in my dealings with the media). I last met him at a *Guardian* lunch in 1983.

James Cameron was highly professional and had great integrity – a man who gave journalism a good name.

In my lecture I want to deal with the relationship between the media and the political process – a relationship so close that sometimes it seems to be incestuous.

I've often thought that at least political leaders and the media had one thing in common – they are more interested in politicians than they are in politics. But clearly both sides in this process have tried to influence the other for their own purposes, and when you describe the political parties and the media you are talking about a struggle for power over other people's minds. Every society, in any period of history, requires consent in order to be governed. Wealth and power are indivisible. If you've got wealth you've got access to power, and if you've got power it's not difficult to make money.

Clearly one form of influence is reaching a position where you can get rid of anybody who is difficult. Mao said that power comes out of the barrel of a gun, so military power creates consent by fear. But of course there are other ways of doing it. Religion is a very powerful way of gaining control, which is why Henry VIII nationalised the Church of England – our oldest nationalised industry. Henry had had a row with the Pope about a number of issues, so he got a priest in every pulpit in every parish on every Sunday to tell the faithful that God wanted you to do what the king wanted you to do – a very sensible policy for him to pursue.

The Conservative party did the same when they nationalised the BBC – they wanted a pundit on every channel every night, telling people there was no alternative to what the government was doing. When you read what John Reith[1] said during the General Strike in 1926, you realise how it was that he won the support of the Conservative government. Reith observed that if the BBC had been in existence there would never have been a French Revolution – such was the sense of power that he felt he had.

Another example of this. When I was Postmaster General I found myself wondering why Charles II had nationalised the Post

---

1 General Manager of the British Broadcasting Company from 1922 to 1926 and the first Director-General of the BBC as a public corporation from 1927 to 1938.

Office. Was he an early socialist? Of course, the reason was that he wanted to open everybody's letters, and the only way he could do that was by having the Royal Mail. So the Royal Mail was the first MI5 – but it was nationalised for the purpose of control.

Today the BBC seems to me to represent the conventional wisdom, whatever that may be at the time. During the period of the declining years of the British Empire, which did not break up until fairly soon after the BBC was founded, it was then a matter of common agreement that the Empire was a good thing. Wandering around Westminster Abbey the other day, I saw a plaque in the cloisters celebrating the work of people of 'the British race' who had run the Empire: so racism was apparently quite OK as long as we did it! The sun never set on the British Empire (because, as an American is said to have observed: 'God didn't trust an Englishman in the dark'), and the whole idea of the Empire was put across as a great humanitarian thing. When the Americans bombed the Sudan in 1998, I remembered that exactly 100 years earlier we had gone into the Sudan and we had killed 11,000 Sudanese. What did the Prime Minister say at the time? Of course, it took a long time for the news to get home, but when Lord Salisbury did speak, he said the Africans would have grounds to thank us for what we had done. What you must remember about empires is that they always grew as a result of a surge of humanitarian feeling that the poor ignorant natives needed us to put them right. Winston Churchill declared in the 1930s that 400 million poor benighted Indians depend upon the British Raj. That was the conventional view and it was reflected by the BBC.

A foreign enemy has always been necessary, and during the Cold War we were told regularly that the Russians were about to invade. Of course, it wasn't really a military threat – rather it was the attempt to convert an ideological threat into a military threat, and that's why so much of McCarthyism developed. I heard Nye Bevan's[2] resignation speech in 1951, when he said three things about the rearmament programme: the Russians don't want to attack us, they can't afford to attack us, and if we start the Cold War there will be a witch hunt. He was right.

Then there is the practice of demonising people who don't go along with the conventional wisdom. I've had experience of demonisation by the press, and when they want to get at you it is a very intimidating experience. My children were shouted at on their way to school, and I received death threats. One man wrote and said he was going to kill me, but foolishly gave his address: he had the great courtesy to write later and say that he was sorry about what he'd done, and recognised it was in bad taste . . .

My dustbin was emptied every morning in a Rover car. I know

---

2 Minister of Health from 1945 to 1951 in the post-war Attlee government, he resigned over the introduction of health service charges introduced in part to fund the Korean war effort.

that the Kensington Borough Council is very efficient, but it did seem rather unlikely that they would send a Rover to remove my black sacks. My son installed a hinged bell, which when the rubbish sacks were lifted would ring in our house: we'd look out and see the Rover car removing the rubbish. Whether that was MI5, or the *Sun* or the *Daily Express*, I do not know. But I assure you: when they turn on you, it is a very, very frightening experience. Some people are actually frightened out of politics by it. Yet if you stay in politics you have to live with it.

I've recently discovered something even worse, and that is being treated as a harmless old gentleman. The British Ambassador to the USA was giving a lecture in Washington the other day and an American friend of mine who attended asked him afterwards whether Mr Benn was still being bloody great nuisance; the ambassador replied that 'Mr Benn is a national treasure.' I was terrified at the thought that the final corruption had happened: I am old, I am a gentleman, but I hope I'm not harmless.

Perhaps the most interesting of all areas of the conventional wisdom is the question of Europe. In 1971 I went to see Rupert Murdoch[1] to try and persuade him to support a referendum. He wouldn't touch the idea – at that time he was 100% in favour of

---

3   Head of the News International group, in which role he has been proprietor of a number of British newspapers including the *Sun* since 1969 and *The Times* since 1981.

entry. When I encountered him the other day while we were both taking the same lift (a bit like meeting the Queen in Tesco) I said, 'I haven't met you since 1971, when you were opposed to a referendum.' The lift doors opened at my floor and Mr Murdoch just had time to reply: 'That wasn't me, that was Larry Lamb.'[4] I now know that editors have great control over their proprietors, which I hadn't realised at the time.

I wrote to Mrs Thatcher in 1975 and asked: 'If the referendum goes the other way, will you accept the result?'

'Certainly not,' she replied.

With a bit of experience you get to realise that these arguments are always interesting and ought to be kept open.

If we look at the growing power of the global media we're moving into an area completely unknown in earlier generations. The mass of news available now means that there is hardly a place in the world where there isn't somebody who can bring you absolutely up to date against a background of gunfire. The nature of the coverage does tend to reflect the interests of whoever runs that particular broadcasting station. That's not surprising: Lord Beaverbrook,[5] when asked by the Royal Commission on the Press

---

4 Editor of the *Sun*, 1969–72 and 1975–81; editor of the *Daily Express* 1983–6.
5 Conservative politician and owner of the *Daily Express* and the London *Evening Standard*.

why he ran his newspapers, said he ran them for propaganda – not for money, but because he believed in the things he believed in.

The media emphasises its own interests. Take the business news. Every hour we're told what's happened to the Dow Jones Industrial Average and the Footsie and the value of the pound against the dollar and the value of the pound against the euro, though I've no idea how many people are hanging on every hour to hear this news. Speaking for myself, I've never been influenced by any of it. Indeed, I've always believed that the most dangerous fundamentalism in the world is the worship of money – a form of worship which today is regarded as quite normal.

The news media continue to be obsessed by business, yet the statistics which really might be interesting you get perhaps once a year if there's a relevant report. One of the local London radio stations the other day reported that 74% of the children in the borough of Tower Hamlets live in poverty. Why isn't that statistic deemed worthy of being broadcast every hour?

The media reflect the interests of those who run them. But all the figures that really would make you sit up and do something are passed over: I've always believed that if the number of accidents on building sites were broadcast on a daily basis for a couple of weeks there would be legislation immediately to deal with the problem.

The news tends to exclude what it doesn't want, such as demonstrations and meetings. I had a phone call the other day from the BBC asking whether I would take part in a programme on the death of public meetings. I replied that I'd love to: I'd done ten meetings of over a thousand people in the last three weeks!

Yet there seems to be a rule in the media that you don't report public meetings. Demonstrations are reported – somebody in a Mrs Thatcher mask, or somebody shouting – but you never ever hear a speech from a public meeting. Why is it that people who take the trouble to participate in public meetings are never heard?

Violence gets coverage. I was with Jack Jones[6] in Blackpool this year at a rally of 2,000 pensioners, and I pointed out to Jack that the meeting would not be reported in the media at all – unless he were to throw a brick through the window of McDonald's: then there would be two bishops on *Newsnight* talking about the rising tide of violence among older people. But Jack didn't throw the brick, and there was no report of the meeting.

The media dramatise everything. If you vote according to your conscience in the House of Commons you're accused of being 'disloyal' to your leader. The whole idea of loyalty is a monarchical idea: you owe your loyalty to somebody above you. In the Labour movement solidarity is where your loyalty lies: you owe your

6 General Secretary of the Transport and General Workers' Union 1969–78 and
chairman of the National Pensioners' Convention since 1992.

loyalty to the people around you, not to the people above you. The media adopt the monarchical view, but when they report that 'there's been a revolt in the House of Commons', the so-called revolt is simply an expression of people's convictions.

All wars and conflicts sell newspapers, but the key question is whether the media are helping as much as they might to bring out into the open what the people ought to know.

Politicians as well as the media underestimate the intelligence of people. One of the reasons people go to meetings is that they actually want to hear an argument at reasonable length rather than rely on a diet of soundbites. I can do a soundbite – I've been trained, I can give you twenty-two seconds on any known subject – because I'd rather I edited it than they did, and the parties use the media to get their case across and try to speak directly to the public. But political leaders have been very slow to understand what the process is about. I have a video of Ramsay MacDonald standing with his hands on his lapels, looking at the camera and addressing it like a public meeting. I did the first television broadcast with Hugh Gaitskell, when he was Chancellor of the Exchequer in 1951. This presented a great problem: how could you present economic problems visually? They built a wall in the studio called the Wall of Economic Growth, and Gaitskell was to climb up a ladder marked Productivity and pick an apple from the Tree of Prosperity. At the critical moment I heard one engineer say to another, 'Are you lighting for or against?'

The first time Nye Bevan did a television broadcast I took him to Broadcasting House and he couldn't sit down: we had to have a stand mike, and Nye walked round and round addressing it.

Clem Attlee was best of all. His replies to questions were so monosyllabic that it was once said of him: 'Conversation should be like a game of tennis, but with Clem it's like tossing biscuits to a dog.' Soon after Labour's defeat in 1951 we had a television interview with him in Walthamstow Town Hall, preparing eighteen questions for a fifteen-minute broadcast. After about twelve minutes we were rapidly running out of questions, but had a final question ready which gave him the opportunity to talk for half and hour and rebut the great charge against him, that he had run away from an economic crisis: 'Mr Attlee, isn't it true that the gold and dollar reserves are lower now than when you left office?' It was an opening that any Chancellor would welcome, but all Clem said was: 'That may very well be so.' End of broadcast.

Nowadays politicians are much cleverer. The whole business of focus groups, spin doctors and rebuttal units proliferates the idea that there is some alternative to getting out and listening to people and talking to people. The idea that you can spin everything to get the right impression has now been seen through, and the machinery of rebuttal – if anybody says anything about anything, the computer will tell you something he said that was different – is simply a sort of mechanism for repudiating any argument without having to listen to it.

Ministers are not allowed to broadcast without clearing it with Number Ten, but there is nothing very new in this: once when Harold Wilson was getting very frustrated with me, he asked to see the text of a speech I was about to give, to which I had to reply that there was no text, but I'd be happy to send him a tape of the speech after I'd delivered it. Nowadays the control of MPs by faxes from the Labour media machine in Millbank Tower is phenomenal. I used to get a fax every day, already personalised to read something like 'TONY BENN WELCOMES COMPULSORY HOMEWORK FOR PENSIONERS'. I was supposed to take it out of the fax machine, and send it on to the *Derbyshire Times*. (On one occasion I made a speech saying that I felt more like an Avon lady than a Member of Parliament. Shortly afterwards I received furious letter from Avon, denouncing me for comparing their ladies with Members of Parliament. But they also they sent me a large box of cosmetics, which I suppose I should have declared in the Register of Members' Interests.)

This control mechanism – this obsession with members being on message – is as great a threat as any criticism I've made about media coverage.

So much for the party. Now we turn to the Government as government.

Knowledge being power, secrecy is an absolutely essential ingredient of government – and not just for security reasons. There are very few *real* secrets. Indeed, I can hardly think of any secrets that I knew. I was aware of what was in the Budget hours in advance of the Chancellor addressing the House of Commons; I sometimes knew what our negotiating position was a day or two before an international conference (particularly if I was taking part in that conference); occasionally I knew who was going to be in the Honours List, and if that got out it would just be a cause of general guffawing. The nearest thing I ever came to knowing a real secret was when I was in charge of the nuclear energy programme and I received one of those documents marked *TOP SECRET – ATOMIC – UK EYES ONLY*, which had to be read while a secret service man sat across the desk watching me. The document was about how you can enrich uranium – and that very week the whole story was in the *New Scientist*, the main difference between their version and the government's being that we knew how to do it, and the *New Scientist* said they thought we knew how to do it.

It is very easy for a minister to confuse national interest with his own political interest. Take the case of *Spycatcher*. The government went to all sorts of lengths to prevent its being published, sending the Cabinet Secretary to Australia in a vain attempt to stop it. Then the book was published in China, and as I sat at home listening to Norwegian radio reading it out, I felt I was in occupied Europe during the war. I went to Speakers' Corner in Hyde Park and read out passages of the book, and as soon as I started reading the cameras which were clustered there to record the event all stopped filming, so frightened were they that if they broadcast what I read they might get into trouble.

During Cold War the Russians jammed the BBC, and that was denounced. We then bombed the television station in Belgrade on the grounds that television is a major instrument in war.

Press officers in Whitehall put tremendous pressure on broadcasters and Number Ten regularly accuses journalists of following their own agenda. Twice a day – at 11 a.m. in Downing Street and 4 p.m. in House of Commons – the spin doctors meet the spin patients, and if a journalist then writes that 'it is understood that the government's mind is moving in this direction', you know he's been told it half an hour before he wrote it.

The relationship between politics and the press from the point of view of the new technology moves the discussion into an even more interesting area. It is possible to get world news coming in almost on an instantaneous basis: I can go to my computer in the morning and pick up what is being said in newspapers all over the world which would not be available to me from Millbank Tower, and this has a profound effect on the balance of power. If you can empower the public with the new media then they are not so dependent on the normal media and are better able to make their own judgements.

Then there is the potential of digital cameras. It is now possible with a tiny digital camera to make a film and edit yourself on a computer.

I should never have done it, but on the last day of the old parliament – my own very last day in the House – I took a digital camera into the chamber of the House of Commons. I put it on my lap, covered with a handkerchief, and photographed the Commons as we normally see it (with a couple of members on each side). At the end of the session I handed the camera to a friend of mine so that I could be filmed lighting up my pipe in the chamber, and I told the attendants: 'If you come to me and say you've got to go, I'd say I was going anyway.'

What should be our priorities? Above all, access for those who do not have the resources to get access now. Individual stories of unemployment, homelessness, strikes, drugs, and so on, could be so easily and at such low cost structured and presented. Public service funding of that type of information would make it much easier for us to understand the world in which we live and not to be surprised by it

The right to free speech is marvellous, but not a lot of use if you haven't got the right to be heard.

I desperately want to hear arguments without interruption. I know you've got to cross-examine people, but you can hardly cross-examine them until you've heard what they have to say. If Moses had come down from Mount Sinai and been interviewed about the Ten Commandments on *Newsnight,* how it might have run?

> - What do you say about the treatment of your mother and
>   father?
> - You should respect –
> - Oh, respect them, should you? What about adultery?
> - Well, they're against –
> - Oh, they're against, are they?

You'd never have heard the Ten Commandments at all.

It's almost impossible to understand an issue if you can't hear a consistent argument. I love listening to people I disagree with: first because it educates me; secondly, you think: Are they right, and if not, how do you deal with it?

Recently the Al Jazeera television station asked to do an interview. Of course, I said: how long will the interview be? Two hours, they said. Recorded? No, it's live. They gave me a very rough time, but at least the audience for that programme – over seventy million people, they told me – heard an argument at length, every single aspect of it.

We're now getting more international viewpoints, and a sense of history underpinning current events. In 1980 I went with my fellow Labour MPs Eric Heffer and Joan Lestor to see the Russian ambassador to protest about the Soviet invasion of Afghanistan. The ambassador was very polite, and declared that Russia had to invade because Britain and the USA were arming exiles to overthrow the government. He didn't mention Osama bin Laden by name, but that was what was happening, and the Taliban were invited to Texas when George Bush was governor to discuss a new pipeline.

At the moment there is a rapid realisation by the media that the arguments about the Afghan war by those who are against it (as I am) have a rather greater credibility than would normally be the case with a war. The BBC will probably get award at Cannes in three or four years time for films about Afghanistan and the Gulf and Kosovo, but it would be helpful if they could produce such films early enough to help to develop the argument while it's actually going on – to enable people to hear different views.

I've often wondered how progress is made and the conclusion I've come to is this. If you raise a progressive idea, or even a new idea, it's ignored; then if you go on, you're absolutely stark staring bonkers; then if you go on after that you're dangerous; then there's a pause; then you can't find anyone who doesn't claim to have thought of it in the first place. That is how progress is made.

Think of the debate on the environment. Ten years ago Swampy was a bearded weirdo who'd be arrested on sight by the police. He'll be in the Honours List next year, after the Prime Minister has made a series of major speeches about the environment. That is how it happens.

How can the media accelerate the process of understanding what is said, so that we don't have the violence which is associated with delay? How can the media help us to move from the initial reporting of an issue to an examination of what people are saying about it, thereby making a satisfactory resolution more realisable?

Members of Parliament and journalists alike should recognise the personal responsibility, the moral responsibility, that both sides have, and to illustrate this I can't do better than read the words of the constitution of UNESCO in 1946:

> The Governments of the States Parties to this Constitution on behalf of their peoples declare:
>
> That since wars begin in the minds of men, it is in the minds of men that the defences of peace must be constructed:
>
> That ignorance of each other's ways and lives has been a common cause, throughout the history of mankind, of that suspicion and mistrust between the peoples of the world through which their differences have all too often broken into war:
>
> That the great and terrible war which has now ended was a war made possible by the denial of the democratic princi-

ples of the dignity, equality and mutual respect of men, and by the propagation, in their place, through ignorance and prejudice, of the doctrine of the inequality of men and races;

That the wide diffusion of culture, and the education of humanity for justice and liberty and peace are indispensable to the dignity of man and constitute a sacred duty which all the nations must fulfil in a spirit of mutual assistance and concern;

That a peace based exclusively upon the political and economic arrangements of governments would not be a peace which could secure the unanimous, lasting and sincere support of the peoples of the world.

Those words seem in a way to encapsulate everything that James Cameron stood for.

When a great man dies, it's often said that we'll never see the like of him again, but when I look at John Pilger or Robert Fisk, to name but two, I believe that such people uphold James Cameron's principles. It is absolutely fundamental that they be able to be heard as they are, and that others who might have equally valuable things to say should be heard too, because what is at stake now, in a world where every mistake could be fatal for the human race, is something we have to keep very much in mind.